Introduction to Philosophy

Revised Edition

Fred Feldman
University of Massachusetts

McGraw-Hill, Inc.
College Custom Series

*New York St. Louis San Francisco Auckland Bogotá
Caracas Lisbon London Madrid Mexico Milan Montreal
New Delhi Paris San Juan Singapore Sydney Tokyo Toronto*

McGraw-Hill's **College Custom Series** consists of products that are produced from camera-ready copy. Peer review, class testing, and accuracy are primarily the responsibility of the author(s).

Introduction to Philosophy

1 2 3 4 5 6 7 8 9 0 Sem Sem 9 0 9 8 7 6 5 4

ISBN 0-07-020502-7

Editor: Gale Murray

Cover Design: Pat Koch

Printer/Binder: Quebecor Printing Semline, Inc.

This book is printed on recycled paper containing a minimum of 50% total recycled fiber with 10% postconsumer de-inked fiber.

CONTENTS

PART III - PHILOSOPHICAL THEOLOGY

PART IV - EPISTEMOLOGY

PREFACE

I want to take this opportunity to say a few words about what's in this book and how it is organized. I also want to describe the criteria that guided me in selecting these items. Finally, I want to mention something about the history of the collection.

I

The first selection (by James L. Christian) is the Introduction to his extremely successful textbook, *philosophy: an introduction to the art of wondering*. In this article, Christian discusses his views about the nature of philosophy. Although I don't entirely agree with what Christian says, I think his remarks provide a very useful basis for a discussion of the nature of philosophy.

The rest of the selections are organized into four sections. The first section concerns the puzzle about *freedom and determinism*.. How is it possible for human beings to act freely if everything we do is caused? The second section contains articles about what I call 'philosophical anthropology'. (Others call this 'the mind-body problem'.) The issue here is *the nature of persons*. Is each person just a physical object—his or her own body? Or is a person more complex than that, containing also a non-physical soul or mind? The third section contains articles about the *existence of God*. The first three essays contain arguments for the existence of God. The final essay of the third section contains an argument against the existence of God, based on the existence of evil in the world. The fourth section of the book is about *knowledge and skepticism*. I have included some classic skeptical arguments designed to show that we cannot know lots of things we may think we know. I have also included some classic attempts to explain how these arguments can be refuted.

II

Now let me turn to the criteria I had in mind as I chose the articles. As I made my selections, I had several different (and not always compatible) aims in mind.

Perhaps my central aim was this: I tried to find articles that contained *clear, vigorous presentations of classic positions* on the issues under consideration in the collection. This aim is well illustrated by the selections in the first section, on freedom and dterminism. Hard determinism is forcefully defended in the article by Paul Ree. Soft determinism is defended with equal clarity and zeal by A.J. Ayer. In his article, Roderick Chisholm presents a magnificently persuasive and lucid account of libertarianism. Richard Taylor's chapter on fatalism is, similarly, clear and vigorous.

Since in my own course I especially like to discuss the arguments philosophers use to attack or defend various doctrines, I also sought out articles that contain *persuasive or interesting argumentation.* David Armstrong's article contains some very serious arguments against Descartes' views about the nature of persons. The articles by Leibniz, Anselm, and Paley contain classic arguments for the existence of God. The article by Mackie contains a remarkably spirited presentation of an argument against the existence of God based on the existence of evil. Taylor's article contains a profoundly puzzling argument for fatalism. Many of the other selections also contain important and interesting arguments. The selection from Sextus Empiricus contains an amazing collection of arguments apparently designed to show that we don't know anywhere near as much as we may think we know.

Another aim here is *diversity.* While I did not try to find articles representing every possible position on each of the issues, I did try to find articles that would illustrate the most important positions. Thus, in the section on free will and determinism, there is an article by a hard determinist (Ree), a soft determinist (Ayer), a libertarian (Chisholm), and a fatalist (Taylor). In the section on philosophical anthropology, there are two articles by dualists (Ryle and Armstrong). In the section on the existence of God, there is an example of a teleological argument (Paley), a cosmological argument (Leibniz), an ontological argument (Anselm), and an argument against the existence of God (Mackie).

While seeking diversity, I also sought to *avoid redundancy.* thus, there are very few cases in which two articles present fundamentally similar lines of thought. Each article here makes a unique contribution to the collection as a whole.

Philosophy does not have to be dull. At its best, philosophical writing can be lively and exciting. Sometimes it can be pretty funny, too. As I made my selections, I sought articles that would be *fun to read.* I think that many of the selections are funny. Many passages in Sextus Empiricus are truly nutty; Gaunilon's reply to Anselm seems to me to be the work of a witty fellow; Taylor's story of Osmo and the amazing book is also amusing. Plato's description of the death of Socrates can hardly be called funny, but it is a marvelous piece of writing— a moving and profound discussion of death, philosophy, and the nature of persons. Descartes' *Meditations* are acknowledged classics of philosophical writing.

A final aim was *historical importance.* I wanted, where possible to choose essays by important figures in the history of philosophy. Equally, where possible I wanted to include essays that are themselves well-known and highly regarded. Where possible, I preferred the *original* presentation of some important doctrine or argument, rather than some derivative version. Considerations of this sort played some role in my choice of the selections from Plato, Descartes, Leibniz, Sextus Empiricus, Anselm, Locke, Berkeley, and Hume.

I have also included one essay that I wrote especially for this volume. I cannot claim that I included it because of its historical importance. The essay has not previously been published. Nor is it outstandingly original. All the main ideas were taken from a series of essays that was published quite a few years ago in the British journal *Mind.* Someone—I don't know who—came up with the puzzle about the great falsifier. Subsequent contributors tried to explain where the argument goes wrong. I have attempted to simplify the puzzle, and to bring it up to date. I certainly do not think that the argument succeeds; on the other hand it is not easy to explain precisely where it goes wrong. It is included primarily because I think readers might have some fun with it.

III

Several years ago, it became necessary for me to revise the curriculum for my course in introduction to philosophy. At first, I thought I would make use of one of the popular anthologies. After reviewing the available choices, I settled on an excellent and very widely used collection. It contained several essays that I wanted to use. Unfortunately, it also contained a very large number of essays that I did not want to use. The book was large, heavy, and expensive. My students justifiably complained. They were required to buy a fairly costly book, even though they were going to read only a small fraction of the essays in that book.

Furthermore, since the book did not contain all the articles I wanted to use in my course, I had to make and distribute copies of a few extra articles. This was a nuisance for me, and an extra expense for my students.

Subsequently, a representative of a local copyshop convinced me that he could produce a much less expensive anthology containing all and only the items I used in my course. This seemed to me to be a great idea, and I signed on. The new anthology was produced, and we used it for a few semesters. In some ways it was a big improvement over the old and too-expensive volume.

Nevertheless, there were still problems. One problem was that the quality of the copying was pretty bad. Another was that the binding was poor. The main problem, however, was that the whole business was entirely illegal. The copyshop had not secured permission to reproduce copywritten materials.

Then a friend told me about McGraw-Hill Custom Publishing. He told me that they could produce a much higher quality anthology at a very low price. He also told me that they would secure all the necessary permissions so that the book would be legal. He also said that their system is flexible, so that if it should later become necessary to alter the contents of the anthology, it could easily be done. This seemed to me to be a great idea and so I agreed to have McGraw-Hill take over the job of producing the anthology for my course. That is how this book came into existence.

The earliest version of this collection contained a certain combination of essays. Students liked some of the essays; they didn't like others. Teaching assistants found it satisfying to teach some of the essays; they did not enjoy teaching others. The successful essays remained; the unsuccessful ones were declared "unfit"—they did not survive. As time went by, new selections were added. In some cases, as I recall, the new selections were originally suggested by teaching assistants.

I am very grateful to all my friends, colleagues, and former teaching assistants who played a role in the construction of this anthology. As in the case of the evolution of plants and animals, some of the facts about the evolution of this book are shrouded in the mists of time. I no longer know who is responsible for the selections that remain in the book. I know that David Cowles has been extremely helpful. I know that I discussed the book on many occasions with Ned Markosian, Eric Moore, Asli Gocer, Kevin Moon, Julie Petty, Neil Feit, Geoff Goddu, and several other former teaching assistants. I wish I could mention here all the people who deserve my thanks. Unfortunately, my memory is not up to the task.

I am also grateful to my friend Michael Fried who encouraged me to let McGraw-Hill produce the book. I am extremely grateful to the editor at McGraw-Hill, Margaret Hollander, who did an extraordinarily good job of putting this collection together quickly and efficiently. I have truly enjoyed working with her on this project.

Fred Feldman
Amherst, Massachusetts
November, 1992

WHAT DO YOU MEAN PHILOSOPHY???

James L. Christian
Santa Ana College

Sometime, at your leisure—if you want to know what philosophy is—go into a large bookstore and browse. Check a variety of books in psychology, anthropology, physics, chemistry, archeology, astronomy, and other nonfiction fields. Look at the last chapter in each book. In a surprising number of cases, you will find that the author has chosen to round out his work with a final summation of what the book is all about. That is, having written a whole book on a specialized subject in which he is probably an authority, he finds that he also has ideas about the larger meaning of the facts that he has written about. The final chapter may be called "Conclusions," "Epilogue," "Postscript," "My Personal View," "Implications," "Comments," "Speculations," or (as in one case) "So What?" But in every instance, the author is trying to elucidate the larger implications of his subject matter and to clarify how he thinks it relates to other fields or to life. He has an urge to tell us the meaning of all his facts taken together. He wants to share with us the philosophic implications of what he has written.

When he does this, the author has moved beyond the role of a field specialist. He is a philosopher.

2 This is a textbook in synoptic° philosophy. It is an invitation to ponder, in the largest possible perspective, the weightier, more stubborn problems of human existence. It is an invitation to think—to wonder, to question, to speculate, to reason, even to fantasize—in the eternal search for wisdom. In a word, synoptic philosophy is an attempt to weave interconnecting lines of illumination between all the disparate realms of human thought in the hope that, like a thousand dawnings, new insights will burst through.

By its very nature, philosophy is a do-it-yourself enterprise. There is a common misunderstanding that philosophy—like chemistry or history—has a content to offer, a content which a teacher is to teach and a student is to learn. This is not the case. There are no facts, no theories, certainly no final truths which go by the name of "philosophy" and which one is supposed to accept and believe. Rather, philosophy is a skill—more akin to mathematics and music; it is something that one *learns to do.*

Philosophy, that is, is a *method.* It is *learning how* to ask and re-ask questions until meaningful answers begin to appear. It is *learning how* to relate materials. It is *learning where* to go for the most dependable, up-to-date information that might shed light on some problem. It is *learning how* to double check fact-claims in order to verify or falsify them. It is *learning how* to reject fallacious fact-claims—to reject them no matter how prestigious the authority who holds them or how deeply one would personally like to believe them.

°Synoptic. From the Greek *sunoptikos*, "seeing the whole together" or "taking a comprehensive view." The attempt to achieve an all-inclusive overview of one's subject matter.

3 The student should be aware that philosophy has never been just one kind of activity with a single approach to a single task. Rather, there have been many kinds of philosophy: the quiet philosophy of the sage who sees much but speaks little because language cannot hold life; the articulate, noisy dialectics of Socrates; the calm, logical apologetics of Aquinas; the mystical philosophy of Plotinus and Chuang-tzu; the mathematical philosophy of Russell and Wittgenstein.

Each school of philosophy has concentrated upon some aspect of man's knowledge. Logical/analytical philosophy has worked long and hard on the confusion which vitiates so much of our thinking and communicating. Pragmatism has concentrated on finding solutions to problems of man's social existence. Existential philosophy has been concerned with making life meaningful to each, unique individual. Activist schools argue that philosophers spend too much time trying to make sense of the world and too little time trying to change it. Several schools of philosophy, Eastern and Western, challenge the individual to turn away from an alienating society and to seek harmony with Nature or Ultimate Reality.

Each kind of philosophy has made an immense contribution to its area of concern. Each was doubtless a part of the *Zeitgeist*—"the spirit of the age"—which gave it birth and to which it spoke.

The present unhappy condition of human knowledge calls for the application of a synoptic methodology. We now possess vast accumulations of specialized knowledge in countless fields, but these fields remain isolated from one another. Yet it is increasingly clear that many of our urgent problems can be understood only when the specialized information from a variety of these separate fields is integrated and "seen together"—synoptically. It is only then that we can develop realistic solutions to these complex problems.

4 It is often said that philosophers engage in two basic tasks: "taking apart"—*analyzing* ideas to discover if we truly know what we think we know (and we don't)—and "putting together"—*synthesizing* all our knowledge to find if we can attain a larger and better view of life (we can).

But in practice philosophers do a lot more than this. They talk a lot. They carry on dialogues with anyone who comes within range. And they argue a great deal. Not the usual kinds of argument in which egos fight to win, but philosophical arguments in which they attempt to clarify the reasoning that lies behind their statements; and no one cares about winning since, in philosophical arguments, everyone wins.

They also ask one another for definitions to be sure they're thinking clearly; and they push one another to pursue the implications of their ideas and statements. They prod themselves and others to examine the basic assumptions upon which their beliefs and arguments rest.

Philosophers are persistent explorers in the nooks and crannies of human knowledge which are commonly overlooked or deliberately ignored. It is an exciting but restless adventure of the mind.

5 Philosophers, however, do not engage in this critical task just to make nuisances of themselves. Indeed, the central aim of philosophers has always been . . . to construct a picture of the whole of reality, in which every element of man's knowledge and every aspect of man's experience will find its proper place. Philosophy, in short, is man's quest for the unity of knowledge: it consists in a perpetual struggle to create the concepts in which the universe can be conceived as a universe and not a multiverse. The history of philosophy is attempt is made to grasp this total unity. . . .

> It cannot be denied that this attempt stands without rival as the most audacious enterprise in which the mind of man has ever engaged. Just reflect for a moment: Here is man, surrounded by the vastness of a universe in which he is only a tiny and perhaps insignificant part—and he wants to *understand* it. . . .
>
> WILLIAM HALVERSON
> *A Concise Introduction to Philosophy*
> (1967, Random House, Inc., p. 18ff)

6 In one respect, philosophic material can be deceptive. Since it deals with life by examining the sort of questions we ask every day, some of the subject matter will have an easy, familiar ring.

The fact is that synoptic philosophy must be as diligently studied as any other subject, not to remember data, but to set the mind in motion toward developing larger concepts, connecting ideas, and seeing through and beyond mere words and facts.

In a sense, intellectual growth *happens to us*; it is not really something that we do. But it happens to us only when our minds are given a chance to operate on their terms. They take their own time to process information and to begin developing a web of interconnecting lines of illumination among their materials. This undertaking is partly conscious, of course; but largely it is an unconscious process. This is why much philosophic insight just happens, as though the light moves from the depths upward and not from the rational conscious downward.

Only disciplined study with an open mind will produce philosophic awareness. Insight and consciousness still come only with relentless labor. In this age of instant everything, there is still no instant wisdom, unfortunately.

7 No two of us possess precisely the same information, or see things from the same viewpoint, or share the same values. Therefore, each of us must do synoptic philosophy in his own unique and personal way. A student entering upon the activity of philosophizing may need to be on guard against developing a world-view which resembles, a bit too closely, the prepackaged philosophy of life belonging to someone else or to some institution. Most of us are philosophically lazy, and it is easy to appropriate another's thoughts and rationalize our theft. The British logician Wittgenstein warned us that "a thought which is not independent is a thought only half understood." Similarly, a philosophy of life that is not the authentic product of one's own experience is a philosophy only half understood.

Nor will any of us succeed in developing a finished philosophy; for as one changes with life, so does one's thinking. A philosophy *of life* must change *with life*. Doing philosophy is an endless activity.

For this reason, this textbook is merely an example of synoptic philosophy. This is the way I have had to do it because of *my* perspectives, *my* interests, *my* areas of knowledge, *my* personal concerns, and *my* limitations. But *your* world-view will be different because it will be *yours,* and *yours alone*.

This is why my attempt to do synoptic philosophy is, at most, a guideline showing how it might be done; at least, the expression of a hope that, someday, in your own way, you will resolve the contradictions of your own existence—both of knowing and of being—and proceed to see life in a larger, more fulfilling way.

PART ONE

THE PROBLEM OF FREEDOM AND DETERMINISM

DETERMINISM AND THE ILLUSION OF MORAL RESPONSIBILITY

Paul Rée

1. Nothing Happens without a Cause

. . .To say that the will is not free means that it is subject to the law of causality. Every act of will is in fact preceded by a sufficient cause. Without such a cause the act of will cannot occur; and, if the sufficient cause is present, the act of will must occur.

To say that the will is free would mean that it is not subject to the law of causality. In that case every act of will would be an absolute beginning [a first cause] and not a link [in a chain of events]: it would not be the effect of preceding causes.

The reflections that follow may serve to clarify what is meant by saying that the will is not free . . . Every object—a stone, an animal, a human being—can pass from its present state to another one. The stone that now lies in front of me may, in the next moment, fly through the air, or it may disintegrate into dust or roll along the ground. If, however, one of these *possible* states is to be *realized,* its sufficient cause must first be present. The stone will fly through the air if it is tossed. It will roll if a force acts upon it. It will disintegrate into dust, given that some object hits and crushes it.

It is helpful to use the terms "potential" and "actual" in this connection. At any moment there are innumerably many potential states. At a given time, however, only *one* can become actual, namely, the one that is triggered by its sufficient cause.

The situation is no different in the case of an animal. The donkey that now stands motionless between two piles of hay may, in the next moment, turn to the left or to the right, or he may jump into the air or put his head between his legs. But here, too, the sufficient cause must first be present if of the *possible* modes of behavior one is to be *realized.*

Let us analyze one of these modes of behavior. We shall assume that the donkey has turned toward the bundle on his right. This turning presupposes that certain muscles were contracted. The cause of this muscular contraction is the excitation of the nerves that lead to them. The cause of this excitation of the nerves is a state of the brain. It was in a state of decision. But how did the brain come to be in that condition? Let us trace the states of the donkey back a little farther.

This selection consists of the major portions of Chapters 1 and 2 of Paul Rée's *Die Illusion der Willensfreiheit,* a work published in Berlin in 1885. The third chapter of Rée's booklet, which is omitted here, is a detailed critique of Kant's views on the subject.

The subtitles in this translation were supplied by the editor; the first and fifth take the place of chapter headings in the original text. Cuts have been indicated by the use of dots. The translator has supplied a few minor emendations; these have been put in square brackets.

A few moments before he turned, his brain was not yet so constituted as to yield the sufficient cause for the excitation of the nerves in question and for the contraction of the muscles; for otherwise the movement would have occurred. The donkey had not yet "decided"to turn. If he then moved at some subsequent time, his brain must in the meantime have become so constituted as to bring about the excitation of the nerves and the movement of the muscles. Hence the brain underwent some change. To what causes is this change to be attributed? To the effectiveness of an impression that acts as an external stimulus, or to a sensation that arose internally; for example, the sensation of hunger and the idea of the bundle on the right, by jointly affecting the brain, change the way in which it is constituted so that it now yields the sufficient cause for the excitation of the nerves and the contraction of the muscles. The donkey now "wants" to turn to the right; he now turns to the right.

Hence, just as the position and constitution of the stone, on the one hand, and the strength and direction of the force that acts upon it, on the other, necessarily determine the kind and length of its flight, so the movement of the donkey—his turning to the bundle on the right—is no less necessarily the result of the way in which the donkey's brain and the stimulus are constituted at a given moment. That the donkey turned toward this particular bundle was determined by something trivial. If the bundle that the donkey did not choose had been positioned just a bit differently, or if it had smelled different, or if the subjective factor—the donkey's sense of smell or his visual organs—had developed in a somewhat different way, then, so we may assume, the donkey would have turned to the left. But the cause was not complete there, and that is why the effect could not occur, while with respect to the other side, where the cause was complete, the effect could not fail to appear.

For the donkey, consequently, just as for the stone, there are innumerably many *potential* states at any moment; he may walk or run or jump, or move to the left, to the right, or straight ahead. But only the one whose sufficient cause is present can ever become *actual.*

At the same time, there is a difference between the donkey and the stone in that the donkey moves because he wants to move, while the stone moves because it is moved. We do not deny this difference. There are, after all, a good many other differences between the donkey and the stone. We do not by any means intend to prove that this dissimilarity does not exist. We do not assert that the donkey is a stone, but only that the donkey's every movement and act of will has causes just as the motion of the stone does. The donkey moves because he wants to move. But that he wants to move at a given moment, and in this particular direction, is causally determined.

Could it be that there was no sufficient cause for the donkey's wanting to turn around—that he simply wanted to turn around? His act of will would then be an absolute beginning. An assumption of that kind is contradicted by experience and the universal validity of the law of causality. By experience, since observation teaches us that for every act of will some causes were the determining factors. By the universal validity of the law of causality, since, after all, nothing happens anywhere in the world without a sufficient cause. Why, then, of all things should a donkey's act of will come into being without a cause? Besides, the state of willing, the one that immediately precedes the excitation of the motor nerves, is no different in principle from other states—that of indifference, of lassitude, or of weariness. Would anyone believe that all of these states exist without a cause? And if one does not believe that, why should just the state of willing be thought to occur without a sufficient cause?

It is easy to explain why it seems to us that the motion of the stone is necessary while the donkey's act of will is not. The causes that move the stone are, after all, external and visible. But the causes of the donkey's act of will are internal and invisible; between us and the locus of their effectiveness lies the skull of the donkey. Let us consider this difference somewhat more closely. The stone lies before us as it is constituted. We can also see the force acting upon it, and from these two factors, the constitution of the stone and the force, there results, likewise visible, the rolling of the stone. The case of the donkey is different. The state of his brain is hidden from our view. And, while the bundle of hay is visible, its effectiveness is not. It is an internal process. The bundle does not come into visible contact with the brain but acts at a distance. Hence the subjective and the objective factor—the brain and the impact that the bundle has upon it—are invisible.

Let us suppose that we could depict the donkey's soul in high relief, taking account of and making visible all those states, attitudes, and feelings that characterize it before the donkey turns. Suppose further that we could see how an image detaches itself from the bundle of hay and, describing a visible path through the air, intrudes upon the donkey's brain and how it produces a change there in consequence of which certain nerves and muscles move. Suppose, finally, that we could repeat this experiment arbitrarily often, that, if we returned the donkey's soul into the state preceding his turning and let exactly the same impression act upon it, we should always observe the very same result. Then we would regard the donkey's turning to the right as necessary. We would come to realize that the brain, constituted as it was at that moment, had to react to such an impression in precisely that way.

In the absence of this experiment it seems as though the donkey's act of will were not causally determined. We just do not see its being causally determined and consequently believe that no such determination takes place. The act of will, it is said, is the cause of the turning, but it is not itself determined; it is said to be an absolute beginning.

The opinion that the donkey's act of will is not causally determined is held not only by the outsider; the donkey himself, had he the gift of reflection, would share it. The causes of his act of will would elude him, too, since in part they do not become conscious at all and in part pass through consciousness fleetingly, with the speed of lightning. If, for example, what tipped the scales was that he was closer by a hair's breadth to the bundle on the right, or that it smelled a shade better, how should the donkey notice something so trivial, something that so totally fails to force itself upon his consciousness?

In *one* sense, of course, the donkey is right in thinking "I could have turned to the left." His state at the moment, his position relative to the bundle, or its constitution need merely have been somewhat different, and he really would have turned to the left. The statement "I could have acted otherwise" is, accordingly, true in this sense: turning to the left is one of the movements possible for me (in contrast, for example, to the movement of flying); it lies within the realm of my possibilities.

We arrive at the same result if we take the law of inertia as our point of departure. It reads: every object strives to remain in its present state. Expressed negatively this becomes: without a sufficient cause no object can pass from its present state to another one. The stone will lie forever just as it is lying now; it will not undergo the slightest change if no causes—such as the weather or a force—act upon it to bring about a change. The donkey's brain will remain in the same state unchanged for all eternity if no causes—the feeling of hunger or fatigue, say, or external impressions—bring about a change.

If we reflect upon the entire life of the donkey *sub specie necessitatis,* we arrive at the following result. The donkey came into the world with certain properties of mind and body, his genetic inheritance. Since the day of his birth, impressions—of the companions with whom he frolicked or worked, his feed, the climate—have acted upon these properties. These two factors, his inborn constitution and the way in which it was formed through the impressions of later life, are the cause of all of his sensations, ideas, and moods, and of all of his movements, even the most trivial ones. If, for example, he cocks his left ear and not the right one, that is determined by causes whose historical development could be traced back ad infinitum; and likewise when he stands, vacillating, between the two bundles. And when action, the act of feeding, takes the place of vacillation, that, too, is determined: the idea of the one bundle now acts upon the donkey's mind, when it has become receptive to the idea of that particular sheaf, in such a way as to produce actions.

2. *Human Beings and the Law of Causality*

Let us now leave the realm of animals and proceed to consider man. Everything is the same here. Man's every feeling is a necessary result. Suppose, for example, that I am stirred by a feeling of pity at this moment. To what causes is it to be attributed? Let us go back as far as possible. An infinite amount of time has elapsed up to this moment. Time was never empty; objects have filled it from all eternity. These objects . . . have continually undergone change. All of these changes were governed by the law of causality; not one of them took place without a sufficient cause.

We need not consider what else may have characterized these changes. Only their *formal* aspect, only this *one* point is of concern to us: no change occurred without a cause.

At some time in the course of this development, by virtue of some causes, organic matter was formed, and finally man. Perhaps the organic world developed as Darwin described it. Be that as it may, it was in any case due to causes that I was born on a particular day, with particular properties of body, of spirit, and of heart. Impressions then acted upon this constitution; I had particular governesses, teachers, and playmates. Teaching and example in part had an effect and in part were lost upon me; the former, when my inborn constitution made me receptive to them, when I had an affinity for them. And that is how it has come to be, through the operation of [a chain of] causes, that I am stirred by a feeling of pity at this moment. The course of the world would have had to be somewhat different if my feelings were to be different now.

It is of no consequence for the present investigation whether the inborn capacity for pity, for taking pleasure in another's pain, or for courage remains constant throughout life or whether teaching, example, and activity serve to change it. In any case the pity or pleasure in another's pain, the courage or cowardice, that a certain person feels or exhibits at a given moment is a necessary result, whether these traits are inborn—an inheritance from his ancestors—or were developed in the course of his own life.

Likewise every intention, indeed, every thought that ever passes through the brain, the silliest as well as the most brilliant, the true as well as the false, exists of necessity. In that sense there is no freedom of thought. It is necessary that I sit in this place at this moment, that I hold my pen in my hand in a particular way, and that I write that every thought is necessary; and if the reader should perchance be of the opinion that this is not the case, i.e., if he should believe that thoughts may not be viewed as effects, then he holds this false opinion of necessity also.

Just as sensations and thoughts are necessary, so, too, is action. It is, after all, nothing other than their externalization, their objective embodiment. Action is born of sensations and thoughts. So long as the sensations are not sufficiently strong, action cannot occur, and when the sensations and thoughts are constituted so as to yield the sufficient cause for it, then it must occur; then the appropriate nerves and muscles are set to work. Let us illustrate this by means of an action that is judged differently at different levels of civilization, namely, murder.[1] Munzinger, for example, says that among the Bogos the murderer, the terror of the neighborhood, who never tires of blood and murder, is a man of respect. Whoever has been raised with such views will not be deterred from murder either by external or by internal obstacles. Neither the police nor his conscience forbids him to commit it. On the contrary, it is his habit to praise murder; his parents and his gods stimulate him to commit it, and his companions encourage him by their example. And so it comes to be that, if there is a favorable opportunity, he does the deed. But is this not terribly trivial? After all, everyone knows that an act of murder is due to *motives!* True, but almost no one (except perhaps a philosopher) knows that an act of murder, and indeed every action, has a *cause.* Motives are a part of the cause. But to admit that there are motives for an action is not yet to recognize that it is causally determined, or to see clearly that the action is determined by thoughts and sensations—which in turn are effects—just as the rolling of a ball is determined by a force. But it is this point, and only this one, to which we must pay heed.

Let us now consider the act of murder from the same point of view in the case of civilized peoples. Someone raised at a higher level of civilization has learned from childhood on to disapprove of murder and to regard it as deserving punishment. God, his parents, and his teachers—in short, all who constitute an authority for him—condemn acts of this kind. It is, moreover, inconsistent with his character, which has been formed in an era of peace. Lastly, too, fear of punishment will deter him. Can murder prosper on such soil? Not easily. Fear, pity, the habit of condemning murder—all these are just so many bulwarks that block the path to such an action. Nevertheless need, passion, or various seductive influences will perhaps remove one after another of these bulwarks. Let us consider the cause of an act of murder more closely. First it is necessary to distinguish between two components, the subjective and the objective, in the total cause. The *subjective* part of the cause consists of the state of the murderer at the moment of the deed. To this we must assign all ideas that he had at the time, the conscious as well as the unconscious ones, his sensations, the temperature of his blood, the state of his stomach, of his liver—of each and every one of his bodily organs. The *objective* component consists of the appearance of the victim, the locality in which the deed took place, and the way it was illuminated. The act of murder was necessarily consummated at that moment because these impressions acted upon a human being constituted in that particular way at the time. "Necessarily" means just that the act of murder is an effect; the state of the murderer and the impressions acting upon it are its cause. If the cause had not been complete, the effect could not have occurred. If, for example, the murderer had felt even a trifle more pity at that moment, if his idea of God or of the consequences that his deed would have here on earth had been somewhat more distinct, or if the moon had been a little brighter, so that more light would have fallen upon the victim's face and his pleading eyes—then, perhaps, the cause of the act of murder would not have become complete, and in consequence the act would not have taken place.

Thus for man, as for animal and stone, there are at any moment innumerably many *potential* states. The murderer might, at the moment when he committed the murder, have climbed a tree instead or stood on his head. If, however, instead of the murder one of these actions were to have become *actual,* then its sufficient cause would have had to be present. He would have climbed a tree if he had had the intention of hiding, or of acting as a lookout, that is to say, if at that moment he had had other ideas and sensations. But this could have been the case only if the events that took place in the world had been somewhat different [stretching back in time] ad infinitum.

3. *Determinism and Will-Power*

But I can, after all, break through the network of thoughts, sensations, and impressions that surrounds me by resolutely saying "I will not commit murder!" No doubt. We must, however, not lose sight of the fact that a resolute "I will" or "I will not" is also, wherever it appears, a necessary result; it does not by any means exist without a cause. Let us return to our examples. Although the Bogo really has reasons only to commit murder, it is nevertheless possible for a resolute "I will not commit murder" to assert itself. But is it conceivable that this "I will not" should occur without a sufficient cause? Fear, pity, or some other feeling, which in turn is an effect, overcomes him and gives rise to this "I will not" before the cause of the murder has yet become complete. Perhaps Christian missionaries have had an influence upon him; hence the idea of a deity that will visit retribution on him for murder comes before his soul, and that is how the "I will not"comes to be. It is easier to detect the causes of the resolute "I will not commit murder" in someone raised at a higher level of civilization; fear, principles, or the thought of God in most cases produce it in time.

A resolute will can be characteristic of a man. No matter how violently jealousy, greed, or some other passion rages within him, he does not want to succumb to it; he does not succumb to it. The analogue of this constitution is a ball that, no matter how violent a force acts upon it, does not budge from its place. A billiard cue will labor in vain to shake the earth. The earth victoriously resists the cue's thrusts with its mass. Likewise man resists the thrusts of greed and jealousy with the mass of his principles. A man of that kind, accordingly, is free—from being dominated by his drives. Does this contradict determinism? By no means. A man free from passion is still subject to the law of causality. He is necessarily free. It is just that the word "free" has different meanings. It may be correctly predicated of man in every sense except a single one: he is not free from the law of causality. Let us trace the causes of his freedom from the tyranny of the passions.

Let us suppose that his steadfastness of will was not inherited, or, if so, merely as a disposition. Teaching, example, and, above all, the force of circumstances developed it in him. From early childhood on he found himself in situations in which he had to control himself if he did not want to perish. Just as someone standing at the edge of an abyss can banish dizziness by thinking "If I become dizzy, then I will plunge," so thinking "If I yield to my excitation—indeed, if I so much as betray it—I will perish" has led him to control of his drives.

It is often thought that those who deny that the will is free want to deny that man has the ability to free himself from being dominated by his drives. However, one can imagine man's power to resist passions to be as great as one wants, even infinitely great; that is to say, a man may possibly resist even the most violent passion: his love of God or his principles have still more power over him than the passion. The question whether even the most resolute act of will is an effect is entirely independent of this.

But is being subject to the law of causality not the weak side of the strong? By no means. Is a lion weak if he can tear a tiger apart? Is a hurricane weak if it can uproot trees? And yet the power by means of which the lion dismembers and the storm uproots is an effect, and not an absolute beginning. By having causes, by being an effect, strength is not diminished.

Just as resolute willing is to be considered an effect, so is irresolute willing. A vacillating man is characterized by the fact that he alternately wants something and then doesn't want it. To say that someone contemplating murder is still vacillating means that at one time the desire for possessions, greed, and jealousy predominate—then he wants to commit murder; at another time fear of the consequences, the thought of God, or pity overcomes him, and then he does not want to commit murder. In the decisive moment, when his victim is before him, everything depends upon which feeling has the upper hand. If at that moment passion predominates, then he wants to commit murder; and then he commits murder.

We see that, from whatever point of view we look at willing, it always appears as a necessary result, as a link [in a chain of events], and never as an absolute beginning.

But can we not prove by means of an experiment that willing is an absolute beginning? I lift my arm because I *want* to lift it . . . Here my *wanting* to lift my arm is the cause of the lifting, but this wanting, we are told, is not itself causally determined; rather, it is an absolute beginning. I simply want to lift my arm, and that is that. We are deceiving ourselves. This act of will, too, has causes; my intention to demonstrate by means of an experiment that my will is free gives rise to my wanting to lift my arm. But how did this intention come"I want to demonstrate my freedom" has the effect that I want to lift my arm. There is a gap in this chain. Granted that my intention to demonstrate that my will is free stands in some relation to my wanting to lift my arm, why do I not demonstrate my freedom by means of some other movement? Why is it *just my arm* that I want to lift? This specific act of will on my part has not yet been causally explained. Does it perhaps not have causes? Is it an uncaused act of will? Let us note first that someone who wishes to demonstrate that his will is free will usually really extend or lift his arm, and in particular his right arm. He neither tears his hair nor wiggles his belly. This can be explained as follows. Of all of the parts of the body that are subject to our voluntary control, there is none that we move more frequently than the right arm. If, now, we wish to demonstrate our freedom by means of some movement, we will automatically make that one to which we are most accustomed . . . Thus we first have a conversation about or reflection on the freedom of the will; this leads to the intention of demonstrating our freedom; this intention arises in an organism with certain [physiological] habits [such as that of readily lifting the right arm], and as a result we want to lift (and then lift) the right arm.

I remember once discussing the freedom of the will with a left-handed man. He asserted "My will is free; I can do what I want." In order to demonstrate this he extended his *left* arm.

It is easy to see, now, what the situation is with regard to the assertion "I can do what I want." In one sense it is indeed correct; in another, however, it is wrong. The *correct* sense is to regard willing as a cause and action as an effect. For example, I can kill my rival if I want to kill him. I can walk to the left if I want to walk to the left. The causes are *wanting* to kill and *wanting* to walk; the effects are killing and walking. In some way every action must be preceded by the act of willing it, whether we are aware of it or not. According to this view, in fact, I can do *only* what I want to do, and only if I want to do it. The *wrong* sense is to regard willing *merely* as a cause, and not at the same time as the effect of something else. But, like everything else, it is cause *as well as effect.* An absolutely initial act of will does not exist. Willing stands in the middle: it brings about killing and walking to the left; it is the effect of thoughts and sensations (which in turn are effects).

4. Ignorance of the Causation of Our Actions

Hence our volition (with respect to some action) is always causally determined. But it seems to be free (of causes); it seems to be an absolute beginning. To what is this appearance due?

We do not perceive the causes by which our volition is determined, and that is why we believe that it is not casually determined at all.

How often do we do something while "lost in thought"! We pay no attention to what we are doing, let alone to the causes from which it springs. While we are thinking, we support our head with our hand. While we are conversing, we twist a piece of paper in our hand. If we then reflect on our behavior—stimulated perhaps by a conversation about the freedom of the will and if we are quite incapable of finding a sufficient cause for it, then we believe that there was no sufficient cause for it at all, that, consequently, we could have proceeded differently at that moment, e.g., supporting our head with the left hand instead of the right . . .

To adduce yet another example: suppose that there are two eggs on the table. I take one of them. Why not the other one? Perhaps the one I took was a bit closer to me, or some other trivial matter, which would be very difficult to discover and is of the kind that almost never enters our consciousness, tipped the scales. If I now look back but do not see why I took that particular egg, then I come to think that I could just as well have taken the other.

Let us replace "I could have taken the other egg" by other statements containing the expression "I could have." For example, I could, when I took the egg, have chopped off my fingers instead, or I could have jumped at my neighbor's throat. Why do we never adduce such statements . . . but always those contemplating an action close to the one that we really carried out? Because at the moment when I took the egg, chopping off my fingers and murder were far from my mind. From this point of view the two aspects of our subject matter—the fact that acts of will are necessary and that they appear not to be necessary—can be perceived especially clearly. *In fact* taking the other egg was at that moment just as impossible as chopping off a finger. For, whether a nuance of a sensation or a whole army of sensations and thoughts is lacking in the complete cause obviously does not matter; the effect cannot occur so long as the cause is incomplete. But it *seems* as though it would have been possible to take the other egg at that moment; if something almost happened, we think that it could have happened.

While in the case of unimportant matters we perhaps do not notice the causes of our act of will and therefore think that it has no causes, the situation is quite different—it will be objected—in the case of important matters. We did not, after all, marry one girl rather than another while "lost in thought." We did not close the sale of our house while "lost in thought." Rather, everyone sees that motives determined such decisions. In spite of this, however, we think "I could have acted differently." What is the source of this error?

In the case of unimportant matters we do not notice the cause of our action at all; in the case of important ones we perceive it, but not adequately. We do, to be sure, see the separate parts of the cause, but the special relation in which they stood to one another at the moment of the action eludes us.

Let us first consider another example from the realm of animals. A vixen vacillated whether to sneak into the chicken coop, to hunt for mice, or to return to her young in her den. At last she sneaked into the chicken coop. Why? Because she wanted to. But why did she want to? Because this act of will on her part resulted from the relation in which her hunger, her fear of the watchdog, her maternal instinct, and her other thoughts, sensations, and impressions stood to one another at that time. But a vixen with the gift of reflection would, were she to look back upon her action, say "I could have willed differently." For, although she realizes that hunger influenced her act of will, the *degree* of hunger on the one hand, and of fear and maternal instinct on the other, present at the moment of the action elude her. Having become a different animal since the time of the action, perhaps because of it, she thinks—by way of a kind of optical illusion—that she was that other animal already then. It is the same in the case of man. Suppose, for example, that someone has slain his rival out of jealousy. What does he himself, and what do others, perceive with respect to this action? We see that on the one hand jealousy, the desire for possessions, hatred, and rage were present in him, and on the other fear of punishment, pity, and the thought of God. We do not, however, see the particular relation in which hatred and pity, and rage and fear of punishment, stood to one another at the moment of the deed. If we could see this, keep it fixed, and recreate it experimentally, then everyone would regard this action as an effect, as a necessary result.

Let us now, with the aid of our imagination, suppose that the sensations and thoughts of the murderer at the moment of the deed were spread out before us, clearly visible as if on a map. From this reflection we shall learn that *in fact* we are lacking such an overview, and that this lack is the reason why we do not ascribe a cause (or "necessity") to the action.

The kaleidoscopically changing sensations, thoughts, and impressions would, in order for their relation to one another to become apparent, have to be returned to the state in which they were at the moment of the deed, and then made rigid, as if they were being nailed to their place. But beyond that, the thoughts and sensations would have to be spatially extended and endowed with a colored surface; a stronger sensation would have to be represented by a bigger lump. A clearer thought would have to wear, say, a bright red color, a less clear one a gray coloration. Jealousy and rage, as well as pity and the thought of God, would have to be plastically exhibited for us in this way. We would, further, have to see how the sight of the victim acts upon these structures of thoughts and sensations, and how there arises from these two factors first the desire to commit murder and then the act of murder itself.

Moreover, we would have to be able to repeat the process, perhaps as follows: we return the murderer to the state of mind that he had some years before the act of murder; we equip his mind with precisely the same thoughts and sensations, and his body with the same constitution. Then we let the very same impressions act upon them; we bring him into contact with the same people, let him read the same books, nourish him with the same food, and, finally, we will place the murdered person, after having called him back to life, before the murderer with the very same facial expression, in the same illumination and at the same distance. Then, as soon as the parts of the cause have been completely assembled, we would always see that the very same effect occurs, namely, wanting to commit, and then committing, murder.

Finally, too, we would have to vary the experiment, in the manner of the chemists; we would have to be able now to weaken a sensation, now to strengthen it, and to observe the result that this produces.

If these conditions were fulfilled, if we could experimentally recreate the process and also vary it, if we were to see its components and, above all, their relation to one another with plastic clarity before us—on the one hand, the *degree* of jealousy and of rage present at the moment; on the other, the *degree* of fear of punishment and of pity—then we would acknowledge that wanting to commit murder and committing murder are necessary results. But as it is we merely see that, on the one hand, jealousy and related feelings, and, on the other, pity and the idea of God, were present in the murderer. But, since we do not see the particular relation in which the sensations and thoughts stood to one another at the moment of the deed, we simply think that the *one* side could have produced acts of will and actions as well as the *other,* that the murderer could, at the moment when he wanted to commit and did commit murder, just as well have willed and acted differently, say compassionately.

It is the same if we ourselves are the person who acts. We, too, think "I could have willed differently." Let us illustrate this by yet another example. Yesterday afternoon at 6:03 o'clock I sold my house. Why? Because I wished to do so. But why did I wish to do so? Because my intention to change my place of residence, and other circumstances, caused my act of will. But was I compelled to will? Could I not have postponed the sale or forgone it altogether? It seems so to me, because I do not see the particular relation in which my thoughts, sensations, and impressions stood to one another yesterday afternoon at 6:03 o'clock.

Thus: we do not see the sufficient cause (either not at all, in the case of unimportant matters; or inadequately, in the case of important ones); consequently it does not exist for us; consequently we think that our volition and our actions were not causally determined at all, that we could just as well have willed and acted differently. No one would say "I could have willed differently" if he could see his act of will and its causes displayed plastically before him, in an experiment permitting repetition.

But who are the mistaken "we" of whom we are speaking here? Patently the author does not consider himself to be one of them. Does he, then, set himself, along with a few fellow philosophers, apart from the rest of mankind, regarding them as ignorant of the truth? Well, it really is not the case that mankind has always concerned itself with the problem of the freedom of the will and only a small part arrived at the result that the will is not free; rather, in precivilized ages no one, and in civilized ages almost no one, concerned himself with this problem. But of the few who did address themselves to this question, as the history of philosophy teaches us, almost all recognized that there is no freedom of the will. The others became victims of the illusion described above, without ever coming to grips with the problem in its general form (is the will subject to the law of casually or not?) . . .

5. *Determinism is Inconsistent with Judgements of Moral Responsibility*

We hold ourselves and others responsible without taking into account the problem of the freedom of the will.

Experience shows that, if someone has lied or murdered, he is told that he has acted reprehensibly and deserves punishment. Whether his action is uncaused or whether, like the other processes in nature, it is subject to the law of causality—how would people come to raise such questions in the ordinary course of their lives? Or has anyone ever heard of a case in which people talking about an act of murder, a lie, or an act of self-sacrifice discussed these actions in terms of the freedom of the will? It is the same if we ourselves are the person who acted. We say to ourselves "Oh, if only I had not done this! Oh, if only I had acted differently!" or "I have acted laudably, as one should act." At best a philosopher here or there chances upon the question whether our actions are causally determined or not, certainly not the rest of mankind.

Suppose, however, that someone's attention is directed to the fact that the will is not free. At first it will be very difficult to make this plausible to him. His volition is suspended from threads that are too nearly invisible, and that is why he comes to think that it is not causally determined at all. At last, however—so we shall assume—he does come to recognize that actions are effects, that their causes are thoughts and impressions, that these must likewise be viewed as effects, and so on. How will he then judge these actions? Will he continue to maintain that murder is to be punished by reprisal and that benevolent actions are to be considered *meritorious*? By no means. Rather, the first conclusion that he will—validly—draw from his newly acquired insight is that we cannot hold anyone responsible. *"Tout comprendre c'est tout pardonner";* no one can be made to answer for an *effect.*

In order to illustrate this important truth, that whoever considers intentions to be effects will cease to assign merit or blame for them, let us resume discussion of the examples above. From early childhood on the Bogo has learned to praise murder. The praiseworthiness of such an action already penetrated the consciousness of the child as a secondary meaning of the word "murder," and afterward it was confirmed by every impression: his gods and his fellow men praise murder. In consequence he involuntarily judges acts of murder to be praiseworthy, no matter whether it was he himself or someone else who committed them. Let us assume, now, that a philosopher had succeeded in persuading the Bogos that the act of murder and the intention to practice cruelty are causally determined. Then their judgment would undergo an essential modification.

To conceive of actions and intentions as causally determined, after all, means the following. We go back in the history of the individual, say to his birth, and investigate which of his characteristics are inborn and to what causes they are due.[2] Then, ever guided by the law of causality, we trace the development or transformation of these properties; we see how impressions, teachings, and examples come to him and, if his inborn constitution has an affinity for them, are taken up and transformed by it, otherwise passing by without leaving a trace. Finally we recognize that the keystone, the necessary result of this course of development, is the desire to commit murder and the act of murder.

A Bogo who looks upon murder and the intention to practice cruelty in this way—that is, as an effect—will say that it is impossible to regard them as meritorious.

But will he now look upon these actions with apathy, devoid of all feeling? By no means. He will still consider them to be pleasant or unpleasant, agreeable or disagreeable.

When the action is directed against himself, he will perceive it as pleasant or as unpleasant; the prospect of being murdered is unpleasant for everyone, whether he considers the action to be causally determined or uncaused.

Similarly our liking or dislike for the character of a human being will persist even if we regard it as the result of causes. To say that I find someone agreeable means that I am drawn to him; I like him. Of a landscape, too, one says that it is agreeable, and, just as this liking cannot be diminished even if we consider the trees, meadows, and hills to be the result of causes, *so* our liking for the character of a human being is not diminished if we regard it *sub specie necessitatis.* Hence to the Bogo who has come to see that murder is causally determined it is still agreeable or disagreeable. Usually he will consider it to be agreeable. He will say that it warms the cockles of his heart to observe such an action; it accords with his wild temperament, as yet untouched by civilization. Therefore he will, in view of the necessity, suspend only the specifically moral practice of regarding it as meritorious. But his liking may become love, and even esteem and reverence. It will be objected, however, that "I revere a mode of behavior" entails "I consider it meritorious for a person to behave in that way," and similarly for esteem. To be sure, the words "reverence" and "esteem" *frequently* have this meaning, and to *the extent that they do* a determinist would cease using them. But all words that denote human feelings have not only one, but several meanings. They have, if I may express it in that way, a harem of meanings, and they couple now with this one, now with that one. So, if I "revere" someone, it means also that I esteem him, that he impresses me, and that I wish to be like him. . . Reverence and esteem in *this* sense can coexist with determinism.

Hence the Bogo who conceives of the intention to practice cruelty and the act of murder as effects can nevertheless consider them to be agreeable or disagreeable, and in a certain sense he can also have esteem and reverence for them, but he will not regard them as meritorious.

Let us now consider the act of murder at high levels of civilization. Civilization, as it progressed, stigmatized murder and threatened penalties for it on earth and in heaven. This censure already penetrates the consciousness of the child as a secondary meaning of the word "murder" and afterward is confirmed through every impression. All the people whom one knows, all the books that one reads, the state with its institutions, pulpit and stage always use "murder" in a censorious sense. That is how it comes to be that we involuntarily declare an act of murder to be blameworthy, be it that others or that we ourselves, driven by passion, committed it. Whether the action was determined by causes or uncaused—that question is raised neither by the person who acted nor by the uninvolved observers. But if it is raised, if someone considers the act of murder *sub specie necessitatis,* then he ceases to regard it as blameworthy. He will then no longer want to see punishment in the proper sense—suffering as retribution—meted out for it, but merely punishment as a safety measure.[3] The feelings of liking and dislike, however, will continue to exist even then. On the whole, someone raised at a high level of civilization will have a feeling of dislike for acts of murder; he will not feel drawn to whoever commits it; he will not like him. For such an act does not accord with his temperament, which was formed as he was engaged in non-violent occupations. In spite of the recognition that the action was necessary, this dislike can at times grow to revulsion, and even to contempt—given that the latter notion is stripped of the specifically moral elements that it contains (the attribution of blame). It will then mean something like this: I do not want to be like that person.

The situation is the same in the case of benevolent actions and those performed out of a sense of duty; we cease to regard them as meritorious if we consider them to be effects. Let us look more closely at actions performed out of a sense of duty. To say that someone acts out of a sense of duty means that he performs an action, perhaps contrary to his inclinations, because his conscience commands him to do it. But how does conscience come to issue such commandments? As follows: with some actions (and intentions) there is linked for us from early childhood on a categorical "thou shalt do (or have) them"; for example, "you *should* help everyone as much as possible." If someone then makes this habitual judgment into the guiding principle of his behavior, if he helps a person because his conscience commands "thou *shalt* help thy fellow man," then he is acting "out of a sense of duty" . . . If we want to consider such an action from the point of view of eternity and necessity, we shall have to proceed as follows : we investigate (1) the constitution of the child who receives the teaching "thou shalt help," (2) the constitution of those who give it to him. The child absorbing this doctrine has some inborn constitution of nerves, of blood, of imagination, and of reason. The commandment "thou shalt help" is impressed upon this substance with some degree of insistence; the deity, heaven, hell, approval of his fellow men and of his own conscience these ideas are presented to him, depending upon his teachers, as being more or less majestic and inspiring. And the child transforms them with greater or lesser intensity, depending upon his receptivity. The ultimate constitution of a man, the preponderance within him of the sense of duty over his own desires, is in any case a necessary result, a product of his inborn constitution and the impressions received. To someone who contemplates this, such a temperament may, to be sure, still seem agreeable (perhaps because he himself is or would like to be similarly constituted), but no one can regard as *meritorious* behavior that he conceives to be an *effect.*

But what if we ourselves are the person who acted? Then the circumstances are analogous; then, too, liking and dislike remain, while the attribution of merit or blame (the "pangs of conscience") disappears.

Our own action, too, can remain agreeable or become disagreeable for us after it has occurred. It is agreeable if the disposition from which we acted persists after the action; it will become disagreeable if we change our frame of mind. Suppose, for example, that we have acted vengefully and are still in the same mood; then the act of revenge is still agreeable, whether we conceive it to be an effect or not. If, however, a feeling of pity takes the place of our desire for revenge, then we come to dislike our action; we cannot stand our earlier self—the less so, the more pronounced our feeling of pity is. The reflection that the action is an effect in no way affects this feeling of dislike, perhaps of disgust, or even of revulsion for ourselves. We say to ourselves that the desire for revenge was, to be sure, necessarily stronger than the ideas and impressions that stood in its way, hence the action took place necessarily, too; but now it happens that pity is necessarily present, and, along with it, regrets that we acted as we did. . . .

6. Can We Abandon Judgements of Moral Responsibility?

But is it really possible to shake off feelings of guilt so easily? Do they disappear, like a spook, when the magic word *effect* is pronounced? Is the situation with respect to this feeling not quite like that with regard to dislike? It was, to be sure, necessary that I took revenge, but now I necessarily feel dislike for my own action, along with guilt. I can no more prevent the onset of the one feeling than of the other. But if the feeling of guilt asserts itself in spite of the recognition that actions are effects, should we not suspect that our holding others responsible, too, will persist in spite of this insight? Did we commit an error somewhere? Is it that responsibility and necessity do not exclude each other? The situation is as follows. The reason why we assign moral praise to some actions and moral censure to others has already been mentioned repeatedly. Censure already penetrates the consciousness of the child as a secondary meaning of the words "murder," "theft," "vengefulness," and "pleasure in another's pain," and praise as a secondary meaning of the words "benevolence" and "mercy." That is why censure seems to him to be a constituent part of murder, and praise, of benevolence. At a later point in his life, perhaps in his twentieth year, the insight comes to him from somewhere that all actions are effects and therefore cannot earn merit or blame. What can this poor little insight accomplish against the accumulated habits of a lifetime of judging? The habit of mind of assigning blame for actions like murder makes it very difficult to think of them without this judgment. It is all very well for reason to tell us that we may not assign blame for such actions, since they are effects of our habit of judging, which has become a feeling, will see to it that it is done anyway. But—let habit confront habit! Suppose that, whenever someone involuntarily wants to assign blame or merit for an action, he ascends to the point of view of eternity and necessity. He then regards the action as the necessary result of [a chain of events stretching back into] the infinite past. Through that way of looking at things the *instinctive* association between the action and the judgement will be severed, if not the first time, then perhaps by the thousandth. Such a man will shed the habit of assigning blame or merit for any action whatsoever.

In fact, of course, human beings almost never behave like that; this way of looking at things is completely foreign to them. Furthermore, human beings determine their actions by considering whether they will make them happy or unhappy; but shedding the habit of making judgments of moral responsibility] would hardly increase their happiness . . .

The situation with respect to a person's character is no different from that with respect to his individual actions. *Customarily* one assigns blame or merit, whether to himself or to others, for a single action: a single act of cheating or of giving offense. But *sometimes* we go back from the action to its source, to a person's character. In reality, of course, character, in its broadest as well as its smallest traits, is just as necessary as an individual action; it is the product of [a chain of events stretching back into] the infinite past, be it that it was inherited in its entirety or that it was formed in part during the individual's lifetime. But with regard to character, too, hardly anyone adopts this point of view. Just as in the case of particular actions, character is regarded neither as free nor as necessary; that is to say, people do not raise the question at all whether the law of causality is applicable also to actions and character. Hence one assigns blame and merit for character as for actions, though they are effects; for one does not see that they are effects. If one sees this, if one regards character *sub specie necessitatis,* then he ceases to assign blame or merit for it. Liking and dislike, on the other hand, nevertheless persist even then: a character closely related to mine will garner my liking, my love, and perhaps even, in the sense mentioned above, my esteem and reverence—whether I conceive of it as an effect or not.

Hence we assign blame or merit for character and actions out of the habit of judging, without concerning ourselves with the question whether they are causally determined or not. We cease to assign blame or merit for character and actions as soon as we recognize that they are causally determined (if we ignore the remnants of our habits).

Let us recapitulate: the character, the intentions, and the actions of every human being are effects, and it is impossible to assign blame or merit for effects.

NOTES:

1.The German here is *Raubmord,* a compound noun denoting a combination of murder and robbery (with overtones of pillage and rape). In his discussion Ree will focus now on the one aspect, now on the other. To avoid lengthy periphrasis in English, the action in question has been uniformly termed murder. The Bogos to whom Ree refers in the next sentence are a tribe occupying a district in the highlands north of Abyssinia. Werner Munzinger (1832-1875) was a Swiss explorer and linguist who spent many years in Eritrea, Abyssinia, and the Sudan. He described the customs of the Bogos in his book *Uber die Sitten und das Recht der Bogos,* published in 1859.

2. An investigation as detailed as that is, of course, never possible in practice.

3. Punishments are causes that prevent the repetition of the action punished.

FREEDOM AND NECESSITY

A. J. Ayer

When I am said to have done something of my own free will it is implied that I could have acted otherwise; and it is only when it is believed that I could have acted otherwise that I am held to be morally responsible for what I have done. For a man is not thought to be morally responsible for an action that it was not in his power to avoid. But if human behavior is entirely governed by causal laws, it is not clear how any action that is done could ever have been avoided. It may be said of the agent that he would have acted otherwise if the causes of his action had been different, but they being what they were, it seems to follow that he was bound to act as he did. Now it is commonly assumed both that men are capable of acting freely, in the sense that is required to make them morally responsible, and that human behavior is entirely governed by causal laws: and it is the apparent conflict between these two assumptions that gives rise to the philosophical problem of the freedom of the will.

Confronted with this problem, many people will be inclined to agree with Dr. Johnson: 'Sir, we *know* our will is free, and *there's* an end on't.' But, while this does very well for those who accept Dr. Johnson's premiss, it would hardly convince anyone who denied the freedom of the will. Certainly, if we do know that our wills are free, it follows that they are so. But the logical reply to this might be that since our wills are not free, it follows that no one can know that they are: so that if anyone claims, like Dr. Johnson, to know that they are, he must be mistaken. What is evident, indeed, is that people often believe themselves to be acting freely; and it is to this 'feeling' of freedom that some philosophers appeal when they wish, in the supposed interests of morality, to prove that not all human action is causally determined. But if these philosophers are right in their assumption that a man cannot be acting freely if his action is causally determined, then the fact that someone feels free to do, or not to do, a certain action does not prove that he really is so. It may prove that the agent does not himself know what it is that makes him act in one way rather than another: but from the fact the a man is unaware of the causes of his action, it does not follow that no such causes exist.

So much may be allowed to the determinist; but his belief that all human actions are subservient to causal laws still remains to be justified. If, indeed, it is necessary that every event should have a cause, then the rule must apply to human behavior as much as to anything else. But why should it be supposed that every event must have a cause The contrary is not unthinkable. Nor is the law of universal causation a necessary presupposition of scientific thought. The scientist may try to discover causal laws, and in many cases he succeeds; but sometimes he has to be content with statistical laws, and sometimes he comes upon events which, in the present state of his knowledge, he is not able to subsume under any law at all. In the case of these events he assumes that if he knew more he would he able to discover some law, whether causal or statistical, which would enable him to account for them. And this assumption cannot be disproved. For however far he may have carried his investigation, it is always open to him to carry it further; and it is always conceivable that if he called it further he would discover the connection which had hitherto escaped him. Nevertheless, it is also conceivable that the events with which he is concerned are not systematically connected with any others: so that the reason why he does not discover the sort of laws that he requires is simply that they do not obtain.

Now in the case of human conduct the search for explanations has not in fact been altogether fruitless. Certain scientific laws have been established; and with the help of these laws we do make a number of successful predictions about the ways in which different people will behave. But these predictions do not always cover every detail We may be able to predict that in certain circumstances a particular man will be angry, without being able to prescribe the precise form that the expression of his anger will take. We may be reasonably sure that he will shout, but not sure how loud his shout will be, or exactly what words he will use. And it is only a small proportion of human actions that we are able to forecast even so precisely as this. But that, it may be said, is because we have not carried our investigations very far. The science of psychology is still in its infancy and, as it is developed, not only will more human actions be explained, but the explanations will go into greater detail. The ideal of complete explanation may never in fact be attained: but it is theoretically attainable. Well, this may be so: and certainly it is impossible to show *a priori* that it is not so: but equally it cannot be shown that it is. This will not, however, discourage the scientist who, in the field of human behavior, as elsewhere, will continue to formulate theories and test them by the facts. And in this he is justified. For since he has no reason *a priori* to admit that there is a limit to what he can discover, the fact that he also cannot be sure that there is no limit does not make it unreasonable for him to devise theories, nor, having devised them, to try constantly to improve them.

But now suppose it to be claimed that, so far as men's actions are concerned, there is a limit: and that this limit is set by the fact of human freedom. An obvious objection is that in many cases in which a person feels himself be free to do, or not to do, a certain action, we are even now able to explain, in causal terms, why it is that he acts as he does. But it might be argued that even if men are sometimes mistaken in believing that they act freely, it does not follow that they are always so mistaken. For it is not always the case that when a man believes that he has acted freely we are in fact able to account for his action in causal terms. A determinist would say that we should be able to account for it if we had more knowledge of the circumstances, and had been able to discover the appropriate natural laws. But until those discoveries have been made, this remains only a pious hope. And may it not be true that, in some cases at least, the reason why we can give no causal explanation is that no causal explanation is available; and that this is because the agent's choice was literally free, as he himself felt it to be?

The answer is that this may indeed be true, inasmuch as it is open to anyone to hold that no explanation is possible until some explanation is actually found. But even so it does not give the moralist what he wants. For he is anxious to show that men are capable of acting freely in order to infer that they can be morally responsible for what they do. But if it is a matter of pure chance that a man should act in one way rather than another, he may be free but he can hardly be responsible. And indeed when a man's actions seem to us quite unpredictable, when, as we say, there is no knowing what he will do, we do not look upon him as a moral agent. We look upon him rather as a lunatic.

To this it may be objected that we are not dealing fairly with the moralist. For when he makes it a condition of my being morally responsible that I should act freely, he does not wish to imply that it is purely a matter of chance that I act as I do. What he wishes to imply is that my actions are the result of my own free choice: and it is because they are the result of my own free choice that I am held to be morally responsible for them.

But now we must ask how it is that I come to make my choice. Either it is an accident that I choose to act as I do or it is not. If it is an accident, then it is merely a matter of chance that I did not choose otherwise; and if it is merely a matter of chance that I did not choose otherwise, it is surely irrational to hold me morally responsible for choosing as I did. But if it is not an accident that I choose to do one thing rather than another, then presumably there is some causal explanation of my choice: and in that case we are led back to determinism.

Again, the objection may be raised that we are not doing justice to the moralist's case. His view is not that it is a matter of chance that I choose to act as I do, but rather that my choice depends upon my character. Nevertheless he holds that I can still be free in the sense that he requires; for it is I who am responsible for my character. But in what way am I responsible for my character? Only, surely, in the sense that there is a causal connection between what I do now and what I have done in the past. It is only this that justifies the statement that I have made myself what I am: and even so this is an over-simplification, since it takes no account of the external influences to which I have been subjected. But, ignoring the external influences, let us assume that it is in fact the case that I have made myself what I am. Then it is still legitimate to ask how it is that I have come to make myself one sort of person rather than another. And if it be answered that it is a matter of my strength of will, we can put the same question in another form by asking how it is that my will has the strength that it has and not some other degree of strength. Once more, either it is an accident or it is not. If it is an accident, then by the same argument as before, I am not morally responsible, and if it is not an accident we are led back to determinism.

Furthermore, to say that my actions proceed from my character or, more colloquially, that I act in character, is to say that my behavior is consistent and to that extent predictable: and since it is, above all, for the actions that I perform in character that I am held to be morally responsible, it looks as if the admission of moral responsibility, so far from being incompatible with determinism, tends rather to presuppose it. But how can this be so if it is a necessary condition of moral responsibility that the person who is held responsible should have acted freely? It seems that if we are to retain this idea of moral responsibility, we must either show that men can be held responsible for actions which they do not do freely, or else find some way of reconciling determinism with the freedom of the will.

It is no doubt with the object of effecting this reconciliation that some philosophers have defined freedom as the consciousness of necessity and by so doing they are able to say not only that a man can be acting freely when his action is causally determined, but even that his action must he causally determined for it to be possible for him to be acting freely. Nevertheless this definition has the serious disadvantage that it gives to the word 'freedom' a meaning quite different from any that it ordinarily bears. It is indeed obvious that if we are allowed to give the word 'freedom' any meaning that we please, we can find a meaning that will reconcile it with determinism: but this is no more a solution of our present problem than the fact that the word 'horse' could be arbitrarily used to mean what is ordinarily meant by sparrow is a proof that horses have wings. For suppose that I am compelled by another person to do something 'against my will'. In that case, as the word freedom is ordinarily used, I should not be said to the acting freely: and the fact that I am fully aware of the constraint to which I am subjected makes no difference to the matter. I do not become free by becoming conscious that I am not. It may, indeed, be possible to show that my being aware that my action is causally determined is

3 Cont

not incompatible with my acting freely: but it by no means follows that it is in this that my freedom consists. Moreover, I suspect that one of the reasons why people are inclined to define freedom as the consciousness of necessity is that they think that if one is conscious of necessity one may somehow be able to master it. But this is a fallacy. It is like someone's saying that he wishes he could see into the future, because if he did he would know what calamities lay in wait for him and so would be able to avoid them. But if he avoids the calamities then they don't lie in the future and it is not true that he foresees them. And similarity if I am able to master necessity, in the sense of escaping the operation of a necessary law, then the law in question is not necessary. And if the law is not necessary, then neither my freedom nor anything else can consist in my knowing that it is.

Let it be granted, then, that when we speak of reconciling freedom with determinism we are using the word 'freedom' in an ordinary sense. It still remains for us to make this usage clear: and perhaps the best way to make it clear is to show what it is that freedom, in this sense, is contrasted with. Now we began with the assumption that freedom is contrasted with causality: so that a man cannot be said to be acting freely if his action is causally determined. But this assumption has led us into difficulties and I now wish to suggest that it is mistaken. For it is not, I think, causality that freedom is to be contrasted with, but constraint. And while it is true that being constrained to do an action entails being caused to do it, I shall try to show that the converse does not hold. I shall try to show that from the fact that my action is causally determined it does not necessarily follow that I am constrained to do it and this is equivalent to saying that it does not necessarily follow that I am not free.

4 If I am constrained, I do not act freely. But in what circumstance can I legitimately be said to be constrained? An obvious instance is the case in which I am compelled by another person to do what he wants. In a case of this sort the compulsion need not be such as to deprive one of the power of choice. It is not required that the other person should have hypnotized me, or that he should make it physically impossible for me to go against his will. It is enough that he should induce me to do what he wants by making it clear to me that, if I do not, he will bring about some situation that I regard as even more undesirable than the consequence of the action that he wishes me to do. Thus, if the man points a pistol at my head I may still choose to disobey him: but this does not prevent its being true that if I do fall in with his wishes he can legitimately be said to have compelled me. And if the circumstances are such that no reasonable person would be expected to choose the other alternative, then the action that I am made to do is not one for which I am held to be morally responsible.

A similar but somewhat different case is that in which another person has obtained a habitual ascendancy over me. Where this is so, there may be no question of my being induced to act as the other person wishes by being confronted with a still more disagreeable alternative: for if I am sufficiently under his influence this special stimulus will not be necessary. Nevertheless I do not act freely, for the reason that I have been deprived of the power of choice. And this means that I have acquired so strong a habit of obedience that I no longer go through any process of deciding whether or not to do what the other person wants. About other matters I may still deliberate; but as regards the fulfilment of this other person's wishes, my own deliberations have ceased to be a causal factor in my behaviour. And it is in this sense that I may be said to be constrained. It is not, however, necessary that such constraint should take the form of subservience to another person. A kleptomaniac is not a free agent, in respect of his stealing, because he does not go through any process of deciding whether or not to steal. Or rather, if he does go through such a process, it is irrelevant to his behavior. Whatever he resolved to do, he would steal all the same. And it is this that distinguishes him from the ordinary thief.

But now it may be asked whether there is any essential difference between these cases and those in which the agent is commonly thought to be free. No doubt the ordinary thief does go through a process of deciding whether or not to steal, and no doubt it does affect his behavior. If he resolved to refrain from stealing, he could carry his resolution out. But if it be allowed that his making or not making this resolution is causally determined, then how can he be any more free than the kleptomaniac? It may be true that unlike the kleptomaniac he could refrain from stealing if he chose: but if there is a cause, or set of causes, which necessitate his choosing as he does, how can he be said to have the power of choice ? Again, it may be true that no one now compels me to get up and walk across the room: but if my doing so can be causally explained in terms of my history or my environment, or whatever it may be, then how am I any more free than if some other person had compelled me? I do not have the feeling of constraint that I have when a pistol is manifestly pointed at my head; but the chains of causation by which I am bound are no less effective for being invisible.

The answer to this is that the cases I have mentioned as examples of constraint do differ from the others: and they differ just in the ways that I have tried to bring out. If I suffered from a compulsion neurosis, so that I got up and walked across the room, whether I wanted to or not, or if I did so because somebody else compelled me, then I should not be acting freely. But if I do it now, I shall be acting freely, just because these conditions do not obtain; and the fact that my action may nevertheless have a cause is, from this point of view, irrelevant. For it is not when my action has any cause at all, but only when it has a special sort of cause, that it is reckoned not to be free.

But here it may be objected that, even if this distinction corresponds to ordinary usage, it is still very irrational. For why should we distinguish, with regard to a person's freedom, between the operations of one sort of cause and those of another? Do not all causes equally necessitate? And is it not therefore arbitrary to say that a person is free when he is necessitated in one fashion but not when he is necessitated in another?

That all causes equally necessitate is indeed a tautology, if the word 'necessitate' is taken merely as equivalent to 'cause:' but if, as the objection requires, it is taken as equivalent to constrain or compel, then I do not think that this proposition is true. For all that is needed for one eventually to be the cause of another is that, in the given circumstances, the event which is said to be the effect would not have occurred if it had not been for the occurrence of the event which is said to be the cause, or *vice versa*, according as causes are interpreted as necessary, or sufficient, conditions: and this fact is usually deducible from some causal law which states that whenever an event of the one kind occurs then, given suitable conditions, an event of the other kind will occur in a certain temporal or spatio-temporal relationship to it. In short, there is an invariable concomitance between the two classes of events; but there is no compulsion, in any but a metaphorical sense. Suppose, for example, that a psycho-analyst is able to account for some aspect of my behavior by referring it to some lesion that I suffered in my childhood. In that case, it may be said that my childhood experience, together with certain other events, necessitates my behaving as I do. But all that this involves is that it is found to be true in general that when people have had certain experiences as children, they subsequently behave in certain specifiable ways; and my case is just another instance of this general law. It is in this way indeed that my behavior is explained. But from the fact that my behavior is capable of being explained, in the sense that it can be subsumed under some natural law, it does not follow that I am acting under constraint.

If this is correct, to say that I could have acted otherwise is to say, first, that I should have acted otherwise if I had so chosen; secondly, that my action was voluntary in the sense in which the actions, say, of the kleptomaniac are not; and thirdly, that nobody compelled me to choose as I did: and these three conditions may very well be fulfilled. When they are fulfilled, I may be said to have acted freely. But this is not to say that it was a matter of chance that I acted as I did, or, in other words, that my action could not be explained. And that my actions should be capable of being explained is all that is required by the postulate of determinism.

If more than this seems to be required it is, I think, because the use of the very word determinism is in some degree misleading. For it tends to suggest that one event is somehow in the power of another, whereas the truth is merely that they are actually correlated. And the same applies to the use, in this context, of the word 'necessity' and even of the the word cause' itself. Moreover, there are various reasons for this. One is the tendency to confuse causal with logical necessitation, and so to infer mistakenly that the effect is contained in the cause. Another is the uncritical use of a concept of force which is derived from primitive experiences of pushing and striking. A third is the survival of an animistic conception of causality, in which all causal relationships are modelled on the example of one person's exercising authority over another. As a result we tend to form an imaginative picture of an unhappy effect trying vainly to escape from the clutches of an overmastering cause. But, I repeat, the fact is simply that when an event of one type occurs, an event of another type occurs also, in a certain temporal or spatio-temporal relation to the first. The rest is only metaphor. And it is because of the metaphor, and not because of the fact, that we come to think that there is an antithesis between causality and freedom.

Nevertheless, it may be said, if the postulate of determinism is valid, then the future can be explained in terms of the past: and this means that if one knew enough about the past one would be able to predict the future. But in that case what will happen in the future is already decided. And how then can I be said to be free? What is going to happen is going to happen and nothing that I do can prevent it. If the determinist is right, I am the helpless prisoner of fate.

But what is meant by saying that the future course of events is already decided? If the implication is that some person has arranged it, then the proposition is false. But if all that is meant is that it is possible, in principle, to deduce it from a set of particular facts about the past, together with the appropriate general laws, then, even if this is true, it does not in the least entail that I am the helpless prisoner of fate. It does not even entail that my actions make no difference to the future: for they are causes as well as effects, so that if they were different their consequences would be different also. What it does entail is that my behavior can be predicted: but to say that my behavior can be predicted is not to say that I am acting under constraint. It is indeed true that I cannot escape my destiny if this is taken to mean no more than that I shall do what I shall do. But this is a tautology, just as it is a tautology that what is going to happen is going to happen and such tautologies as these prove nothing whatsoever about the freedom of the will.

HUMAN FREEDOM AND THE SELF

Roderick M. Chisholm
Brown University

'A staff moves a stone, and is moved by a hand, which is moved by a man.'
Aristotle, *Physics*, 256a.

1. The metaphysical problem of human freedom might be summarized in the following way: Human beings are responsible agents; but this fact appears to conflict with a deterministic view of human action (the view that every event that is involved in an act is caused by some other event); and it also appears to conflict with an indeterministic view of human action (the view that the act, or some event that is essential to the act, is not caused at all.) To solve the problem, I believe, we must make somewhat far-reaching assumptions about the self or the agent--about the man who performs the act.

Perhaps it is needless to remark that, in all likelihood, it is impossible to say anything significant about this ancient problem that has not been said before.[1]

2. Let us consider some deed, or misdeed, that may be attributed to a responsible agent: one man, say, shot another. If the man was responsible for what he did, then, I would urge, what was to happen at the time of the shooting was something that was entirely up to the man himself. There was a moment at which it was true, both that he could have fired the shot and also that he could have refrained from firing it. And if this is so, then, even though he did fire it, he could have done something else instead. (He didn't find himself firing the shot "against his will", as we say.) I think we can say, more generally, then, that if a man is responsible for a certain event or a certain state of affairs (in our example, the shooting of another man), then that event or state of affairs was brought about by some act of his, and the act was something that was in his power either to perform or not to perform.

But now if the act which he *did* perform was an act that was also in his power *not* to perform, then it could not have been caused or determined by any event that was not itself within his power either to bring about or not to bring about. For example, if what we say he did was really something that was brought about by a second man, one who forced his hand upon the trigger, say, or who, by means of hypnosis, compelled him to perform the act, then since the act was caused by the *second* man it was nothing that was within the power of the *first* man to prevent. And precisely the same thing is true, I think, if instead of referring to a second man who compelled the first one, we speak instead of the *desires* and *beliefs* which the first man happens to have had. For if what we say he did was really something that was brought about by his own beliefs and desires, if these beliefs and desires in the particular situation in which he happened to have found himself caused him to do just what it was that we say he did do, then, since *they* caused it, *he* was unable to do anything other than just what it was that he did do.It makes no difference whether the cause of the deed was internal or external; if the cause was some state or event for which the man himself was mistakenly calling his act. If a flood caused the poorly constructed dam to break, then, given the flood and the constitution of the dam, the break, we may say, *had* to occur and nothing could have happened in its place. And if the flood of desire caused the weak-willed man to give in, then he, too, had to do just what it was that he did do and he was no more responsible than was the dam for the results that followed. (It is true, of curse, that if the man is responsible for the beliefs and desires that he happens to have, then he may also be responsible for the things they lead him to do. But the question now becomes: *is* he responsible for the beliefs and desires he happens to have? If he is, then there was a time when they were within his power either to acquire or not to acquire and we are left, therefore, with our general point.)

One may object: But surely if there were such a thing as a man who is really *good*, then he would be responsible for things that he would do; yet, he would be unable to do anything other than just what it is that he does do, since, being good, he will always choose to do what is best. The answer, I think, is suggested by a comment that Thomas Reid makes upon an ancient author. The author had said of Cato,"He was good because he could not be otherwise", and Reid observes: "This saying, if understood literally and strictly, is not the praise of Cato, but of his constitution, which was no more the work of Cato than his existence".[2] If Cato was himself responsible for the good things that he did, then Cato, as Reid suggests, was such that, although he had the power to do what was not good, he exercised his power only for that which was good.

All of this, if it is true, may give a certain amount of comfort to those who are tender-minded. But we should remind them that it also conflicts with a familiar view about the nature of God—with the view that St.Thomas Aquinas expresses by saying that 'every movement both of the will and of nature proceeds from God as the Prime Mover'.[3] If the act of the sinner *did* proceed from God as the Prime Mover, then God was in the position of the second agent we just discussed—the man who forced the trigger finger, or the hypnotist—and the sinner, so-called, was *not* responsible for what he did. (This may be a bold assertion, in view of the history of western theology, but I must say that I have never encountered a single good reason for denying it.)

There is one standard objection to all of this and we should consider it briefly.

3. The objection takes the form of a stratagem—one designed to show that determinism (and divine providence) is consistent with human responsibility. The stratagem is one that was used by Jonathan Edwards and by many philosophers in the present century, most notably, G.E. Moore. [4]

One proceeds as follows. The expression

(a) He could have done otherwise,

it is argued, means no more nor less than

(b) If he had chosen to do otherwise, then he would have done otherwise.

(In place of 'chosen', one might say 'tried', 'set out', 'decided', 'undertaken', or 'willed'.) The truth of statement (b), it is then pointed out, is consistent with determinism (and with divine providence), for even if all of the man's actions were causally determined, the man could still be such that, *if* he had chosen otherwise, then he would have done otherwise. What the murderers saw, let us suppose, along with his beliefs and desires, *caused* him to fire the shot, yet he was such that *if,* just then, he had chosen or decided *not* to fire the shot, then he would not have fired it. All of this is certainly possible. Similarly, we could say, of the dam, that the flood caused it to break and also that the dam was such that, *if* there had been no flood or any similar pressure, then the dam would have remained intact. And therefore, the argument proceeds, if (b) is consistent with determinism, and if (a) and (b) say the same thing, then (a) is also consistent with determinism; hence we can say that the agent *could* have done otherwise even though he was caused to do what he did do, and therefore determinism and moral responsibility are compatible.

Is the argument sound? The conclusion follows from the premises, but the catch, I think, lies in the first premiss, the one saying that statement (a) tells us no more nor less than what statement (b) tells us. For (b), it would seem, could be true while (a) is false. That is to say, our man might be such that, if he had chosen to do otherwise, then he would have done otherwise, and yet *also* such that he could not have done otherwise. Suppose, after all that our murderer could not have *chosen,* or could not have *decided*, to do otherwise. Then the fact that he happens also to be a man such that, if he had chosen not to shoot he would not have shot, would make no difference. For if he could *not* have chosen *not* to shoot, then he could not have done anything other than just what it was that he did do. In a word: from our statement (b) above ('If he had chosen to do otherwise, then he would have done otherwise'), we cannot make an inference to (a) above ('He could have done otherwise') unless we can *also* assert:

(c) He could have chosen to do otherwise.

And therefore, if we must reject this third statement (c), then, even though we may be justified in asserting (b), we are not justified in asserting (a). If the man could not have chosen to do otherwise, then he could not have done otherwise—*even if* he was such that, if he *had* chosen to do otherwise, then he would have done otherwise.

The stratagem in question, then, seems to me not to work, and I would say, therefore, that the ascription of responsibility conflicts with a deterministic view of action.

4. Perhaps there is less need to argue that the ascription of responsibility also conflicts with an indeterministic view of action—with the view that the act, or some event that is essential to the act, is not caused at all. If the act—the firing of the shot—was not caused at all, if it was fortuitous or capricious, happening so to speak out of the blue, then, presumably, no one—and nothing—was responsible for the act. Our conception of action, therefore, should be neither deterministic nor indeterministic. Is there any other possibility?

5. We must not say that every event involved in the act is caused by some other event; and we must not say that the act is something that is not caused at all. The possibility that remains, therefore, is this: We should say that at least one of the events that are involved in the act is caused, not by any other events, but by something else instead. And this something else can only be the agent—the man. If there is an event that is caused, not by other events, but by the man, then there are some events involved in the act that are not caused by other events. But if the event in question is caused by the man then it *is* caused and we are not committed to saying that there is something involved in the act that is not caused at all.

But this, of course, is a large consequence, implying something of considerable importance about the nature of the agent or the man.

6. If we consider only inanimate natural objects, we may say that causation, if it occurs, is a relation between *events* or *states of affairs*. The dam's breaking was an event that was caused by a set of other events--the dam being weak, the flood being strong, and so on. But if a man is responsible for a particular deed, then, if what I have said is true, there is some event, or set of events, that is caused, *not* by other events or states of affairs, but by the agent, whatever he may be.

I shall borrow a pair of medieval terms, using them, perhaps, in a way that is slightly different from that for which they were originally intended. I shall say that when one event or state of affairs (or set of events or states of affairs) causes some other event or state of affairs, then we have an instance of *transeunt* causation. And I shall say that when an *agent*, as distinguished from an event, causes an event or state of affairs, then we have an instance of *immanent* causation.

The nature of what is intended by the expression 'immanent causation' may be illustrated by this sentence from Aristotle's *Physics*: 'Thus, a staff moves a stone, and is moved by a hand, which is moved by a man.'(VII, 5, 256a, 6-8) If the man was responsible, then we have in this illustration a number of instances of causation—most of them transeunt but at least one of them immanent. What the staff did to the stone was an instance of transeunt causation, and thus we may describe it as a relation between events: 'the motion of the staff caused the motion of the stone.' And similarly for what the hand did to the staff:'the motion of the hand caused the motion of the staff'. And, as we know from physiology, there are still other events which caused the motion of the hand. Hence we need not introduce the agent at this particular point, as Aristotle does—we *need* not, though we *may*. We *may* say that the hand was moved by the man, but we may *also* say that the motion of the hand was caused by the motion of certain muscles; and we may say that the motion of the muscles was caused by certain events that took place within the brain. But some event, and presumably one of those that took place within the brain, was caused by the agent and not by any other events.

There are, of course, objections to this way of putting the matter; I shall consider the two that seem to me to be most important.

7. One may object, firstly: 'If the *man* does anything, then as Aristotle's remark suggests, what he does is to move the *hand*. But he certainly does not *do* anything to his brain—he may not even know that he *has* a brain. and if he doesn't do anything to the brain and if the motion of the hand was caused by something that happened within the brain, then there is no point in appealing to "immanent causation" as being something incompatible with "transeunt causation" for the whole thing, after all, is a matter of causal relations among events or states of affairs.'

The answer to this objection, I think, is this: It is true that the agent does not *do* anything with his brain, or to his brain, in the sense in which he *does* something with his hand and does something to the staff. But from this it does not follow that the agent was not the immanent cause of something that happened within his brain.

We should note a useful distinction that has been proposed by Professor A. I. Melden, namely, the distinction between 'making something A happen' and 'doing A'.[5] If I reach for the staff and pick it up, then one of the things that I do is just that: reach for the staff and pick it up. And if it is something that I do then there is a very clear sense in which it may be said to be something that I know that I do. If you ask me, 'Are you doing something, or trying to do something, with the staff?', I will have no difficulty in finding an answer. But in doing something with the staff, I also make various things happen which are not in this same sense things that I do. I will make various air-particles move, I will free a number of blades of grass from the pressure that had been upon them, and I may cause a shadow to move from one place to another. If these are merely things that I make happen, as distinguished from things that I do, then I may know nothing whatever about them; I may not have the slightest idea that, in moving the staff, I am bringing about any such things as the motion of air-particles, shadows, and blades of grass.

We may say, in answer to the first objection, therefore, that it is true that our agent does nothing to his brain or with his brain; but from this it does not follow that the agent is not the immanent cause of some event within his brain;for the brain event may be something which, like the motion of the air-particles, he made happen in picking up the staff. The only difference between the two cases is this: in each case, he made something happen when he picked up the staff; but in the one case—the motion of the air-particles or of the shadows—it was the motion of the staff that caused the event to happen; and in the other case—the event that took place in the brain—it was this event that caused the motion of the staff.

The point is, in a word, that whenever a man does something A, then (by 'immanent causation') he makes a certain cerebral event happen, and this cerebral event (by 'transeunt causation') makes A happen.

8. The second objection is more difficult and concerns the very concept of 'immanent causation', or causation by an agent, as this concept is to be interpreted here. The concept is subject to a difficulty which has long been associated with that of the prime mover unmoved. We have said that there must be some event A, presumably some cerebral event, which is caused not by any other event, but by the agent. Since A was not caused by any other event, then the agent himself cannot be said to have undergone any change or produced any other event (such as 'an act of will' or the like) which brought A about. But if, when the agent made A happen, there was no event involved other than A itself, no event which could be described as *making* A happen, what did the agent's causation consist of? What, for example, is the difference between A's just happening, and the agents' *causing* A to happen? We cannot attribute the difference to any event that took place within the agent. And so far as the event A itself is concerned, there would seem to be no discernible difference. Thus Aristotle said that the activity of the prime mover is nothing in addition to the motion that it produces, and Suarez said that 'the action is in reality nothing but the effect as it flows from the agent.' [6] Must we conclude, then, that there is no more to the man's action in causing event A than there is to the event A's happening by itself? Here we would seem to have a distinction without a difference—in which case we have failed to find a *via media* between a deterministic and an indeterministic view of action.

The only answer, I think, can be this: that the difference between the man's causing A, on the one hand, and the event A just happening, on the other, lies in the fact that, in the first case but not the second, the event A *was* caused and was caused by the man. There was a brain event A; the agent did, in fact, cause the brain event, but there was nothing that he did to cause it.

The answer may not entirely satisfy and it will be likely to provoke the following question: 'But what are you really *adding* to the assertion that A happened when you utter the words, "The agent *caused* A to happen"?' As soon as we have put the question this way, we see,

I think, that whatever difficulty we may have encountered is one that may be traced to the concept of causation generally, whether 'immanent' or 'transeunt'. The problem, in other words, is not a problem that is peculiar to our conception of human action. It is a problem that must be faced by anyone who makes use of the concept of causation at all; and therefore I would say, it is a problem for everyone but the complete indeterminist.

For the problem, as we put it, referring just to 'immanent causation', or causation by an agent, was this: 'What is the difference between saying of an event A, that A just happened and saying that someone caused A to happen?' The analogous problem, which holds for 'transeunt causation', or causation by an event, is this:'What is the difference between saying, of two events A and B, that B happened and then A happened, and saying that B's happening was the *cause* of A's happening?' And the only answer that one can give is this: that in the one case the agent was the cause of A's happening and in the other case event B was the cause of A's happening. The nature of transeunt causation is no more clear than is that of immanent causation.

9. But we may plausibly say—and there is a respectable philosophical tradition to which we may appeal—that the notion of immanent causation, or causation by an agent, is in fact more clear than that of transeunt causation, or causation by an event, and that it is only by understanding our own causal efficacy, as agents, that we can grasp the concept of *cause* at all. Hume may be said to have shown that we do not derive the concept of *cause* from what we perceive of external things. How, then, do we derive it? The most plausible suggestion, it seems to me, is that of Reid, once again: namely that 'the conception of an efficient cause may very probably be derived from the experience we have had. . .of our own power to produce certain effects'. [7] If we did not understand the concept of immanent causation, we would not understand that of transeunt causation.

10. It may have been noted that I have avoided the term 'free will' in all of this. For even if there is such a faculty as 'the will', which somehow sets our acts agoing, the question of freedom, as John Locke said, is not the question '*whether the will be free*'; it is the question '*whether a man be free*'.[8] For if there is a 'will', as a moving faculty, the question is whether the man is free to will to do these things that he does will to do—and also whether he is free *not* to will any of those things that he does will to do, and again, whether he is free to will any of those things that he does not will to do. Jonathan Edwards tried to restrict himself to the question—'Is the man free to do what it is that he wills?'—but the answer to this question will not tell us whether the man is responsible for what it is that he *does* will to do. Using still another pair of medieval terms, we may say that the metaphysical problem of freedom does not concern the *actus imperatus;* it does not concern the question whether we are free to accomplish whatever it is that we will or set out to do; it concerns the *actus elicitus,* the question whether we are free to will or to set out to do those things that we do will or set out to do.

11. If we are responsible, and if what I have been trying to say is true, then we have a prerogative which some would attribute only to God: each of us, when we act is a prime mover unmoved. In doing what we do, we cause certain events to happen, and nothing—or no one—causes us to cause those events to happen.

12. If we are thus prime movers unmoved and if our actions, or those for which we are responsible, are not causally determined, then they are not causally determined by our *desires.*

And this means that the relation between what we want or what we desire, on the one hand, and what it is that we do, on the other, is not as simple as most philosophers would have it.

We may distinguish between what we might call the 'Hobbist approach' and what we might call the 'Kantian approach' to this question. The Hobbist approach is the one that is generally accepted at the present time, but the Kantian approach, I believe, is the one that is true. According to Hobbism, if we *know*, of some man, what his beliefs and desires happen to be and how strong they are, if we know what he feels certain of, what he desires more than anything else, and if we know the state of his body and what stimuli he is being subjected to, then we may *deduce*, logically, just what it is that he will do—or, more accurately, just what it is that he will try, set out, or undertake to do. Thus Professor Melden has said that 'the connection between wanting and doing is logical'. [9] But according to the Kantian approach to our problem, and this is the one that I would take, there is no such logical connection between wanting and doing, nor need there even be a causal connection. No set of statements about a man's desires, beliefs, and stimulus situation at any time implies any statement telling us what the man will try, set out, or undertake to do at that time. As Reid put it, though we may 'reason from men's motives to their actions and, in many cases with great probability', we can never do so 'with absolute certainty'.[10]

This means that, in one very strict sense of the terms, there can be no science of man. If we think of science as a matter of finding out what laws happen to hold, and if the statement of a law tells us what kinds of events are caused by what other kinds of events, then there will be human actions which we cannot explain by subsuming them under any laws. We cannot say, 'It is causally necessary that, given such and such desires and beliefs, and being subject to such and such stimuli the agent will do so and so'. For at times the agent, if he chooses, may rise above his desires and do something else instead.

But all of this is consistent with saying that, perhaps more often than not, our desires do exist under conditions such that those conditions necessitate us to act. And we may also say, with Leibniz, that at other times our desires may 'incline without necessitating'.

13. Leibniz's phrase presents us with our final philosophical problem. What does it mean to say that a desire or a motive, might 'incline without necessitating'? There is a temptation, certainly, to say that 'to incline' means to cause and that 'not to necessitate' means not to cause, but obviously we cannot have it both ways.

Nor will Leibniz's own solution do. In his letter to Coste, he puts the problem as follows: 'When a choice is proposed, for example to go out or not to go out, it is a question whether, with all the circumstances, internal and external, motives, perceptions, disposition, impressions, passions, inclinations taken together, I am still in a contingent state, or whether I am necessitated to make the choice, for example, to go out; that is to say, whether this proposition true and determined in fact, *In all these circumstances taken together I shall choose to go out,* is contingent or necessary.'[11] Leibniz's answer might be put as follows: in one sense of the terms 'necessary' and 'contingent' the proposition 'in all these circumstances taken together I shall choose to go out', may be said to be necessary and not contingent. But the sense in which the proposition may be said to be contingent, according to Leibniz, is only this: there is no logical contradiction involved in denying the proposition. And the sense in which it may be said to be necessary is this: since 'nothing ever occurs without cause or determining reason', the proposition is causally necessary. 'Whenever all the circumstances taken together are such that the balance of deliberation is heavier on one side than on the other, it is certain and infallible that that is the side that is going to win out'. But if what we have been saying is true, the proposition 'In all these circumstances taken together I shall choose to go out', may be causally as well as logically contingent. Hence we must find another interpretation for Leibniz's statement that our motives and desires may incline us, or influence us, to choose without thereby necessitating us to choose.

Let us consider a public official who has some moral scruples but who also, as one says, could be had. Because of the scruples that he does have, he would never take any positive steps to receive a bribe—he would not actively solicit one. But his morality has it limits and he is also such that, if we were to confront him with a *fait accompli* or to let him see what is about to happen ($10,000 in cash is being deposited behind the garage), then he would succumb and be unable to resist. The general situation is a familiar one and this is one reason that people pray to be delivered from temptation. (It also justifies Kant's remark: 'And how many there are who may have led a long blameless life, who are only *fortunate* in having escaped so may temptations'.[12] Our relation to the misdeed that we contemplate may not be a matter simply of being able to bring it about or not to bring it about. As St. Anselm noted, there are at least four possibilities. We may illustrate them by reference to our public official and the event which is his receiving the bribe, in the following way: (i) he may be able to bring the event about himself (*facere esse*), in which case he would actively cause himself to receive the bribe; (ii) he may be able to refrain from bringing it about himself (*non facere esse*), in which case he would not himself do anything to insure that he receive the bribe; (iii) he may be able to do something to prevent the event from occurring (*facere non esse*), in which case he would make sure that the $10,000 was not left behind the garage; or (iv) he may be unable to do anything to prevent the event from occurring (*non facere non esse*), in which case, though he may not solicit the bribe, he would allow himself to keep it. [13] We have envisaged our official as a man who can resist the temptation to (i) but cannot resist the temptation to (iv)); he can refrain from bringing the event about himself, but he cannot bring himself to do anything to prevent it.

Let us think of 'inclination without necessitation', then, in such terms as these. First we may contrast the two propositions:

(1) He can resist the temptation to do something in order to make A happen;

(2) He can resist the temptation to allow A to happen (i.e. to do nothing to prevent A from happening).

We may suppose that the man has some desire to have A happen and thus has a motive for making A happen. His motive for making A happen, I suggest, is one that *necessitates* provided that, because of the motive, (1) is false; he cannot resist the temptation to do something in order to make A happen. His motive for making A happen is one that *inclines* provided that, because of the motive, (2) is false; like our public official, he cannot bring himself to do anything to prevent A from happening. and therefore we can say that this motive for making A happen is one that *inclines but does not necessitate* provided that, because of the motive, (1) is true and (2) is false; he can resist the temptation to make it happen but he cannot resist the temptation to allow it to happen.

NOTES:

1. The general position to be presented here is suggested in the following writings, among others: Aristotle: *Eudemian Ethics*, bk ii, ch. 6; *Nicomachean Ethics*, bk. iii, ch. 1-5; Thomas Reid, *Essays on the Active Powers of Man*; C.A. Campbell, 'Is "Free Will" a Pseudo-Problem?' *Mind*, 1951, 441-65; Roderick M. Chisholm, 'Responsibility and Avoidability'; and Richard Taylor, 'Determination and the Theory of Agency', in *Determinism and Freedom in the Age of Modern Science,* ed. Sidney Hook (New York,1958).

2. Thomas Reid, *Essays on the Active Powers of Man,* essay IV, ch. 4 (*Works*, 600)

3. Summa Theologica, First Part of the Second Part, qu VI ('On the Voluntary and Involuntary').

4. Jonathan Edwards, Freedom of the Will (New Haven, 1957); G.E. Moore, Ethics (Home University Library, 1912), ch. 6.

5. A.I. Melden, *Free Action* (London, 1961), especially ch 3. Mr. Melden's own views, however, are quite the contrary of those that are proposed here.

6. Aristotle, *Physics,* bk. III, ch. 3; Suarez, *Disputations Metaphysicae*, Disputation 18, s. 10.

7. Reid, *Works*, 524.

8. *Essay Concerning Human Understanding*, bk. II, ch.21.

9. Melden, 166.

10. Reid, *Works*, 608, 612.

11.'Lettre a Mr. Coste de la Necessite et de la Contingence' (1707) in *Opera Philosophica,* ed. Erdmann, 447-9.

12. In the Preface to the *Metaphysical Elements of Ethics,* in *Kant's Critique of Practical Reason and Other Works on the Theory of Ethics*, ed. I. K. Abbott (London, 1959), 303.

13. Cf. D.P. Henry, 'Saint Anselm's *De "Grammatica"*', *Philosophical Quarterly*, X (1960). 145-6. St Anselm noted that (i) and (iii), respectively, may be thought of as forming the upper left and the upper right corners of a square of opposition, and (ii) and (iv) the lower left and the lower right.

DETERMINISM AND THE CASE OF THE GREAT FALSIFIER

Fred Feldman
University of Massachusetts

Determinists hold that that since every event has a cause, nobody ever could have done otherwise than whatever he or she in fact did. They conclude from this that nobody is ever morally responsible for anything. This view is morally pernicious. It makes people feel that they are fully justified in doing whatever they like. It should be refuted.

Fortunately, it is possible to refute determinism. Indeed, the refutation can be carried out by any reasonable person. All it takes is a few moments' careful thought. In this paper, I refute determinism.

1. **Universal causation and universal predictability.** One of the central tenets of determinism is the view that every event has a cause. When we say that an event has a cause, we imply that there was some other event (or combination of events) that occurred prior to the event in question, and which was causally sufficient for the event in question. Thus, if I say that the explosion of the Challenger Space Shuttle had a cause, then I imply that there was some event (or combination of events) that occurred before the explosion, and that this prior event (or combination of events) was causally sufficient for the explosion. Once the prior events had taken place, the Shuttle *had to* explode. Those prior events *made* the Shuttle explode.

In the case of the Space Shuttle explosion, the cause must have been a very complex combination of factors. I suppose that the stiff, cold o-rings played a very important role in that causal combination. But, of course, so did the enormous pressure inside the boosters, and the presence of huge tanks of extremely flammable fuel nearby. But if the explosion indeed had a cause (as I'm sure it did) then that cause must have been some such combination of factors. Perhaps some elements of the cause were occurring just instants before the explosion. For example, one part of the cause was this: nobody on the ground, and none of the computers on board, shut down the rockets at any time prior to the explosion.

After the explosion, NASA scientists were able to figure out why the Challenger exploded. They determined that the combination of defective o-rings, excessive internal pressure, nearby fuel tanks, and other factors, caused the explosion. It can be seen, then, that when the NASA scientists *explain* why the Challenger exploded, they do this by citing the cause of the explosion. In such a case, for obvious reasons, the explanation is said to be a "causal explanation." We can explain why an event occurs by saying what caused it to occur.

A despondent NASA scientist might wish that he had known about the causal conditions prior to the explosion of the Challenger. 'If only I had known,' he might say, 'I could have prevented the explosion'. Assuming that the scientist in question had the appropriate authority, his claim seems right. Suppose he had reason to believe, just before liftoff, that the o-rings were cold and inflexible. Suppose he also knew that, if the Challenger took off, the pressure in

Reprinted with permission of Fred Feldman.

the rocket would be excessive, and that hot gases would burn through the o-rings and expose the fuel tanks to extreme heat. He could then predict that, if the Challenger took off, it would explode. Undoubtedly, he would then see to it that the Challenger did not take off. In this case, a sufficiently knowledgeable person, knowing that the causes of an explosion were about to take place, could easily predict that, if they did take place, then the explosion would be sure to follow.

In general, it seems that causation and predictability go hand-in-hand. Suppose there is some event, E. Suppose that some prior event, C, in fact caused E. Then it appears that a sufficiently knowledgeable person would have been able to predict the occurrence of E. All he or she would have to know is that C has already occurred, and that C is causally sufficient for E.

Let us say that an event, E, is "in principle predictable" provided that if a person knew all the relevant laws of nature, and all the relevant antecedent conditions, then he or she would be able to predict that E would occur. While the explosion of the Challenger was (so far as I know) not predicted, it was in principle predictable. If anyone had known about the o-rings and the pressure and the applicable laws of nature, he or she would have been able to predict that the rocket would explode. Alas, no one had the requisite knowledge. (Or, if someone did have the knowledge, he or she was unfortunately not in a position to stop the launch anyway.)

It should be clear that if every event has a cause, then every event is in principle predictable. For consider some arbitrary event, E. Suppose it has a cause, C. Then imagine a person knowing in advance that C is occurring and that C is causally sufficient for E. He or she can predict that E will occur.

Of course I don't mean to suggest that every event is such that if it has a cause, then in fact someone did predict it—the vast majority of events are utterly outside the ken of every human being. We don't know that they have occurred, and we don't know what caused them. Even if we restrict ourselves to events within the ken of human beings, we have to recognize that in most cases, nobody knows the cause or the relevant causal law. All I mean to assert is that if an event is caused, then it is *in principle* predictable—that is, if someone had known about the cause of that event, and had also known about the relevant causal law, then he or she would have been able to predict that the event itself would occur.

From this principle, we may infer that if some event is in principle unpredictable, then that event must be uncaused. For if the event is in principle unpredictable, then, no matter how much someone knows about the antecedent conditions and laws of nature, he or she would still be unable to predict that the event would occur. (That's what 'in principle unpredictable' means.) If there were a cause for the event, the person would know about it and the relevant laws, and could predict the event. Since he or she knows everything about the antecedent conditions but still can't predict, there must be no cause.

2. **Some events are in principle unpredictable**. Quite a lot of ordinary human action is in principle predictable. Suppose I know that an ordinary man has been dropped, without a parachute, from a high-flying airplane. Suppose I also know about the law of gravity. I can predict that he will fall.

Insofar as psychology is a genuine science, it can make somewhat more interesting predictions about human behavior. I suppose that the day may come when fully informed psychologists, knowing quite a bit about the causes of human action, will be able to predict all sorts of things about what we do. Thus, I grant that quite a lot of human behavior is in principle predictable.

However, it seems to me clear that at least some human behavior is in principle unpredictable. Imagine the following scenario:

> A team of high-powered neurophysiologists are gathered in a laboratory. They have mountains of the most up-to-date equipment, including CAT Scanners, EEG Monitors, etc. Before them stands a short, slender man wearing a turban. On his shirt are the letters 'GF'. The slender man is The Great Falsifier—a man who claims to be able to falsify predictions.
>
> These people are engaged in a sort of competition. The Great Falsifier is going to raise a finger. The neurophysiologists will then be permitted to study the Great Falsifier's brain and nervous system until they are prepared to make a prediction about his next finger movement. They will then announce their prediction. Then, at the sound of a bell, the Great Falsifier will either move his finger to the left, or he will move it to the right—in either case, he will try to falsify the prediction made by the neurophysiologists.
>
> When all is ready, the Great Falsifier is instructed to raise the index finger of his right hand. He holds his finger about a foot in front of his nose. The neuro-physiologists then go to work. They attach their electrodes to the Great Falsifier's scalp; they monitor his brain waves; they do a real-time assay of the levels of all relevant hormones in his brain. They then fire up their computer. They input all the information they have gained as a result of their testing. They study the computer's output carefully. They discuss the results. At last, they make their prediction: 'At the sound of the bell, you will move your finger to the right.' Moments later, the bell rings. The Great Falsifier moves his finger to the left, thereby once again falsifying the neurophysiologists' prediction.
>
> The test is repeated over and over again. Each time the neurophysiologists study the Great Falsifier's brain and nervous system carefully. Each time they make a prediction about the impending finger-wiggling behavior of the Great Falsifier. Each time, at the sound of the bell, the Great Falsifier falsifies their prediction.

The case of the Great Falsifier of course does not establish that all acts of finger wiggling are in principle unpredictable. Indeed, it does not even establish that all acts of finger wiggling done by the Great Falsifier are in principle unpredictable. The conclusion is somewhat more modest than that. The case is intended to establish that there is a certain narrow and specifiable sort of finger wiggling behavior that is in principle unpredictable. The sort in question occurs when (a) there are no unusual constraints placed on the Great Falsifier's fingers, (b) someone has made a unified, contingent prediction about his impending finger wiggling behavior, and (c) the Great Falsifier has been given a complete, honest statement of the prediction. Finger wiggling behavior occurring in these circumstances is in principle unpredictable.

It is clear, I think, that there are certain circumstances in which not even the Great Falsifier will be able to falsify finger wiggling predictions. For example, suppose that the Great Falsifier's finger has been securely tied to a metal bar, and the bar is attached to a powerful electric motor. Suppose the motor is set up in such a way that, when the bell rings, it will move the bar to the right. Then the Great Falsifier's finger will move to the right, too. In any case such as this, we say that there are "unusual constraints" placed on the Great Falsifier's fingers. Such cases don't count.

More subtle cases are also ruled out. Suppose ten or twelve of the neurophysiologists get frustrated after several hundred failures, and decide to hold a gun to the head of the Great Falsifier. They threaten to kill him if he refuses to move his finger to the right. The threats of the neurophysiologists place an "unusual constraint" on the Great Falsifier. The fact that his behavior under duress is predictable is irrelevant.

Secondly, the prediction must be unified and contingent. To see why this is important, imagine that the neurophysiologists make this prediction: 'Either you will move your finger to the right, or else you won't.' It should be obvious that no matter what the Great Falsifier does, he cannot falsify this prediction. Even if he explodes in a puff of smoke, the prediction will turn out to have been correct. Any such prediction fails to be contingent. A contingent finger wiggling prediction is one such as: 'You will move your finger to the right' or 'You will move your finger to the left' or 'You will refuse to move your finger altogether.'

We also have to rule out as irrelevant cases such as this: suppose half of the neurophysiologists predict that the Great Falsifier will move his finger to the right, and half of them predict that he will not move it to the right. Obviously, then, half of the neurophysiologists will have predicted correctly. The predictions are not "unified." Thus, the case is irrelevant. You can't expect anyone to falsify *all* the predictions made about him, if all the actions available to him have been predicted.

Another sort of case must be ruled out. Suppose the neurophysiologists reach the conclusion that the Great Falsifier is going to move his finger to the right at the sound of the bell. They then make their "prediction". They say, 'You will move to the left.' Then, of course, in his attempt to falsify what he takes to be their prediction, the Great Falsifier will move his finger to the right. Two points must be made here. First, the case is irrelevant, since the neurophysiologists haven't given an honest account of their prediction. Second, a moment's reflection will reveal that, if the neurophysiologists had given an honest account of their prediction, the Great Falsifier would have been able to falsify that, too.

It may be important to mention that certain sorts of remark are not predictions at all. For example, suppose the neurophysiologists say this: 'If we predict that you will move your finger to the right, then you will move it to the left; and if we predict that you will move it to the left, then you will move it to the right.'

This remark is not a finger wiggling prediction at all. It is, rather, a "second order" statement about what would happen if a proper, "first order" prediction were made. It is, in effect, an admission that whatever prediction they make, the Great Falsifier will falsify it. If such a remark were made, the proper response by the Great Falsifier should be this: 'I think you are right. I will indeed falsify any finger wiggling prediction you may make. Would you now like to make such a prediction?'

3. **The refutation of determinism**. Let's use the term "nominal" for finger wiggling behavior performed by the Great Falsifier in circumstances in which (a) there are no unusual constraints on his fingers, and (b) a unified, contingent finger wiggling prediction has been made, and (c) the Great Falsifier has been given an honest statement of the prediction.

The argument then is this:

1. At least some of the Great Falsifier's nominal finger wiggling behavior is in principle unpredictable.

2. If at least some of the Great Falsifier's nominal finger wiggling behavior is in principle unpredictable, then at least some human action is uncaused.

3. If at least some human action is uncaused, then determinism is false.

4. Therefore, determinism is false.

The explanation of premise (1) was given in Section 2 above. The explanation of premise (2) was given in Section 1 above. Premise (3) follows immediately from the formulation of Determinism. It is obvious that the argument is valid. Therefore, determinism has been refuted.

4. **Some further thoughts.** The moral of the story, I think, is that there is an important sense in which it is correct to say that "knowledge is power." If sufficiently well-informed others observe our behavior, they may be able to predict how we will behave. Many have thought that this shows that we have no control over our behavior.

However, if these others tell us of their predictions, we may be able to falsify them. Of course, it would be absurd to say that we can falsify *every* prediction about which we learn. If someone predicts that I will fall when dropped out of an airplane, I cannot falsify his prediction. If someone predicts that my heart will beat, or that I will want to breathe, then I will not even attempt to falsify his prediction. But in a wide variety of interesting cases, if I know that someone has predicted that I will behave in a certain way, I will be able to falsify his prediction. This shows that at least some of my behavior is genuinely "up to me."

I am inclined to believe, furthermore, that even when I don't know about another's prediction about my behavior, at least some of my behavior is still "up to me." You can test this for yourself. Hold your finger up in front of your nose. Imagine that someone has predicted that you will move it to the right. Surely, it is perfectly clear to you that you can falsify this prediction. Isn't it obvious that you can move your finger to the left? Now imagine that someone has predicted that you will move your finger to the left. Surely, in this case, it is perfectly clear to you that you can move your finger to the right. Thus, you are in some respects like the Great Falsifier. If you know about it, you too are able to falsify any nominal finger wiggling prediction made about yourself. This is just a complicated way of saying that, when you are under no unusual constraints, you are free to move your finger to the left, and you are free to move it to the right.

Obviously, we all hope that our freedom extends to more interesting acts than mere finger wigglings! One would prefer to have freedom with respect to many acts of moral significance. My own view is that we all do have such wide-ranging freedom. However, I have not here attempted to prove this more interesting point. My purpose here has been rather more modest. I have attempted to show nothing more than that determinism is false. And I have done it.

FATE

Richard Taylor

We all, at certain moments of pain, threat, or bereavement, are apt to entertain the idea of fatalism, the thought that what is happening at a particular moment is unavoidable, that we are powerless to prevent it. Sometimes we find ourselves in circumstances not of our own making, in which our very being and destinies are so thoroughly anchored that the thought of fatalism can be quite overwhelming, and sometimes consoling. One feels that whatever then happens, however good or ill, will be what those circumstances yield, and we are helpless. Soldiers, it is said, are sometimes possessed by such thoughts. Perhaps all men would feel more inclined to them if they paused once in a while to think of how little they ever had to do with bringing themselves to wherever they have arrived in life, how much of their fortunes and destinies were decided for them by sheer circumstance, and how the entire course of their lives is often set, once and for all, by the most trivial incidents, which they did not produce and could not even have foreseen. If we are free to work out our destinies at all, which is doubtful, we have a freedom that is at best exercised within exceedingly narrow paths. All the important things—when we are born, of what parents, into what culture, whether we are loved or rejected, whether we are male or female, our temperament, our intelligence or stupidity, indeed everything that makes for the bulk of our happiness and misery—all these are decided for us by the most casual and indifferent circumstances. by sheer coincidences, chance encounters, and seemingly insignificant fortuities. One can see this in retrospect if he searches, but few search. The fate that has given us our very being has given us also our pride and conceit. and has thereby formed us so that, being human, we congratulate ourselves on our blessings, which we call our achievements, blame the world for our blunders, which we call our misfortunes, and scarcely give a thought to that impersonal fate which arbitrarily dispenses both.

FATALISM AND DETERMINISM

Determinism, it will be recalled, is the theory that all events are rendered unavoidable by their causes. The attempt is sometimes made to distinguish this from fatalism by saying that, according to the fatalist, certain events are going to happen *no matter what,* or in other words, regardless of causes. But this is enormously contrived. It would be hard to find in the whole history of thought a single fatalist, on that conception of it.

Fatalism is the belief that whatever happens is unavoidable. That is the clearest expression of the doctrine, and provides the basis of the attitude of calm acceptance that the fatalist is thought, quite correctly, to embody. One who endorses the claim of universal causation, then, and the theory of the causal determination of all human behavior, is a kind of fatalist—or at least he should be, if he is consistent. For that theory, as we have seen, once it is clearly spelled out and not hedged about with unresolved "ifs," does entail that whatever happens is rendered inevitable by the causal conditions preceding it, and is therefore unavoidable. One can indeed think of verbal formulas for distinguishing the two theories, but if we think of a fatalist as one who has a certain attitude, we find it to be the attitude that a thoroughgoing determinist should, in consistency, assume. That some philosophical determinists are not fatalists does not so much illustrate a great difference between fatalism and determinism, but rather the humiliation to one's pride that a fatalist position can deliver, and the comfort that can sometimes be found in evasion.

FATALISM WITH RESPECT TO THE FUTURE AND THE PAST

A fatalist, then, is someone who believes that whatever happens is and always was unavoidable. He thinks it is not up to him what will happen a thousand years hence, next year, tomorrow, or the very next moment. Of course he does not pretend always to *know* what is going to happen. Hence, he might try sometimes to read signs and portents, as meteorologists and astrologers do, or to contemplate the effects upon him of the various things that might, for all he knows, be fated to occur. But he does not suppose that whatever happens could ever have really been avoidable.

A fatalist thus thinks of the future in the way we all think of the past, for all men are fatalists as they look *back* on things. To a large extent we know what has happened—some of it we can even remember—whereas the future is still obscure to us, and we are therefore tempted to invest it, in our imagination, with all sorts of "possibilities." The fatalist resists this temptation, knowing that mere ignorance can hardly give rise to any genuine possibility in things. He thinks of both past and future "under the aspect of eternity," the way God is supposed to view them. We all think of the past this way, as something settled and fixed, to be taken for what it is. We are never in the least tempted to try to modify it. It is not in the least up to us what happened last year, yesterday, or even a moment ago, any more than are the motions of the heavens or the political developments in Tibet. If we are not fatalists, then we might think that past things once *were* up to us, to bring about or prevent, as long as they were still future—but this expresses our attitude toward the future, not the past.

Such is surely our conception of the whole past, whether near or remote. But the consistent fatalist thinks of the future in the same way. We say of past things that they are no longer within our power. The fatalist says they never were.

THE SOURCES OF FATALISM

A fatalistic way of thinking most often arises from theological ideas, or from what are generally thought to be certain presuppositions of science and logic. Thus, if God is really all-knowing and all-powerful, it is not hard to suppose that He has arranged for everything to happen just as it is going to happen, that He already knows every detail of the whole future course of the world, and there is nothing left for you and me to do except watch things unfold, in the here or hereafter. But without bringing God into the picture, it is not hard to suppose, as we have seen, that everything that happens is wholly determined by what went before it, and hence that whatever happens at any future time is the only thing that can then happen, given what precedes it. Or even disregarding that, it seems natural to suppose that there is a body of truth concerning what the future holds, just as there is such truth concerning what is contained in the past, whether or not it is known to any man or even to God, and hence, that everything asserted in that body of truth will assuredly happen, in the fullness of time, precisely as it is described therein.

No one needs to be convinced that fatalism is the only proper way to view the past. That it is also the proper way to view the future is less obvious, due in part, perhaps, to our vastly greater ignorance of what the future holds. The consequences of holding such fatalism are obviously momentous. To say nothing of the consolation of fatalism, which enables a person to view all things as they arise with the same undisturbed mind with which he contemplates even the most revolting of history's horrors, the fatalist teaching also relieves one of all tendency toward both blame and approbation of others and of both guilt and conceit in himself. It promises that a perfect understanding is possible, and removes the temptation to view things in terms of human wickedness and moral responsibility. This thought alone, once firmly grasped, yields a sublime acceptance of all that life and nature offer, whether to oneself or one's fellows; and although it thereby reduces one's pride, it simultaneously enhances the feelings, opens the heart, and expands the understanding.

DIVINE OMNISCIENCE

Suppose for the moment, just for the purpose of discussion, that God exists and is omniscient. To say that God is omniscient means that He knows everything that is true. He cannot, of course, know that which is false. Concerning any falsehood, an omniscient being can know that it is false; but then it is a truth that is known, namely, the truth that the thing in question *is* a falsehood. So if it is false that the moon is a cube, then God can, like you or me, know that this is false; but He cannot know the falsehood itself, that the moon is a cube.

Thus, if God is omniscient He knows, as you probably do, the date of your birth. He also knows, as you may not, the hour of your birth. Furthermore, God knows, as you assuredly do not, the date, and indeed the moment, of your conception—for there is such a truth, and we are supposing that God knows every truth. Moreover, He knows, as you surely do not, the date of your death, and even the exact moment, and the circumstances thereof—whether at that moment, known already to Him, you die as the result of accident, a fatal malady, suicide, murder, whatever. And, still assuming God exists and knows everything, He knows whether any ant walked across my desk last night, and if so, what ant it was, where it came from, how long it was on the desk, how it came to be there, and so on, to every truth about this insect that there is. Similarly, of course, He knows when some ant will again appear on my desk, if ever. He knows the number of hairs on my head, notes the fall of every sparrow, knows why it fell, and why it was going to fall. These are simply a few of the consequences of the omniscience that we are for the moment assuming. A more precise way of expressing all this is to say that God knows, concerning any statement whatever that anyone could formulate, that it is true, in case it is, and otherwise, that it is false. And let us suppose that God, at some time or other, or perhaps from time to time, vouchsafes some of his knowledge to men, or perhaps to certain chosen men. Thus prophets arise, proclaiming the coming of certain events, and things do then happen as they have foretold. Of course it is not surprising that they should, on the supposition we are making; namely, that the foreknowledge of these things comes from God, who is omniscient.

Vivian Hurst

THE STORY OF OSMO

Now then, let us make one further supposition, which will get us squarely into the philosophical issue these ideas are intended to introduce. Let us suppose that God has revealed a particular set of facts to a chosen scribe who, believing (correctly) that they came from God, wrote them all down. The facts in question then turned out to be all the more or less significant episodes in the life of some perfectly ordinary man named Osmo. Osmo was entirely unknown to the scribe, and in fact to just about everyone, but there was no doubt concerning whom all these facts were about, for the very first thing received by the scribe from God, was: "He of whom I speak is called Osmo." When the revelations reached a fairly voluminous bulk and appeared to be completed, the scribe arranged them in chronological order and assembled them into a book. He at first gave it the title *The Life of Osmo, as Given by God,* but thinking that people would take this to be some sort of joke, he dropped the reference to God.

The book was published, but attracted no attention whatsoever, because it appeared to be nothing more than a record of the dull life of a very plain man named Osmo. The scribe wondered, in fact, why God had chosen to convey such a mass of seemingly pointless trivia.

The book eventually found its way into various libraries, where it gathered dust until one day a high school teacher in Indiana, who rejoiced under the name of Osmo, saw a copy on the shelf. The title caught his eye. Curiously picking it up and blowing the dust off, he was thunderstruck by the opening sentence: "Osmo is born in Mercy Hospital in Auburn, Indiana, on June 6, 1942, of Finnish parentage, and after nearly losing his life from an attack of pneumonia at the age of five, he is enrolled in the St. James school there." Osmo turned pale. The book nearly fell from his hands. He thumbed back in excitement to discover who had written it. Nothing was given of its authorship nor for that matter, of its publisher. His questions of the librarian produced no further information, he being as ignorant as Osmo of how the book came to be there.

So Osmo, with the book pressed tightly under his arm. dashed across the street for some coffee, thinking to compose himself and then examine this book with care. Meanwhile he glanced at a few more of its opening remarks, at the things said there about his difficulties with his younger sister, how he was slow in learning to read, of the summer on Mackinac Island, and so on. His emotions now somewhat quieted, Osmo began a close reading. He noticed that everything was expressed in the present tense, the way newspaper headlines are written. For example, the text read, "Osmo is born in Mercy Hospital," instead of saying he *was* born there, and it recorded that he quarrels with his sister, is a slow student, is fitted with dental braces at age eight, and so on, all in the journalistic present tense. But the text itself made quite clear approximately when all these various things happened, for everything was in chronological order, and in any case each year of its subject's life constituted a separate chapter, and was so titled—"Osmo's Seventh Year," "Osmo's Eighth Year," and so on through the book.

Osmo became absolutely engrossed, to the extent that he forgot his original astonishment, bordering on panic, and for a while even lost his curiosity concerning authorship. He sat drinking coffee and reliving his childhood, much of which he had all but forgotten until the memories were revived by the book now before him. He had almost forgotten about the kitten, for example, and had entirely forgotten its name, until he read, in the chapter called "Osmo's Seventh Year," this observation: "Sobbing, Osmo takes Fluffy, now quite dead, to the garden, and buries her next to the rose bush." Ah yes! And then there was Louise, who sat next to him in the eighth grade—it was all right there. And how he got caught smoking one day. And how he felt when his father died. On and on. Osmo became so absorbed that he quite forgot the business of the day, until it occurred to him to turn to Chapter 26, to see what might be said there, he having just recently turned twenty-six. He had no sooner done so than his panic returned, for lo! what the book said was true! That it rains on his birthday for example, that his wife fails to give him the binoculars he had hinted he would like, that he receives a raise in salary shortly thereafter, and so on. Now how in God's name, Osmo pondered, could anyone know that, apparently before it had happened? For these were quite recent events, and the book had dust on it. Quickly moving on, Osmo came to this: "Sitting and reading in the coffee shop across from the library, Osmo, perspiring copiously, entirely forgets, until it is too late, that he is supposed to collect his wife at the hairdresser's at four." Oh my god! He had forgotten all about that. Yanking out his watch, Osmo discovered that it was nearly five o clock—too late. She would be on her way home by now, and in a very sour mood.

Osmo's anguish at this discovery was nothing, though, compared to what the rest of the day held for him. He poured more coffee, and it now occurred to him to check the number of chapters in this amazing book. Only twenty-nine ! But surely, he thought, that doesn't mean anything. How anyone could have gotten all this stuff down so far was puzzling enough, to be sure, but no one on God's earth could possibly know in advance how long this or that man is going to live. (Only God could know that sort of thing, Osmo reflected.) So he read along; though not without considerable uneasiness and even depression, for the remaining three chapters were on the whole discouraging. He thought he had gotten that ulcer under control, for example. And he didn't see any reason to suppose his job was going to turn out that badly, or that he was really going to break a leg skiing; after all, he could just give up skiing. But then the book ended on a terribly dismal note. It said: "And Osmo, having taken Northwest flight 569 from O'Hare, perishes when the aircraft crashes on the runway at Fort Wayne, with considerable loss of life, a tragedy rendered the more calamitous by the fact that Osmo had neglected to renew his life insurance before the expiration of the grace period." And that was all. That was the end of the book.

So *that's* why it had only twenty-nine chapters. Some idiot thought he was going to get killed in a plane crash. But, Osmo thought, he just wouldn't get on that plane. And this would also remind him to keep his insurance in force. (About three years later our hero, having boarded a flight for St. Paul, went berserk when the pilot announced they were going to land at Fort Wayne instead. According to one of the stewardesses, he tried to hijack the aircraft and divert it to another airfield. The Civil Aeronautics Board cited the resulting disruptions as contributing to the crash that followed as the plane tried to land.)

FOUR QUESTIONS

Osmo's extraordinary circumstances led him to embrace the doctrine of fatalism. Not quite completely, perhaps, for there he was, right up to the end, trying vainly to buck his fate—trying, in effect, to make a fool of God, though he did not know this, because he had no idea of the book's source. Still, he had the overwhelming evidence of his whole past life to make him think that everything was going to work out exactly as described in the book. It always had. It was, in fact, precisely this conviction that terrified him so'

But now let us ask these questions, in order to make Osmo's experiences more relevant to our own. First, why did he become, or nearly become, a fatalist? Second, just what did his fatalism amount to? Third, was his belief justified in terms of the evidence he had? And finally, is that belief justified in terms of the evidence we have—or in other words, should we be fatalists too?

This last, of course, is the important metaphysical question, but we have to approach it through the others.

Why did Osmo become a fatalist? Osmo became a fatalist because there existed a set of true statements about the details of his life, both past and future, and he came to know what some of these statements were and to believe them, including many concerning his future. That is the whole of it.

No theological ideas entered into his conviction, nor any presuppositions about causal determinism, the coercion of his actions by causes, or anything of this sort. The foundations of Osmo's fatalism were entirely in logic and epistemology, having only to do with truth and knowledge. Ideas about God did not enter in, for he never suspected that God was the ultimate source of those statements. And at no point did he think God was *making* him do what he did. All he was concerned about was that someone seemed somehow to *know* what he had done and was going to do.

What, then, did Osmo believe? He did not, it should be noted, believe that certain things were going to happen to him, *no matter what.* That does not express a logically coherent belief. He did not think he was in danger of perishing in an airplane crash even in case he did not get into any airplane, for example, or that he was going to break his leg skiing, whether he went skiing or not. No one believes what he considers to be plainly impossible. If anyone believes that a given event is going to happen, he does not doubt that those things necessary for its occurrence are going to happen too. The expression, "no matter what," by means of which some philosophers have sought an easy and even childish refutation of fatalism, is accordingly highly inappropriate in any description of the fatalist conviction.

Osmo's fatalism was simply the realization that the things described in the book were unavoidable.

Of course we are all fatalists in this sense about some things, and the metaphysical question is whether this familiar attitude should not be extended to everything. We know the sun will rise tomorrow, for example, and there is nothing we can do about it. Each of us knows he is sooner or later going to die, too, and there is nothing to be done about that either. We normally do not know just when, of course, but it is mercifully so! For otherwise we would simply sit checking off the days as they passed, with growing despair, like a man condemned to the gallows and knowing the hour set for his execution. The tides ebb and flow, and heavens revolve, the seasons follow in order, generations arise and pass, and no one speaks of taking preventive measures. With respect to those things each of us recognizes as beyond his control, we are of necessity fatalists.

The question of fatalism is simply: Of all the things that happen in the world, which, if any, are avoidable? And the philosophical fatalist replies: None of them. They never were. Some of them only seemed so.

Was Osmo's fatalism justified? Of course it was. When he could sit right there and read a true description of those parts of his life that had not yet been lived, it would be idle to suggest to him that his future might, nonetheless, contain alternative possibilities. The only doubts Osmo had were whether those statements could really be true. But here he had the proof of his own experience, as one by one they were tested. Whenever he tried to prevent what was set forth, he of course failed. Such failure, over and over, of even the most herculean efforts, with never a single success, must surely suggest, sooner or later, that he was *destined* to fail. Even to the end, when Osmo tried so desperately to save himself from the destruction described in the book, his effort was totally in vain—as he should have realized it was going to be had he really known that what was said there was true. No power in heaven or earth can render false a statement that is true. It has never been done, and never will be.

Is the doctrine of fatalism, then, true? This amounts to asking whether our circumstances are significantly different from Osmo's. Of course we cannot read our own biographies the way he could. Only men who become famous ever have their lives recorded, and even so, it is always in retrospect. This is unfortunate. It is too bad that someone with sufficient knowledge—God, for example—cannot set down the lives of great men in advance, so that their achievements can be appreciated better by their contemporaries, and indeed, by their predecessors—their parents, for instance. But mortals do not have the requisite knowledge, and if there is any god who does, he seems to keep it to himself.

None of this matters, as far as our own fatalism is concerned. For the important thing to note is that, of the two considerations that explain Osmo's fatalism, only one of them was philosophically relevant, and that one applies to us no less than to him. The two considerations were: (1) there existed a set of true statements about his life, both past and future, and (2) he came to know what those statements were and to believe them. Now the second of these two considerations explains why, as a matter of psychological fact, Osmo became fatalistic, but it has nothing to do with the validity of that point of view. Its validity is assured by (1) alone. It was not the fact that the statements happened to be written down that rendered the things they described unavoidable: that had nothing to do with it at all. Nor was it the fact that, because they had been written, Osmo could read them. His reading them and coming to believe them likewise had nothing to do with the inevitability of what they described. This was ensured simply by there being such a set of statements, whether written or not, whether read by anyone or not, and whether or not known to be true. All that is required is that they should *be* true.

Each of us has but one possible past, described by that totality of statements about us in the past tense, each of which happens to be true. No one ever thinks of rearranging things there; it is simply accepted as given. But so also, each of us has but one possible future, described by that totality of statements about oneself in the future tense, each of which happens to be true. The sum of these constitutes one's biography. Part of it has been lived. The main outlines of it can still be seen, in retrospect, though most of its details are obscure. The other part has not been lived, though it most assuredly is going to be, in exact accordance with that set of statements just referred so. Some of its outlines can already be seen, in prospect, but it is on the whole more obscure than the part belonging to the past. We have at best only premonitory glimpses of it. It is no doubt for this reason that not all of this part, the part that awaits us, is perceived as given, and men do sometimes speak absurdly of altering it—as though what the future holds, as identified by any true statement in the future tense. might after all *not* hold.

Osmo's biography was all expressed in the present tense because all that mattered was that the things referred to were real events; it did not matter to what part of time they belonged. His past consisted of those things that preceded his reading of the book, and he simply accepted it as given. He was not tempted to revise what was said there, for he was sure it was true. But it took the book to make him realize that his future was also something given. It was equally pointless for him to try to revise what was said there, for it, too, was true. As the past contains what has happened, the future contains what will happen, and neither contains, in addition to these things, various other things that did not and will not happen.

Of course we know relatively little of what the future contains. Some things we know. We know the sun will go on rising and setting, for example, that taxes will be levied and wars rage, that men will continue to be callous and greedy, and that people will be murdered and robbed. It is just the details that remain to be discovered. But the same is true of the past; it is only a matter of degree. When I meet a total stranger I do not know, and will probably never know, what his past has been, beyond certain obvious things—that he had a mother, and things of this sort. I know nothing of the particulars of that vast realm of fact that is unique to his past. And the same for his future, with only this difference—that *all* men are strangers to me as far as their futures are concerned, and here I am even a stranger to myself.

Yet there is one thing I know concerning any stranger's past and the past of everything under the sun; namely, that whatever it might hold, there is nothing anyone can do about it now. What has happened cannot be undone. The mere fact that it has happened guarantees this.

And so it is, by the same token, of the future of everything under the sun. Whatever the future might hold, there is nothing anyone can do about it now. What will happen cannot be altered. The mere fact that it is going to happen guarantees this.

THE LAW OF THE EXCLUDED MIDDLE

The presupposition of fatalism is therefore nothing but the commonest presupposition of all logic and inquiry; namely, that there is such a thing as truth, and that this has nothing at all to do with the passage of time. Nothing *becomes* true or *ceases* to be true; whatever is truth at all simply *is* true.

It comes to the same thing, and is perhaps more precise, to say that every meaningful statement, whether about oneself or anything else, is either true or else it is false; that is, its denial is true. There is no middle ground. The principle is thus appropriately called the law of excluded middle. It has nothing to do with what tense a statement happens to express, nor with the question of whether anyone, man or god, happens to know whether it is true or false.

Thus no one knows whether there was an ant on my desk last night, and no one ever will. But we do know that either this statement is true or else its denial is true - there is no third alternative. If we say it *might* be true, we mean only that we do not happen to know. Similarly, no one knows whether or not there is going to be an ant there tonight, but we do know that either it will or else it will not be there.

In a similar way we can distinguish two mutually exclusive but exhaustive classes of statements about any man; namely, the class of all those that are true, and the class of all that are false. There are no others in addition to these. Included in each are statements never asserted or even considered by anyone, but such that, if anyone were to formulate one of them, it would either be a true statement or a false one.

Consider, then, that class of statements about some particular person--yourself, let us suppose—each of which happens to be true. Their totality constitutes your biography. One combination of such statements describes the time, place, and circumstances of your birth. Another combination describes the time, place, and circumstances of your death. Others describe in detail the rises and falls of your fortunes, your achievements and failures, your joys and sorrows - absolutely everything that is true of you.

Some of these things you have already experienced, others await you. But the entire biography is there. It is not written, and probably never will be; but it is nevertheless there, all of it. If, like Osmo, you had some way of discovering those statements in advance, then like him you could hardly help becoming a fatalist. But foreknowledge of the truth would not create any truth, nor invest your philosophy with truth, nor add anything to the philosophical foundations of the fatalism that would then be so apparent to you. It would only serve to make it apparent.

OBJECTIONS

This thought, and the sense of its force, have tormented and frightened men from antiquity, and thinkers whose pride sometimes exceeds their acumen and their reverence for truth have attempted every means imaginable to demolish it. There are few articles of faith upon which virtually all men can agree, but one of them is certainly the belief in their cherished free will. Any argument in opposition to the doctrine of fate, however feeble, is immediately and uncritically embraced, as though the refutation of fatalism required only the denial of it, supported by reasons that would hardly do credit to a child. It will be worthwhile, therefore, to look briefly at some of the arguments most commonly heard.

1. One can neither foresee the future nor prove that there is any god, or even if there is, that he could know in advance the free actions of men.

   The reply to this is that it is irrelevant. The thesis of fatalism rests on no theory of divination and on no theology. These ideas were introduced only illustratively.

2. True statements are not the causes of anything. Statements only entail; they do not cause, and hence threaten no man's freedom.

   But this, too, is irrelevant, for the claim here denied is not one that has been made.

3. The whole argument just conflates fact and necessity into one and the same thing, treating as unavoidable that which is merely true. The fact that a given thing is going to happen implies only that it is going to happen, not that it has to. Someone might still be able to prevent it - though of course no one will. For example, President Kennedy was murdered. This means it was true that he was going to be murdered. But it does not mean his death at that time and place was unavoidable. Someone *could* have rendered that statement false; though of course no one did.

   That is probably the commonest "refutation" of fatalism ever offered. But how strong is the claim that something *can* be done, when in fact it never *has* been done in the whole history of the universe, in spite, sometimes, of the most strenuous efforts? No one has ever rendered false a statement that was true, however hard some men have tried. When an attempt, perhaps a heroic attempt, is made to avoid a given calamity, and the thing in question happens anyway, at just the moment and in just the way it was going to happen, we have reason to doubt that it could have been avoided. And in fact great effort was made to save President Kennedy, for example, from the destruction toward which he was heading on that fatal day, a whole legion of bodyguards having no other mission. And it failed. True, we can say that *if* more strenuous precautions had been taken, the event would not have happened. But to this we must add, *true*, they were not taken, and hence *true*, they were not going to be taken—and we have on our hands again a true statement of the kind that no man has ever had the slightest degree of success in rendering false.

4. The fatalist argument just rests on a "confusion of modalities." The fact that something is true entails only that its denial is false not that its denial is impossible. All that is impossible is that both should he true, or both false. Thus, if the president is going to be murdered, it is certainly false that he is not—but not impossible. What is impossible is that he will be both murdered and spared.

   Here again we have only a distracting irrelevancy, similar to the point just made. The fatalist argument has nothing to do with impossibility in those senses familiar to logic. It has to do with unavoidability. It is in other words concerned with human abilities. The fact that a statement is true does not, to be sure, entail that it is necessary, nor do all false statements express impossibilities. Nonetheless, no man is able to avoid what is truly described, however contingently, in any statement, nor to bring about what is thus falsely described. Nor can anyone convert the one to the other, making suddenly true that which was false, or vice versa. It has never been done, and it never will be. It would be a conceit indeed for someone now to suggest that he, alone among men, might be able to accomplish that feat. This inability goes far beyond the obvious impossibility of making something both true and false at once. No metaphysics turns on that simple point.

5. Perhaps it would be best, then, to discard the presupposition underlying the whole fatalist philosophy; namely, the idea that statements are true in advance of the things they describe. The future is the realm of possibilities, concerning any of which we should neither say it is true that it will happen, nor that it is false.

But, in reply, this desperate move is nothing but arbitrary fiction, resorted to for no other reason than to be rid of the detested doctrine of fatalism. What is at issue here is the very law of excluded middle, which, it is suggested, we shall be allowed to affirm only up to that point at which it threatens something dear. We shall permit it to hold for one part of time, but suddenly retract it in speaking of another, even though the future is continuously being converted to the past through sheer temporal passage.

Most surely, if the statement, made now, that President Kennedy has been murdered, is a true one, then the prediction, made before the event, that he was going to be murdered, was true too. The two statements have exactly the same content, and are in fact one and the same statement, except for the variation of tense. The fact that this statement is more easily known in retrospect than in prospect casts no doubt on its truth, but only illustrates a familiar fact of epistemology. A prediction, to be sure, must await fulfillment, but it does not thereupon for the first time acquire its truth. Indeed, had it not been true from the start it could not have been fulfilled, nor its author congratulated for having it right. Fulfillment is nothing but the occurrence of what is correctly predicted.

The law of excluded middle is not like a blank check, into which we can write whatever values we please, according to our preferences. We can no more make ourselves metaphysically free and masters of our desires by adding qualifications to this law than a poor man can make himself rich just by adding figures to his bankbook. The law pronounces every meaningful statement true, or, if not true, then false. It leaves no handy peg between these two on which one may hang his beloved freedom of will for safekeeping, nor does it say anything whatever about time.

Every single philosophical argument against the teaching of fatalism rests upon the assumption that we are free to pursue and realize various alternative future possibilities—the very thing, of course, that is at issue. When some of these possibilities have become realized and moved on into the past, the supposed alternative possibilities usually appear to have been less real than they had seemed: but this somehow does not destroy the fond notion that they were there. Metaphysics and logic are weak indeed in the face of an opinion nourished by invincible pride, and most men would sooner lose their very souls than be divested of that dignity which they imagine rests upon their freedom of will.

INVINCIBLE FATE

We shall say, therefore, of whatever happens, that it was going to be that way. And this is a comfort, both in fortune and in adversity. We shall say of him who turns out bad and mean, that he was going to; of him who turns out happy and blessed, that he was going to; neither praising nor berating fortune, crying over what has been, lamenting what was going to be, or passing moral judgments.

Shall we, then, sit idly by, passively observing the changing scene without participation, never testing our strength and our goodness, having no hand in what happens, or in making things come out as they should? This is a question for which each will find his own answer. Some men do little or nothing with their lives. and might as well never have lived, they make such waste of it. Others do much, and the lives of a few even shine like the stars. But we knew this before we ever began talking about fate. In time we will all know of which sort we were destined to be.

PART TWO

PHILOSOPHICAL ANTHROPOLOGY

PHAEDO

Plato

PERSONS OF THE DIALOGUE

PHAEDO, *who is the narrator of the Dialogue to Echecrates of Philius*
SOCRATES
ATTENDANT OF THE PRISON
APPOLLODORUS
SIMMIAS
CEBES
CRITO

SCENE:- *The Prison of Socrates*

PLACE OF THE NARRATION:- *Phlius*

*****

Simmias & Socrates

And now, O my judges, I desire to prove to you that the real philosopher has reason to be of good cheer when he is about to die, and that after death he may hope to obtain the greatest good in the other world. And how this may be, Simmias and Cebes, I will endeavour to explain. For I deem that the true votary of philosophy is likely to be misunderstood by other men; they do not perceive that he is always pursuing death and dying; and if this be so, and he has had the desire of death all his life long, why when his time comes should he repine at that which he has been always pursuing and desiring?

The true philosopher is always dying:- why then should he avoid the death which he desires?

Simmias said laughingly: Though not in a laughing humour, you have made me laugh, Socrates; for I cannot help thinking that the many when they hear your words will say how truly you have described philosophers, and our people at home will likewise say that the life which philosophers desire is in reality death, and that they have found them out to be deserving of the death which they desire.

'How they will laugh when they hear this!'

And they are right, Simmias, in thinking so, with the exception of the words they have found them out; for they have not found out either what is the nature of that death which the true philosopher deserves, or how he deserves or desires death. But enough of them:--let us discuss the matter among ourselves. Do we believe that there is such a thing as death?

Yes, they do not under stand the nature of death, or why the philos opher desires or deserves it.

To be sure, replied Simmias.

Is it not the separation of soul and body? And to be dead is the completion of this; when the soul exists in herself, and is released from the body and the body is released from the soul, what is this but death?

Just so, he replied.

From *The Dialogues of Plato,* translated by B. Jowett, 1892.

Simmias and Socrates

SOCRATES
SIMMIAS

There is another question, which will probably throw light on our present enquiry if you and I can agree about it:—Ought the philosopher to care about the pleasures—if they are to be called pleasures—of eating and drinking?

Certainly not, answered Simmias.

Life is best when the soul is most freed from the concerns of the body, and is alone and by herself.

And what about the pleasures of love—should he care for them?

By no means.

And will he think much of the other ways of indulging the body, for example, the acquisition of costly raiment, or sandals, or other adornments of the body? Instead of caring about them, does he not rather despise anything more than nature needs? What do you say?

I should say that the true philosopher would despise them.

Would you not say that he is entirely concerned with the soul and not with the body? He would like, as far as he can, to get away from the body and to turn to the soul.

Quite true.

In matters of this sort philosophers, above all other men, may be observed in every sort of way to dissever the soul from the communion of the body.

Very true.

Whereas, Simmias, the rest of the world are of opinion that to him who has no sense of pleasure and no part in bodily pleasure, life is not worth having; and that he who is indifferent about them is as good as dead.

That is also true.

The senses are untrustworthy guides: they mislead the soul in the search for truth.

What again shall we say of the actual acquirement of knowledge?—is the body, if invited to share in the enquiry, a hinderer or a helper? I mean to say, have sight and hearing any truth in them? Are they not, as the poets are always telling us, inaccurate witnesses? and yet, if even they are inaccurate and indistinct, what is to be said of the other senses?—for you will allow that they are the best of them?

Certainly, he replied.

Then when does the soul attain truth?—for in attempting to consider anything in company with the body she is obviously deceived.

True.

Then must not true existence be revealed to her in thought, if at all?

Yes.

And thought is best when the mind is gathered into herself and none of these things trouble her—neither sounds nor sights nor pain nor any pleasure,—when she takes leave of the body, and has as little as possible to do with it, when she has no bodily sense or desire, but is aspiring after true being?

Certainly.

And therefore the philos-opher runs away from the body.

And in this the philosopher dishonours the body; his soul runs away from his body and desires to be alone and by herself?

That is true.

Well, but there is another thing, Simmias: Is there or is there not an absolute justice?

The doctrine of ideas

SOCRATES, SIMMIAS.

Another argument. The absolute truth of justice, beauty, and other ideas is not perceived by the senses, which only introduce a disturbing element.

Assuredly there is.

And an absolute beauty and absolute good?

Of course.

But did you ever behold any of them with your eyes?

Certainly not.

Or did you ever reach them with any other bodily sense?—and I speak not of these alone, but of absolute greatness, and health, and strength, and of the essence or true nature of everything. Has the reality of them ever been perceived by you through the bodily organs? or rather, is not the nearest approach to the knowledge of their several natures made by him who so orders his intellectual vision as to have the most exact conception of the essence of each thing which he considers?

Certainly.

And he attains to the purest knowledge of them who goes to each with the mind alone, not introducing or intruding in the act of thought sight or any other sense together with reason, but with the very light of the mind in her own clearness searches into the very truth of each; he who has got rid, as far as he can, of eyes and ears and, so to speak, of the whole body, these being in his opinion distracting elements which when they infect the soul hinder her from acquiring truth and knowledge—who, if not he, is likely to attain to the knowledge of true being?

What you say has a wonderful truth in it, Socrates, replied Simmias.

The soul in herself must perceive things in themselves.

And when real philosophers consider all these things, will they not be led to make a reflection which they will express in words something like the following? 'Have we not found,' they will say, 'a path of thought which seems to bring us and our argument to the conclusion, that while we are in the body, and while the soul is infected with the evils of the body, our desire will not be satisfied? and our desire is of the truth. For the body is a source of endless trouble to us by reason of the mere requirement of food; and is liable also to diseases which overtake and impede us in the search after true being: it fills us full of loves, and lusts, and fears, and fancies of all kinds, and endless foolery, and in fact, as men say, takes away from us the power of thinking at all. Whence come wars, and fightings, and factions? whence but from the body and the lusts of the body? Wars are occasioned by the love of money, and money has to be acquired for the sake and in the service of the body; and by reason of all these impediments we have no time to give to philosophy; and, last and worst of all, even if we are at leisure and betake ourselves to some speculation, the body is always breaking in upon us, causing turmoil and confusion in our enquiries, and so amazing us that we are prevented from seeing the truth. It has been proved to us by experience that if we would have pure knowledge of anything we must be quit of the body—the soul in herself must behold things in themselves: and then we shall attain the wisdom which we desire, and of which we say that we are lovers; not while we live, but after death; for if while in company with the body, the soul cannot have pure knowledge, one of two things follows—either knowledge is not to be attained at all, or, if at all, after death. For then, and not till then, the soul will

The true philosopher

SOCRATES, SIMMIAS.

be parted from the body and exist in herself alone. In this present life, I reckon that we make the nearest approach to knowledge when we have the least possible intercourse or communion with the body, and are not surfeited with the bodily nature, but keep ourselves pure until the hour when God himself is pleased to release us. And thus having got rid of the foolishness of the body we shall be pure and hold converse with the pure, and know of ourselves the clear light everywhere, which is no other than the light of truth.' For the impure are not permitted to approach the pure. These are the sort of words, Simmias, which the true lovers of knowledge cannot help saying to one another, and thinking. You would agree; would you not?

Undoubtedly, Socrates.

But, O my friend, if this be true, there is great reason to hope that, going whither I go, when I have come to the end of my journey, I shall attain that which has been the pursuit of my life. And therefore I go on my way rejoicing, and not I only, but every other man who believes that his mind has been made ready and that he is in a manner purified.

Certainly, replied Simmias.

Purification is the separation of the soul from the body.

And what is purification but the separation of the soul from the body, as I was saying before; the habit of the soul gathering and collecting herself into herself from all sides out of the body; the dwelling in her own place alone, as in another life, so also in this, as far as she can;—the release of the soul from the chains of the body?

Very true, he said.

And this separation and release of the soul from the body is termed death?

To be sure, he said.

And the true philosophers, and they only, are ever seeking to release the soul. Is not the separation and release of the soul from the body their especial study?

That is true.

And, as I was saying at first, there would be a ridiculous contradiction in men studying to live as nearly as they can in a state of death, and yet repining when it comes upon them.

Clearly.

And the true philosophers, Simmias, are always occupied in the practice of dying, wherefore also to them least of all men is death terrible. Look at the matter thus:—if they have been in every way the enemies of the body, and are wanting to be alone with the soul, when this desire of theirs is granted, how inconsistent would they be if they trembled and repined, instead of rejoicing at their departure to that place where, when they arrive, they hope to gain that which in life they desire—and this was wisdom—and at the same time to be rid of the company of their enemy. Many a man has been willing to go to the world below animated by the hope of seeing there an earthly love, or wife, or son, and conversing with them. And will he who is a true lover of wisdom, and is strongly persuaded in like manner that only in the world below he can worthily enjoy her, still repine at death? Will he not depart with joy? Surely he will, O

The exchange of virtue

SOCRATES, SIMMIAS.

my friend, if he be a true philosopher. For he will have a firm conviction that there, and there only, he can find wisdom in her purity. And if this be true, he would be very absurd, as I was saying, if he were afraid of death.

The true philosopher who has been always trying to disengage himself from the body will rejoice in death.

He would indeed, replied Simmias.

And when you see a man who is repining at the approach of death, is not his reluctance a sufficient proof that he is not a lover of wisdom, but a lover of the body, and probably at the same time a lover of either money or power, or both?

Quite so, he replied.

And is not courage, Simmias, a quality which is specially characteristic of the philosopher?

Certainly.

There is temperance again, which even by the vulgar is supposed to consist in the control and regulation of the passions, and in the sense of superiority to them—is not temperance a virtue belonging to those only who despise the body, and who pass their lives in philosophy?

He alone possesses the true secret of virtue, which in ordinary men is merely based on a calculation of lesser and greater evils.

Most assuredly.

For the courage and temperance of other men, if you will consider them, are really a contradiction.

How so?

Well, he said, you are aware that death is regarded by men in general as a great evil.

Very true, he said.

And do not courageous men face death because they are afraid of yet greater evils?

That is quite true.

Then all but the philosophers are courageous only from fear and because they are afraid; and yet that a man should be courageous from fear, and because he is a coward, is surely a strange thing.

Ordinary men are courageous only from cowardice; temperate from intemperance.

Very true.

And are not the temperate exactly in the same case? They are temperate because they are intemperate—which might seem to be a contradiction, but is nevertheless the sort of thing which happens with this foolish temperance. For there are

pleasures which they are afraid of losing; and in their desire to keep them, they abstain from some pleasures, because they are overcome by others; and although to be conquered by pleasure is called by men intemperance, to them the conquest of pleasure consists in being conquered by pleasure. And that is what I mean by saying that, in a sense they are made temperate through intemperance.

Such appears to be the case.

Yet the exchange of one fear or pleasure or pain for another fear or pleasure or pain, and of the greater for the less, as if they were coins, is not the exchange of virtue. O my blessed Simmias, is there not one true coin for which all things ought to be exchanged?—and that is wisdom; and only in exchange for this, and in company with this, is anything truly bought or sold, whether courage or temperance or justice. And is not all true virtue the companion of wisdom, no

True virtue is inseperable from wisdom.

The incredulity of Cebes

SOCRATES, CEBES.

matter what fears or pleasures or other similar goods or evils may or may not attend her? But the virtue which is made up of these goods, when they are severed from wisdom and exchanged with one another, is a shadow of virtue only, nor is there any freedom or health or truth in her; but in the true exchange there is a purging away of all these things, and temperance, and justice, and courage, and wisdom herself are the purgation of them. The founders of the mysteries would appear to have had a real meaning, and were not talking nonsense when they intimated in a figure long ago that he who passes unsanctified and uninitiated into the world below will lie in a slough, but that he who arrives there after initiation and purification will dwell with the gods. For 'many,' as they say in the mysteries, 'are the thyrsus-bearers, but few are the mystics,'—meaning, as I interpret the words, 'the true philosophers.' In the number of whom, during my whole life, I have been seeking, according to my ability, to find a place;—whether I have sought in a right way or not, and whether I have succeeded or not, I shall truly know in a little while, if God will, when I myself arrive in the other world—such is my belief. And therefore I maintain that I am right, Simmias and Cebes, in not grieving or repining at parting from you and my masters in this world, for I believe that I shall equally find good masters and friends in another world. But most men do not believe this saying; if then I succeed in convincing you by my defence better than I did the Athenian judges, it will be well.

The thyrsus-bearers and the mystics

Cebes answered: I agree, Socrates, in the greater part of what you say. But in what concerns the soul, men are apt to be incredulous; they fear that when she has left the body her place may be nowhere, and that on the very day of death she may perish and come to an end—immediately on her release from the body, issuing forth dispersed like smoke or air and in her flight vanishing away into nothingness.If she could only be collected into herself after she has obtained release from the evils of which you were speaking, there would be good reason to hope, Socrates, that what you say is true. But surely it requires a great deal of argument and many proofs to show that when the man is dead his soul yet exists, and has any force or intelligence.

Fears are enter tained lest the soul when she dies should be scattered to the winds.

True, Cebes, said Socrates; and shall I suggest that we converse a little of the probabilities of these things?

I am sure, said Cebes, that I should greatly like to know your opinion about them.

I reckon, said Socrates, that no one who heard me now, not even if he were one of my old enemies, the Comic poets, could accuse me of idle talking about matters in which I have no concern:—If you please, then, we will proceed with the enquiry.

The discuss-ion suited to the occasion.

Suppose we consider the question whether the souls of men after death are or are not in the world below. There comes into my mind an ancient doctrine which affirms that they go from hence into the other world, and returning hither, are born again from the dead. Now if it be true that the living come from the dead, then our souls must exist in the other world, for if not, how could they have been born again? And this would be conclusive, if there were any real evidence

The alternation of all existence

SOCRATES, CEBES.

that the living are only born from the dead; but if this is not so, then other arguments will have to be adduced.

Very true, replied Cebes.

Then let us consider the whole question, not in relation to man only, but in relation to animals generally, and to plants, and to everything of which there is generation, and the proof will be easier. Are not all things which have opposites generated out of their opposites? I mean such things as good and evil, just and unjust—and there are innumerable other opposites which are generated out of opposites. And I want to show that in all opposites there is of necessity a similar alternation; I mean to say, for example, that anything which becomes greater must become greater after being less.

All things which have opposites are generated out of opposites

True.

And that which becomes less must have been once greater and then have become less.

Yes.

And the weaker is generated from the stronger, and the swifter from the slower.

Very true.

And the worse is from the better, and the more just is from the more unjust.

Of course.

And is this true of all opposites? and are we convinced that all of them are generated out of opposites?

Yes.

And in this universal opposition of all things, are there not also two intermediate processes which are ever going on, from one to the other opposite, and back again; where there is a greater and a less there is also an intermediate process of increase and diminution and that which grows is said to wax, and that which decays to wane?

And there are intermediate processes or passages into and out of one another, such as increase and diminution, division and composition, and the like.

Yes, he said.

And there are many other processes, such as division and composition, cooling and heating, which equally involve a passage into and out of one another. And this necessarily holds of all opposites even though not always expressed in words—they are really generated out of one another, and there is a passing or process from one to the other of them?

Very true, he replied.

Well, and is there not an opposite of life, as sleep is the opposite of waking?

True, he said.

And what is it?

Death, he answered.

And these, if they are opposites, are generated the one from the other, and have their two intermediate processes also?

Of course.

Now, said Socrates, I will analyze one of the two pairs of opposites which I have mentioned to you, and also its intermediate processes, and you shall analyze

Life and death like waking and sleeping

SOCRATES, CEBES

the other to me. One of them I term sleep, the other waking. The state of sleep is opposed to the state of waking, and out of sleeping waking is generated, and out of waking,sleeping; and the process of generation is in the one case falling asleep, and in the other waking up. Do you agree?

Life is opposed to death, as waking is to sleeping, and in like manner they are generated from one another.

I entirely agree.

Then, suppose that you analyze life and death to me in the same manner. Is not death opposed to life?

Yes.

And they are generated one from the other?

Yes.

What is generated from the living?

The dead.

And what from the dead?

I can only say in answer—the living.

Then the living, whether things or persons, Cebes, are generated from the dead?

That is clear, he replied.

Then the inference is that our souls exist in the world below?

That is true.

And one of the two processes or generations is visible—for surely the act of dying is visible?

Surely, he said.

What then is to be the result? Shall we exclude the opposite process? and shall we suppose nature to walk on one leg only? Must we not rather assign to death some corresponding process of generation?

Certainly, he replied.

And what is that process?

Return to life.

And return to life, if there be such a thing, is the birth of the dead into the world of the living?

Quite true.

Then here is a new way by which we arrive at the conclusion that the living come from the dead, just as the dead come from the living: and this, if true, affords a most certain proof that the souls of the dead exist in some place out of which they come again.

Yes, Socrates, he said; the conclusion seems to flow necessarily out of our previous admissions.

If there were no compens-ation or return in nature, all things would pass into the state of death.

And that these admissions were not unfair, Cebes, he said, may be shown, I think, as follows: If generation were in a straight line only, and there were no compensation or circle in nature, no turn or return of elements into their opposites, then you know that all things would at last have the same form and pass into the same state, and there would be no more generation of them.

What do you mean? he said.

A simple thing enough, which I will illustrate by the case of sleep, he replied. You know that if there were no alternation of sleeping and waking, the tale of

The circle of nature

SOCRATES, CEBES, SIMMIAS

The sleeping Endymion would be unmeaning in a world of sleepers.

the sleeping Endymion would in the end have no meaning, because all other things would be asleep too, and he would not be distinguishable from the rest. Or if there were composition only, and no division of substances, then the chaos of Anaxagoras would come again. And in like manner, my dear Cebes, if all things which partook of life were to die, and after they were dead remained in the form of death, and did not come to life again, all would at last die, and nothing would be alive—what other result could there be? For if the living spring from any other things, and they too die, must not all things at last be swallowed up in death?

There is no escape, Socrates, said Cebes; and to me your argument seems to be absolutely true.

Yes, he said, Cebes, it is and must be so, in my opinion; and we have not been deluded in making these admissions; but I am confident that there truly is such a thing as living again, and that the living spring from the dead, and that the souls of the dead are in existence, and that the good souls have a better portion than the evil.

*****

SOCRATES, CEBES

The soul and the ideas belong to the class of the unchanging which is also the unseen.

Then now let us return to the previous discussion. Is that idea or essence, which in the dialectical process we define as essence or true existence—whether essence of equality, beauty, or anything else—are these essences, I say, liable at times to some degree of change? or are they each of them always what they are, having the same simple self-existent and unchanging forms, not admitting of variation at all, or in any way, or at any time?

They must be always the same, Socrates, replied Cebes.

And what would you say of the many beautiful—whether men or horses or garments or any other things which are named by the same names and may be called equal or beautiful,—are they all unchanging and the same always, or quite the reverse? May they not rather be described as almost always changing and hardly ever the same, either with themselves or with one another?

The latter, replied Cebes; they are always in a state of change.

And these you can touch and see and perceive with the senses, but the unchanging things you can only perceive with the mind— they are invisible and are not seen?

That is very true, he said.

Well then, added Socrates, let us suppose that there are two sorts of existences—one seen, the other unseen.

Let us suppose them.

The seen is the changing, and the unseen is the unchanging?

That may be also supposed.

And, further, is not one part of us body, another part soul?

To be sure.

And to which class is the body more alike and akin?

Clearly to the seen—no one can doubt that.

The nature of the soul

SOCRATES, CEBES.

And is the soul seen or not seen?

Not by man, Socrates.

And what we mean by 'seen' and 'not seen' is that which is or is not visible to the eye of man?

Yes, to the eye of man.

And is the soul seen or not seen?

Not seen.

Unseen then?

Yes.

Then the soul is more like to the unseen, and the body to the seen?

That follows necessarily, Socrates.

The soul which is unseen, when she makes use of the bodily senses, is dragged down into the region of the changeable, and must return into herself before she can attain to true wisdom.

And were we not saying long ago that the soul when using the body as an instrument of perception, that is to say, when using the sense of sight or hearing or some other sense (for the meaning of perceiving through the body is perceiving through the senses)—were we not saying that the soul too is then dragged by the body into the region of the changeable, and wanders and is confused; the world spins round her, and she is like a drunkard, when she touches change?

Very true.

But when returning into herself she reflects, then she passes into the other world, the region of purity, and eternity, and immortality, and unchangeableness, which are her kindred, and with them she ever lives, when she is by herself and is not let or hindered; then she ceases from her erring ways, and being in communion with the unchanging is unchanging. And this state of the soul is called wisdom?

That is well and truly said, Socrates, he replied.

And to which class is the soul more nearly alike and akin, as far as may be inferred from this argument, as well as from the preceding one?

The soul is of the nature of the unchange-able, the body of the chang-ing; the soul rules, the body serves; the soul is in the likeness of the divine, the body of the mortal.

I think, Socrates, that, in the opinion of every one who follows the argument, the soul will be infinitely more like the unchangeable—even the most stupid person will not deny that.

And the body is more like the changing?

Yes.

Yet once more consider the matter in another light: When the soul and the body are united, then nature orders the soul to rule and govern, and the body to obey and serve. Now which of these two functions is akin to the divine? and which to the mortal? Does not the divine appear to you to be that which naturally orders and rules, and the mortal to be that which is subject and servant?

True.

And which does the soul resemble?

The soul resembles the divine, and the body the mortal—there can be no doubt of that, Socrates.

Then reflect, Cebes: of all which has been said is not this the conclusion?—that the soul is in the very likeness of the divine, and immortal, and intellectual, and uniform, and indissoluble, and unchangeable; and that the body is in the very

The passing of the soul

likeness of the human, and mortal, and unintellectual, and multiform, and dissoluable, and changeable. Can this, my dear Cebes, be denied?

SOCRATES, CEBES

It cannot.

But if it be true, then is not the body liable to speedy dissolution? and is not the soul almost or altogether indissoluble?

Certainly.

Even from the body something may be learned about the soul; for the corpse of a man lasts for some time, and when embalmed, in a manner for ever.

And do you further observe, that after a man is dead, the body, or visible part of him, which is lying in the visible world, and is called a corpse, and would naturally be dissolved and decomposed and dissipated, is not dissolved or decomposed at once, but may remain for some time, nay even for a long time, if the constitution be sound at the time of death, and the season of the year favourable? For the body when shrunk and embalmed, as the manner is in Egypt, may remain almost entire through infinite ages; and even in decay, there are still some portions, such as the bones and ligaments, which are practically indestructible:—Do you agree?

Yes.

And is it likely that the soul, which is invisible, in passing to the place of the true Hades, which like her is invisible, and pure, and noble, and on her way to the good and wise God, whither, if God will, my soul is also soon to go,—that the soul, I repeat, if this be her nature and origin, will be blown away and destroyed immediately on quitting the body, as the many say? That can never be, my dear Simmias and Cebes. The truth rather is, that the soul which is pure at departing and draws after her no bodily taint, having never voluntarily during life had connection with the body, which she is ever avoiding, herself gathered into herself;—and making such abstraction her perpetual study—which means that she has been a true disciple of philosophy; and therefore has in fact been always engaged in the practice of dying? For is not philosophy the study of death?—

How unlikely then that the soul should at once pass away

Certainly—

*****

A man of sense ought not to say, nor will I be very confident, that the description which I have given of the soul and her mansions is exactly true. But I do say that, inasmuch as the soul is shown to be immortal, he may venture to think, not improperly or unworthily, that something of the kind is true. The venture is a glorious one, and he ought to comfort himself with words like these, which is the reason why I lengthen out the tale. Wherefore, I say, let a man be of good cheer about his soul, who having cast away the pleasures and ornaments of the body as alien to him and working harm rather than good, has sought after the pleasures of knowledge; and has arrayed the soul, not in some foreign attire, but in her own proper jewels, temperance, and justice, and courage, and nobility, and truth—in these adorned she is ready to go on her journey to the world below, when her hour comes. You, Simmias and Cebes, and all other men, will

SOCRATES, CRITO

These descriptions are not true to the letter, but something like them is true.

SOCRATES, CRITO

depart at some time or other. Me already, as a tragic poet would say, the voice of fate calls. Soon I must drink the poison; and I think that I had better repair to the bath first, in order that the women may not have the trouble of washing my body after I am dead.

When he had done speaking, Crito said: And have you any commands for us, Socrates—anything to say about your children, or any other matter in which we can serve you?

Nothing particular, Crito, he replied: only, as I have always told you, take care of yourselves; that is a service which you may be ever rendering to me and mine and to all of us, whether you promise to do so or not. But if you have no thought for yourselves, and care not to walk according to the rule which I have prescribed for you, not now for the first time, however much you may profess or promise at the moment, it will be of no avail.

We will do our best, said Crito: And in what way shall we bury you?

In any way that you like; but you must get hold of me, and take care that I do not run away from you. Then he turned to us, and added with a smile:—I cannot make Crito believe that I am the same Socrates who have been talking and conducting the argument; he fancies that I am the other Socrates whom he will soon see, a dead body—and he asks, How shall he bury me? And though I have spoken many words in the endeavour to show that when I have drunk the poison I shall leave you and go to the joys of the blessed,—these words of mine, with which I was comforting you and myself, have had, as I perceive, no effect upon Crito. And therefore I want you to be surety for me to him now, as at the trial he was surety to the judges for me: but let the promise be of another sort; for he was surety for me to the judges that I would remain, and you must be my surety to him that I shall not remain, but go away and depart; and then he will suffer less at my death, and not be grieved when he sees my body being burned or buried. I would not have him sorrow at my hard lot, or say at the burial, Thus we lay out Socrates, or, Thus we follow him to the grave or bury him; for false words are not only evil in themselves, but they infect the soul with evil. Be of good cheer then, my dear Crito, and say that you are burying my body only, and do with that whatever is usual, and what you think best.

The dead body which remains is not the true Socrates.

When he had spoken these words, he arose and went into a chamber to bathe; Crito followed him and told us to wait. So we remained behind, talking and thinking of the subject of discourse, and also of the greatness of our sorrow; he was like a father of whom we were being bereaved, and we were about to pass the rest of our lives as orphans. When he had taken the bath his children were brought to him—(he had two young sons and an elder one); and the women of his family also came, and he talked to them and gave them a few directions in the presence of Crito; then he dismissed them and returned to us.

He takes leave of his family.

The humanity of the jailer.

Now the hour of sunset was near, for a good deal of time had passed while he was within. When he came out, he sat down with us again after his bath, but not much was said. Soon the jailer, who was the servant of the Eleven, entered and stood by him, saying:—To you, Socrates, whom I know to be the noblest and gentlest and best of all who ever came to this place, I will not impute the angry

Socrates is ready to depart

feelings of other men, who rage and swear at me, when, in obedience to the authorities, I bid them drink the poison—indeed, I am sure that you will not be angry with me; for others, as you are aware, and not I, are to blame. And so fare you well, and try to bear lightly what must needs be—you know my errand. Then bursting into tears he turned away and went out.

SOCRATES CRITO, THE JAILER.

Socrates looked at him and said: I return your good wishes, and will do as you bid. Then turning to us, he said, How charming the man is: since I have been in prison he has always been coming to see me, and at times he would talk to me, and was as good to me as could be, and now see how generously he sorrows on my account. We must do as he says, Crito; and therefore let the cup be brought if the poison is prepared: if not, let the attendant prepare some.

Crito would detain Socrates a little while.

Yet, said Crito, the sun is still upon the hill-tops, and I know that many a one has taken the draught late, and after the announcement has been made to him, he has eaten and drunk, and enjoyed the society of his beloved; do not hurry—there is time enough.

Socrates thinks that there is nothing to be gained by delay.

Socrates said: Yes, Crito, and they of whom you speak are right in so acting, for they think that they will be gainers by the delay; but I am right in not following their example, for I do not think that I should gain anything by drinking the poison a little later; I should only be ridiculous in my own eyes for sparing and saving a life which is already forfeit. Please then to do as I say, and not to refuse me.

The poison is brought.

Crito made a sign to the servant, who was standing by; and he went out, and having been absent for some time, returned with the jailer carrying the cup of poison. Socrates said: You, my good friend, who are experienced in these matters, shall give me directions how I am to proceed. The man answered: You have only to walk about until your legs are heavy, and then to lie down, and the poison will act. At the same time he handed the cup to Socrates, who in the easiest and gentlest manner, without the least fear or change of colour or feature, looking at the man with all his eyes, Echecrates, as his manner was, took the cup and said: What do you say about making a libation out of this cup to any god? May I, or not? The man answered: We only prepare, Socrates, just so much as we deem enough. I understand, he said: but I may and must ask the gods to prosper my journey from this to the other world—even so—and so be it according to my prayer. Then raising the cup to his lips, quite readily and cheerfully he drank off the poison. And hitherto most of us had been able to control our sorrow; but now when we saw him drinking, and saw too that he had finished the draught, we could no longer forbear, and in spite of myself my own tears were flowing fast; so that I covered my face and wept, not for him, but at the thought of my own calamity in having to part from such a friend. Nor was I the first; for Crito, when he found himself unable to restrain his tears, had got up, and I followed; and at that moment, Apollodorus, who had been weeping all the time, broke out in a loud and passionate cry which made cowards of us all. Socrates alone retained his calmness: What is this strange outcry? he said. I sent away the women mainly in order that they might not misbehave in this way, for I have been told that a man should die in peace. Be quiet then, and have patience.

He drinks the poison.

The company of friends are unable to control themselves

Says Socrates 'A man should die in peace.'

The end

When we heard his words we were ashamed, and refrained our tears; and he walked about until, as he said, his legs began to fail, and then he lay on his back, according to the directions, and the man who gave him the poison now and then looked at his feet and legs; and after a while he pressed his foot hard, and asked him if he could feel; and he said, No; and then his leg, and so upwards and upwards, and showed us that he was cold and stiff. And he felt them himself, and said: When the poison reaches the heart, that will be the end. He was beginning to grow cold about the groin, when he uncovered his face, for he had covered himself up, and said—they were his last words—he said: Crito, I owe a cock to Asclepius; will you remember to pay the debt? The debt shall be paid, said Crito; is there anything else? There was no answer to this question; but in a minute or two a movement was heard, and the attendants uncovered him; his eyes were set, and Crito closed his eyes and mouth.

The debt to Asclepius.

Such was the end, Echecrates, of our friend; concerning whom I may truly say, that of all the men of his time whom I have known, he was the wisest and justest and best.

ON THE MIND AND THE BODY

René Descartes

MEDITATION II: Concerning the Nature of the Human Mind and how it is more easily known than the Body

So disquieting are the doubts in which yesterday's meditation has involved me that it is no longer in my power to forget them. Nor do I yet see how they are to be resolved. It is as if I had all of a sudden fallen into very deep water, and am so disconcerted that I can neither plant my feet securely on the bottom nor maintain myself by swimming on the surface. I shall, however, brace myself for a great effort, entering anew on the path which I was yesterday exploring, that is, I shall proceed by setting aside all that admits even of the very slightest doubt, just as if I had convicted it of being absolutely false; and I shall persist in following this path, until I have come upon something certain, or, failing in that, until at least I know, and know with certainty, that in the world there is nothing certain.

Archimedes[1], that he might displace the whole earth, required only that there might be some one point, fixed and immovable, to serve in leverage; so likewise I shall be entitled to entertain high hopes if I am fortunate enough to find some one thing that is certain and indubitable.

I am supposing, then, that all the things I see are false;[2] that of all the happenings my memory has ever suggested to me, none has ever so existed; that I have no senses; that body, shape, extension, movement and location are but mental fictions.What is there, then, which can be esteemed true? Perhaps this only, that nothing whatsoever is certain.

But how do I know that there is not something different from all the things I have thus far enumerated and in regard to which there is not the least occasion for doubt? Is there not some God, or other being by whatever name we call Him, who puts these thoughts into my mind? Yet why suppose such a being? May it not be that I am myself capable of being their author? Am I not myself at least a something? But already I have denied that I have a body and senses. This indeed raises awkward questions. But what is it that thereupon follows? Am I so dependent on the body and senses that without them I cannot exist? Having persuaded myself that outside me there is nothing, that there is no heaven, no Earth, that there are no minds, no bodies, am I thereby committed to the view that I also do not exist? By no means. If I am persuading myself of something in so doing I assuredly do exist. But what if, unknown to me, there be some deceiver, very powerful and very cunning, who is constantly employing his ingenuity in deceiving me? Again, as before, without doubt, if he is deceiving me, I exist. Let him deceive me as much as he will, he can never cause me to be nothing so long as I shall be thinking that I am something. And thus, having reflected well, and carefully examined all

From Meditations II and VI of Descartes' *Meditations on First Philosophy* (first published in 1641), translated by Norman Kemp Smith. Reprinted by permission of The Macmillan Press, Ltd.

things, we have finally to conclude that this declaration, *Ego sum, ego existo,* [I am, I exist] is necessarily true every time I propound it or mentally apprehend it.

But I do not yet know in any adequate manner what I am, I who am certain that I am; and I must be careful not to substitute some other thing in place of myself, and so go astray in this knowledge which I am holding to be the most certain and evident of all that is knowable by me. This is why I shall now meditate anew on what, prior to my venturing on these questionings, I believed myself to be. I shall withdraw those beliefs which can, even in the least degree, be invalidated by the reasons cited, in order that at length, of all my previous beliefs, there may remain only what is certain and indubitable.

What then did I formerly believe myself to be? Undoubtedly I thought myself to be a man. But what is a man? Shall I say a rational animal? No, for then I should have to inquire what is "animal," what "rational;" and thus from the one question I should be drawn on into several others yet more difficult. I have not, at present, the leisure for any such subtle inquiries. Instead, I prefer to meditate on the thoughts which of themselves sprang up in my mind on my applying myself to the consideration of what I am, considerations suggested by my own proper nature. I thought that I possessed a face, hands, arms, and that whole structure to which I was giving the title "body," composed as it is of the limbs discernible in a corpse. In addition, I took notice that I was nourished, that I walked, that I sensed, that I thought, all of which actions I ascribed to the soul. But what the soul might be I did not stop to consider; or if I did, I imaged it as being something extremely rare and subtle, like a wind, a flame or an ether, and as diffused throughout my grosser parts. As to the nature of "body," no doubts whatsoever disturbed me. I had, as I thought, quite distinct knowledge of it; and had I been called upon to explain the manner in which I then conceived it, I should have explained myself somewhat thus: by body I understand whatever can be determined by a certain shape, and comprised in a certain location, whatever so fills a certain space as to exclude from it every other body, whatever can be apprehended by touch, sight, hearing, taste or smell, and whatever can be moved in various ways, not indeed of itself but something foreign to it by which it is touched and impressed. For I nowise conceived the power of self movement, of sensing or knowing, as pertaining to the nature of body: on the contrary I was somewhat astonished on finding in certain bodies faculties such as these.

But what am I now to say that I am, now that I am supposing that there exists a very powerful, and if I may so speak, malignant being, who employs all his powers and skill in deceiving me? Can I affirm that I possess any one of those things which I have been speaking of as pertaining to the nature of body? On stopping to consider them with closer attention, and on reviewing all of them, I find none of which I can say that it belongs to me; to enumerate them again would be idle and tedious. What then, of those things which I have been attributing not to body, but to the soul? What of nutrition or of walking? If it be that I have no body, it cannot be that I take nourishment or that I walk. Sensing? There can be no sensing in the absence of body; and besides I have seemed during sleep to apprehend things which, as I afterwards noted, had not been sensed. Thinking? Here I find what does belong to me: it alone cannot be separated from me. I am, I exist.[3] This is certain. How often? As often as I think. For it might indeed be that if I entirely ceased to think, I should thereupon altogether cease to exist. I am not at present admitting anything which is not necessarily true; and, accurately speaking, I am therefore [taking myself to be] only a thinking thing, that is to say, a mind, an understanding or reason—terms the significance of which has hitherto been unknown to me. I am, then, a real thing, and really existent. What thing ? I have said it, a thinking thing.

And what more am I? I look for aid to the imagination. [But how mistakenly!] I am not that assemblage of limbs we call the human body; I am not a subtle penetrating air distributed throughout all these members; I am not a wind, a fire, a vapor, a breath or anything at all that I can image. I am supposing all these things to be nothing. Yet I find, while so doing, that I am still assured that I am a something.

But may it not be that those very things which, not being known to me, I have been supposing non-existent, are not really different from the self that I know ? As to that I cannot say, and am not now discussing it. I can judge only of things that are known to me. Having come to know that I exist, I am inquiring as to what I am, this I that I thus know to exist. Now quite certainly this knowledge, taken in the precise manner as above, is not dependent on things the existence of which is not yet known to me; consequently and still more evidently it does not depend on any of the things which are feigned by the imagination. Indeed this word *feigning* warns me of my error; for I should in truth be feigning were I to *image* myself to be a something; since imaging is in no respect distinguishable from the contemplating of the shape or image of a *corporeal* thing. Already I know with certainty that I exist, and that all these imaged things, and in general whatever relates to the nature of body, may possibly be dreams merely or deceptions. Accordingly, I see dearly that it is no more reasonable to say, "I will resort to my imagination in order to learn more distinctly what I am," than if I were to say, "I am awake and apprehend something that is real, true; but as I do not yet apprehend it sufficiently well, I will of express purpose go to sleep, that my dreams may represent it to me with greater truth and evidence." I know therefore that nothing of all I can comprehend by way of the imagination pertains to this knowledge I [already] have of myself, and that if the mind is to determine the nature of the self with perfect distinctness, I must be careful to restrain it, diverting it from all such imaginative modes of apprehension.

What then is it that I am? A thinking thing.[4] What is a thinking thing? It is a thing that doubts, understands, affirms, denies, wills, abstains from willing, that also can be aware of images and sensations.

Assuredly if all these things pertain to me, I am indeed a something. And how could it be they should not pertain to me? Am I not that very being who doubts of almost everything, who none the less also apprehends certain things, who affirms that one thing only is true, while denying all the rest, who yet desires to know more, who is averse to being deceived, who images many things, sometimes even despite his will, and who likewise apprehends many things which seem to come by way of the senses? Even though I should be always dreaming, and though he who has created [5] me employs all his ingenuity in deceiving me, is there any one of the above assertions which is not as true as that I am and that I exist? Any one of them which can be distinguished from my thinking? Any one of them which can be said to be separate from the self? So manifest is it that it is I who doubt, I who apprehend I who desire, that there is here no need to add anything by way of rendering it more evident. It is no less certain that I can apprehend images. For although it may happen (as I have been supposing) that none of the things imaged are true, the imaging, and active power, is none the less really in me, as forming part of my thinking. Again, I am the being who senses, that is to say, who apprehends corporeal things, as if by the organs of sense, since I do in truth see light, hear noise, feel heat. These things, it will be said, are false, and I am only dreaming. Even so, it is none the less certain that it seems to me that I see, that I hear, and that I am warmed. This is what in me is rightly called sensing, and as used in this precise manner is nowise other than thinking.

From all this I begin to know what I am somewhat better than heretofore. But it still seems to me—for I am unable to prevent myself continuing in this way of thinking—that corporeal things, which are reconnoitered by the senses, and whose images inform thought, are known with much greater distinctness than that part of myself (whatever it be) which is not imageable—strange though it may be to be thus saying that I know and comprehend more distinctly those things which I am supposing to be doubtful and unknown, and as not belonging to me, than others which are known to me, which appertain to my proper nature and of the truth of which I am convinced— in short are known more distinctly than I know myself. But I can see how this comes about: my mind delights to wander and will not yet suffer itself to be restrained within the limits of truth.

Let us, therefore, once again allow the mind the freest reign, so that when afterwards we bring it, more opportunely, under due constraint, it may be the more easily controlled. Let us begin by considering the things which are commonly thought to be the most distinctly known, viz., the bodies which we touch and see; not, indeed, bodies in general, for such general notions are usually somewhat confused, but one particular body. Take, for example, this piece of wax; it has been but recently taken from the hive; it has not yet lost the sweetness of the honey it contained; it still retains something of the odor of the flowers from which it has been gathered; its color, its shape, its size, are manifest to us; it is hard, cold, easily handled, and when struck upon with the finger emits a sound. In short, all that is required to make a body known with the greatest possible distinctness is present in the one now before us. But behold ! While I am speaking let it be moved toward the fire. What remains of the taste exhales, the odor evaporates, the color changes, the shape is destroyed, its size increases, it becomes liquid, it becomes hot and can no longer be handled, and when struck upon emits no sound. Does the wax, notwithstanding these changes, still remain the same wax? We must admit that it does; no one doubts that it does, no one judges otherwise. What, then, was it I comprehended so distinctly in knowing the piece of wax? Certainly, it could be nothing of all that I was aware of by way of the senses, since all the things that came by way of taste, smell, sight, touch and hearing, are changed, and the wax none the less remains.

Perhaps it has all along been as I am now thinking, viz., that the wax was not that sweetness of honey, nor that pleasing scent of flowers, nor that whiteness, that shape, that sound, but a body which a little while ago appeared to me decked out with those modes, and now appears decked out with others. But what precisely is it that I am here imaging? Let us attentively consider the wax, withdrawing from it all that does not belong to it, that we may see what remains. As we find, what then alone remains is a something extended, flexible and movable. But what is this "flexible," this "movable?" What am I then imaging? That the piece of wax from being round in shape can become square, or from being square can become triangular? Assuredly not. For I am apprehending that it admits of an infinity of similar shapes, and am not able to compass this infinity by way of images. Consequently this comprehension of it cannot be the product of the faculty of imagination.

What, we may next ask, is its extension? Is it also not known [by way of the imagination]? It becomes greater when the wax is melted, greater when the wax is made to boil, and ever greater as the heat increases; and I should not be apprehending what the wax truly is, if I did not think that this piece of wax we are considering allows of a greater variety of extensions than I have ever imaged. I must, therefore, admit that I cannot by way of images comprehend what this wax is, and that it is by the mind alone that I [adequately] apprehend it. I say this particular wax, for as to wax in general that is yet more evident. Now what is this wax which cannot be [adequately] apprehended save by the mind? Certainly the same that I see, touch, image, and in short, the very body that from the start I have been supposing it to be. And what has especially to be noted is that our [adequate] apprehension of it is not a seeing, nor a touching, nor an imaging, and has never been such, although it may formerly have seemed so, but is solely an inspection of the mind which may be imperfect and confused, as it formerly was, or clear and distinct, as it now is, according as my attention is directed less or more to the constituents composing the body.

I am indeed amazed when I consider how weak my mind is and how prone to error. For although I can, dispensing with words, [directly] apprehend all this in myself none the less words have a hampering hold upon me, and the accepted usages of ordinary speech tend to mislead me. Thus when the wax is before us we say that we see it to be the same wax as that previously seen, and not that we judge it to be the same from its retaining the same color and shape. From this I should straightway conclude that the wax is known by ocular vision, independently of a strictly mental inspection, were it not that perchance I recall how when looking from a window at beings passing by on the street below, I similarly say that it is men I am seeing, just as I say that I am seeing the wax. What do I see from the window beyond hats and cloaks, which might cover automatic machines? Yet I judge those to be men. In analogous fashion, what I have been supposing myself to see with the eyes I am comprehending solely with the faculty of judgment, a faculty proper not to my eyes but to my mind.

But aiming as I do at knowledge superior to the common, I should be ashamed to draw grounds for doubt from the forms and terms of ordinary speech. I prefer therefore to pass on, and to ask whether I apprehended the wax on my first seeing it, and while I was still believing that I knew it by way of the external senses, or at least by the *sensus communis,* as they call it, that is to say by the imaginative faculty, more perfectly and more evidently than I now apprehend it after having examined with greater care what it is and in what way it can be known. It would indeed be foolish to have doubts as to the answer to this question. Was there anything in that first apprehension which was distinct? What did I apprehend that any animal might not have seen? When, however, I distinguish the wax from its external forms; when stripped as it were of its vestments I consider it in complete nakedness, it is certain that though there may still be error in my judgment, I could not be thus apprehending it without a mind that is human.

What now shall I say of the mind itself, i.e., of myself? For as yet I do not admit in myself anything but mind. What am I to say in regard to this I which seems to apprehend this piece of wax so distinctly? Do I not know myself much more truly and much more certainly, and also much more distinctly and evidently, than I do the wax ? For if I judge that the wax is or exists because I see it, evidently it follows, with yet greater evidence that I myself am or exist, inasmuch as I am thus seeing it. For though it may be that what I see is not in truth wax, and that I do not even possess eyes with which to see anything, yet assuredly when I see, or (for I no longer allow the distinction) when I think I see, it cannot be that I myself who think am not a something. So likewise, if I judge that the wax exists because I touch it, it will follow that I am; and if I judge that the imagination, or some other cause whatever it be, persuades me that the wax exists, the same conclusion follows [viz., that I am thinking by way of an image and thinking what I thus image to be independently existing]. And what I have here said regarding the piece of wax may be said in respect of all other things which are external to me.

And yet a further point: if the apprehension of the wax has seemed to me more determinate and distinct when sight and touch, and many causes besides, have rendered it manifest to me, how much more evidently and distinctly must I now know myself, since all the reasons which can aid in the apprehension of wax, or of any body whatsoever, afford yet better evidence of the nature of my mind. Besides, in the mind itself there are so many more things which can contribute to the more distinct knowledge of it, that those which come to it by way of the body scarcely merit being taken into account.

Thus, then, I have been brought step by step to the conclusion I set out to establish. For I now know that, properly speaking, bodies are cognized not by the senses or by the imagination, but by the understanding alone. They are not thus cognized because seen or touched, but only in so far as they are apprehended understandingly. Thus, as I now recognize, nothing is more easily or more evidently apprehended by me than my mind. Difficult, however, as it is to rid oneself of a way of thinking to which the mind has been so long accustomed, it is well that I should halt for some time at this point, that by prolonged meditation I may more deeply impress upon myself this new knowledge.

From MEDITATION VI

. . . Now that I begin to know myself better and to discover the Author of my being, I do not in truth think that I ought rashly to admit all the things which the senses may seem to teach; but neither do I think that they should all be called in doubt.

In the first place, since I know that all the things I clearly and distinctly apprehend can be created by God exactly as I apprehend them, my being able to apprehend one thing apart from another is, in itself, sufficient to make me certain that the one is different from the other, or at least that it is within God's power to posit them separately; and even though I do not comprehend by what power this separation comes about, I shall have no option but to view them as different. Accordingly, simply from knowing that I exist, and that, meantime, I do not observe any other thing as evidently pertaining to my nature, i.e., to my essence, except this only, that I am a thinking thing, I rightly conclude that my essence consists in this alone, that I am a thinking thing (i.e., a substance, the whole nature or essence of which consists in thinking). And although possibly (or rather certainly, as I shall shortly be declaring) I have a body with which I am very closely conjoined, yet since on the one hand I have a clear and distinct idea of myself, in so far as I am only a thinking unextended thing, and on the other hand a distinct idea of the body in so far as it is only an extended unthinking thing, it is certain that I am truly distinct from my body, and can exist without it.[6]

I further find in myself faculties of thinking which are quite special modes of thinking, distinct from myself, viz., the faculties of imaging and sensing; I can clearly and distinctly apprehend myself as complete without them, but not them without the self, i.e., without an intelligent substance in which they reside. For in the notion we have of them, or (to use the terms of the Schools) in their formal concept, they include some sort of intellection, and I am thereby enabled to recognize that they are at once related to, and distinguished from, the self, as being its modes (just as shapes, movements, and the other modes and accidents of bodies are in respect of the bodies which uphold them).

I am also aware in me of certain faculties, such as the power of changing location, of assuming diverse postures, and the like, which cannot be thought, and cannot therefore exist, any more than can the preceding, apart from some substance in which they reside. But evidently, since the clear and distinct apprehension of these faculties involves the feature of extension, but not any intellection, they must, if they indeed exist, belong to some substance which is corporeal, i.e., extended and unthinking. Now there is, indeed, a certain passive faculty of sense, i.e., of receiving and knowing the ideas of sensible things, but this would be useless to me if there did not also exist in me, or in some other being, an active faculty capable of producing or effecting these ideas. This active faculty cannot, however, be in me—not at least in so far as I am only a thinking thing—since it does not presuppose intellection, and since the ideas present themselves to me without my contributing in any way to their so doing, and often even against my will. This faculty must therefore exist in some substance different from me—a substance that, as already noted, contains, either formally or eminently, all the reality which is objectively [i.e., by way of representation] in the ideas produced by the faculty, and this substance is either body, i.e., corporeal nature, in which there is contained formally, i.e., actually, all that is objectively, i.e., by representation, in those ideas; or it is God Himself, or some creature nobler than body, in which all of it is eminently contained.

But since God is no deceiver, it is evident that He does not of Himself and immediately, communicate those ideas to me. Nor does He do so by way of some creature in which their objective reality is not contained formally [i.e., actually], but only eminently. For as He has given me no faculty whereby I could discover this to be the case, but on the contrary a very strong inclination to believe that those ideas are conveyed to me by corporeal things, I do not see how He could be defended against the charge of deception, were the ideas produced otherwise than by corporeal things. We have, therefore, no option save to conclude that corporeal things do indeed exist.

Yet they are not perhaps exactly such as we apprehend by way of the senses; in many instances they are apprehended only obscurely and confusedly. But we must at least admit that whatever I there clearly and distinctly apprehend, i.e., generally speaking, everything comprised in the object of pure mathematics, is to be found in them. As regards those other things which are only particular, such as that the Sun is of this or that magnitude and shape, and the like, or as regards those things which are apprehended less clearly, such as light, sound, pain and the like, however dubious and uncertain all of these may be, yet inasmuch as God is no deceiver and that there cannot therefore, in the opinions I form, be any falsity for the correction of which He has not given me some faculty sufficient thereto, I may, I believe, confidently conclude that in regard to these things also the means of avoiding error are at my disposal.

Thus there can be no question that all those things in which I am instructed by nature contain some truth; for by nature, considered in general, I now understand no other than either God Himself or the order of created things as instituted by Him, and by my nature in particular I understand the totality of all those things which God has given me.

Now there is nothing which nature teaches me more expressly, or more sensibly, than that I have a body which is adversely affected when I sense pain, and stands in need of food and drink when I suffer hunger or thirst, etc.; and consequently I ought not to doubt there being some truth in all this.

Nature also teaches me by these sensings of pain, hunger, thirst, etc., that I am not lodged in my body merely as a pilot in a ship, but so intimately conjoined, and as it were intermingled with it, that with it I form a unitary whole. Were not this the case, I should not sense pain when my body is hurt, being, as I should then be, merely a thinking thing, but should apprehend the wound in a purely cognitive manner, just as a sailor apprehends by sight any damage to his ship; and when my body has need of food and drink I should apprehend this expressly, and not be made aware of it by confused sensings of hunger, thirst, pain, etc. For these sensings of hunger, thirst, pain, etc., are in truth merely confused modes of thinking, arising from and dependent on the union, and as it were, the intermingling of mind and body.

Because this, nature teaches me that my body exists as one among other bodies, some of which are to be sought after and others shunned. And certainly on sensing colors, sounds, odors, tastes, heat, hardness and the like, I rightly conclude that in the bodies from which these various sensory apprehensions proceed, there are variations corresponding to them, though not perhaps resembling them; and since among these sense-apprehensions some are pleasing to me, and others displeasing, there can be no doubt that my body, or rather my entire self, inasmuch as I am composed of body and mind, can be variously affected, beneficially or harmfully, by surrounding bodies.

Many other things, however, that may seem to have been taught me by nature, are not learned from her, but have gained a footing in my mind only through a certain habit I have of judging inconsiderately. Consequently, as easily happens, the judgments I pass are erroneous.... Thus, although the impression a star makes on my eye is no larger than that made by the flame of a small candle, there is yet in me no real or positive power determining me to believe that the star is no larger than the flame; it is merely that, without reason, I have so judged from my earliest years. And though on approaching fire I sense heat, and on approaching it too closely I sense pain, this is no ground for concluding that something resembling the heat is in the fire and also something resembling the pain, but only that in it there is something, whatever it be, which produces in me these sensations of heat and pain.

So also, although there are spaces in which I find nothing to affect my senses, it does not follow that in them there is no body, for in this, as in many other matters, I have been accustomed to pervert the order of nature. These sensuous apprehensions have been given me by nature only as testifying to my mind what things are beneficial or harmful to the composite whole of which it is a part. For this they are indeed sufficiently clear and distinct. But what I have done is to use them as rules sufficiently reliable to be employed in the immediate determination of the *essence* of bodies external to me; and, as so employed, their testimony cannot be other than obscure and confused.

NOTES:

1. Archimedes: a Greek mathematician, physicist, and inventor, third century B.C.
2. i.e., are not independent existents.
3. *Ego sum, ego existo.*
4. *Res cogitans*; Fr. *une chose qui pense.*
5. Replying to Burman (A.T.v, p. 157; Adam's edition, p. 18), Descartes adds:"Whether this being is indeed God, I cannot yet say. Is the genius who is deluding me the Being who also created me? That I do not yet know and am here speaking only in a confused manner."
6. i.e. should God so provide.

DESCARTES' MYTH

Gilbert Ryle

(1) The Official Doctrine.

THERE is a doctrine about the nature and place of minds which is so prevalent among theorists and even among laymen that it deserves to be described as the official theory. Most philosophers, psychologists and religious teachers subscribe, with minor reservations, to its main articles and, although they admit certain theoretical difficulties in it, they tend to assume that these can be overcome without serious modifications being made to the architecture of the theory. It will be argued here that the central principles of the doctrine are unsound and conflict with the whole body of what we know about minds when we are not speculating about them.

The official doctrine, which hails chiefly from Descartes, is something like this. With the doubtful exceptions of idiots and infants in arms every human being has both a body and a mind. Some would prefer to say that every human being is both a body and a mind. His body and his mind are ordinarily harnessed together, but after the death of the body his mind may continue to exist and function.

Human bodies are in space and are subject to the mechanical laws which govern all other bodies in space. Bodily processes and states can be inspected by external observers. So a man's bodily life is as much a public affair as are the lives of animals and reptiles and even as the careers of trees, crystals and planets.

But minds are not in space, nor are their operations subject to mechanical laws. The workings of one mind are not witnessable by other observers; its career is private. Only I can take direct cognisance of the states and processes of my own mind. A person therefore lives through two collateral histories, one consisting of what happens in and to his body, the other consisting of what happens in and to his mind. The first is public, the second private. The events in the first history are events in the physical world, those in the second are events in the mental world.

It has been disputed whether a person does or can directly monitor all or only some of the episodes of his own private history; but, according to the official doctrine, of at least some of these episodes he has direct and unchallengeable cognisance. In consciousness, self-consciousness and introspection he is directly and authentically apprised of the present states and operations of his mind. He may have great or small uncertainties about concurrent and adjacent episodes in the physical world, but he can have none about at least part of what is momentarily occupying his mind.

It is customary to express this bifurcation of his two lives and of his two worlds by saying that the things and events which belong to the physical world, including his own body, are external, while the workings of his own mind are internal. This antithesis of outer and inner is of course meant to be construed as a metaphor, since minds, not being in space, could not be described as being spatially inside anything else, or as having things going on spatially inside themselves. But relapses from this good intention are common and theorists are found speculating how stimuli, the physical sources of which are yards or miles outside a person's skin, can generate mental responses inside his skull, or how decisions framed inside his cranium can set going movements of his extremities.

Even when 'inner' and 'outer' are construed as metaphors, the problem how a person's mind and body influence one another is notoriously charged with theoretical difficulties. What the mind wills, the legs, arms and the tongue execute; what affects the ear and the eye has something to do with what the mind perceives; grimaces and smiles betray the mind's moods and bodily castigations lead, it is hoped, to moral improvement. But the actual transactions between the episodes of the private history and those of the public history remain mysterious, since by definition they can belong to neither series. They could not be reported among the happenings described in a person's autobiography of his inner life, but nor could they be reported among those described in some one else's biography of that person's overt career. They can be inspected neither by introspection nor by laboratory experiment. They are theoretical shuttlecocks which are forever being bandied from the physiologist back to the psychologist and from the psychologist back to the physiologist.

Underlying this partly metaphorical representation of the bifurcation of a person's two lives there is a seemingly more profound and philosophical assumption. It is assumed that there are two different kinds of existence or status. What exists or happens may have the status of physical existence, or it may have the status of mental existence. Somewhat as the faces of coins are either heads or tails, or somewhat as living creatures are either male or female, so, it is supposed, some existing is physical existing, other existing is mental existing. It is a necessary feature of what has physical existence that it is in space and time, it is a necessary feature of what has mental existence that it is in time but not in space. What has physical existence is composed of matter, or else is a function of matter; what has mental existence consists of consciousness, or else is a function of consciousness.

There is thus a polar opposition between mind and matter, an opposition which is often brought out as follows. Material objects are situated in a common field, known as 'space', and what happens to one body in one part of space is mechanically connected with what happens to other bodies in other parts of space. But mental happenings occur in insulated fields, known as 'minds', and there is, apart maybe from telepathy, no direct causal connection between what happens in one mind and what happens in another. Only through the medium of the public physical world can the mind of one person make a difference to the mind of another. The mind is its own place and in his inner life each of us lives the life of a ghostly Robinson Crusoe. People can see, hear and jolt one another's bodies, but they are irremediably blind and deaf to the workings of one another's minds and inoperative upon them.

What sort of knowledge can be secured of the workings of a mind? On the one side, according to the official theory, a person has direct knowledge of the best imaginable kind of the workings of his own mind. Mental states and processes are (or are normally) conscious states and processes, and the consciousness which irradiates them can engender no illusions and leaves the door open for no doubts. A person's present thinkings, feelings and willings, his perceivings, rememberings and imaginings are intrinsically 'phosphorescent'; their existence and their nature are inevitably betrayed to their owner. The inner life is a stream of consciousness of such a sort that it would be absurd to suggest that the mind whose life is that stream might be unaware of what is passing down it.

True, the evidence adduced recently by Freud seems to show that there exist channels tributary to this stream, which run hidden from their owner. People are actuated by impulses the existence of which they vigorously disavow; some of their thoughts differ from the thoughts which they acknowledge; and some of the actions which they think they will to perform they do not really will. They are thoroughly gulled by some of their own hypocrisies and they successfully ignore facts about their mental lives which on the official theory ought to be patent to them. Holders of the official theory tend, however, to maintain that anyhow in normal circumstances a person must be directly and authentically seized of the present state and workings of his own mind.

Besides being currently supplied with these alleged immediate data of consciousness, a person is also generally supposed to be able to exercise from time to time a special kind of perception, namely inner perception, or introspection. He can take a (non-optical) 'look' at what is passing in his mind. Not only can he view and scrutinize a flower through his sense of sight and listen to and discriminate the notes of a bell through his sense of hearing; he can also reflectively or introspectively watch, without any bodily organ of sense, the current episodes of his inner life. This self-observation is also commonly supposed to be immune from illusion, confusion or doubt. A mind's reports of its own affairs have a certainty superior to the best that is possessed by its reports of matters in the physical world. Sense-perceptions can, but consciousness and introspection cannot, be mistaken or confused.

On the other side, one person has no direct access of any sort to the events of the inner life of another. He cannot do better than make problematic inferences from the observed behaviour of the other person's body to the states of mind which, by analogy from his own conduct, he supposes to be signalised by that behaviour. Direct access to the workings of a mind is the privilege of that mind itself; in default of such privileged access, the workings of one mind are inevitably occult to everyone else. For the supposed arguments from bodily movements similar to their own to mental workings similar to their own would lack any possibility of observational corroboration. Not unnaturally, therefore, an adherent of the official theory finds it difficult to resist this consequence of his premisses, that he has no good reason to believe that there do exist minds other than his own. Even if he prefers to believe that to other human bodies there are harnessed minds not unlike his own, he cannot claim to be able to discover their individual characteristics, or the particular things that they undergo and do. Absolute solitude is on this showing the ineluctable destiny of the soul. Only our bodies can meet.

As a necessary corollary of this general scheme there is implicitly prescribed a special way of construing our ordinary concepts of mental powers and operations. The verbs, nouns and adjectives, with which in ordinary life we describe the wits, characters and higher-grade performances of the people with whom we have do, are required to be construed as signifying special episodes in their secret histories, or else as signifying tendencies for such episodes to occur. When someone is described as knowing, believing or guessing something, as hoping, dreading, intending or shirking something, as designing this or being amused at that, these verbs are supposed to denote the occurrence of specific modifications in his (to us) occult stream of consciousness. Only his own privileged access to this stream in direct awareness and introspection could provide authentic testimony that these mental-conduct verbs were correctly or incorrectly applied. The onlooker, be he teacher, critic, biographer or friend, can never assure himself that his comments have any vestige of truth. Yet it was just because we do in fact all know how to make such comments, make them with general correctness and correct them when they turn out to be confused or mistaken, that philosophers found it necessary to construct their theories of the nature and place of minds. Finding mental conduct concepts being regularly and effectively used, they properly sought to fix their logical geography. But the logical geography officially recommended would entail that there could be no regular or effective use of these mental-conduct concepts in our descriptions of, and prescriptions for, other people's minds.

(2) The Absurdity of the Official Doctrine.

Such in outline is the official theory. I shall often speak of it, with deliberate abusiveness, as 'the dogma of the Ghost in the Machine'. I hope to prove that it is entirely false, and false not in detail but in principle. It is not merely an assemblage of particular mistakes. It is one big mistake and a mistake of a special kind. It is, namely, a category mistake. It represents the facts of mental life as if they belonged to one logical type or category (or range of types or categories), when they actually belong to another. The dogma is therefore a philosopher's myth. In attempting to explode the myth I shall probably be taken to be denying well-known facts about the mental life of human beings, and my plea that I aim at doing nothing more than rectify the logic of mental-conduct concepts will probably be disallowed as mere subterfuge.

I must first indicate what is meant by the phrase 'Category-mistake'. This I do in a series of illustrations.

A foreigner visiting Oxford or Cambridge for the first time is shown a number of colleges, libraries, playing fields, museums, scientific departments and administrative offices. He then asks 'But where is the University? I have seen where the members of the Colleges live, where the Registrar works, where the scientists experiment and the rest. But I have not yet seen the University in which reside and work the members of your University.' It has then to be explained to him that the University is not another collateral institution, some ulterior counterpart to the colleges, laboratories and offices which he has seen. The University is just the way in which all that he has already seen is organized. When they are seen and when their co-ordination is understood, the University has been seen. His mistake lay in his innocent assumption that it was correct to speak of Christ Church, the Bodleian Library, the Ashmolean Museum *and* the University, to speak, that is, as if 'the University' stood for an extra member of the class of which these other units are members. He was mistakenly allocating the University to the same category as that to which the other institutions belong.

The same mistake would be made by a child witnessing the march-past of a division, who, having had pointed out to him such batteries, squadrons, etc., asked when the division was going to appear. He would be supposing that a division was a counterpart to the units already seen, partly similar to them and partly unlike them. He would be shown his mistake by being told that in watching the battalions, batteries and squadrons and such battalions, marching past he had been watching the division marching past. The march-past was not a parade of battalions, batteries, squadrons *and* a division; it was a parade of the battalions, batteries and squadrons *of* a division.

One more illustration. A foreigner watching his first game of cricket learns what are the functions of the bowlers, the batsmen, the fielders, the umpires and the scorers. He then says 'But there is no one left on the field to contribute the famous element of team-spirit. I see who does the bowling, the batting and the wicketkeeping; but I do not see whose role it is to exercise *esprit de corps*.' Once more, it would have to be explained that he was looking for the wrong type of thing. Team-spirit is not another cricketing operation supplementary to all of the other special tasks. It is, roughly, the keenness with which each of the special tasks is performed, and performing a task keenly is not performing two tasks. Certainly exhibiting team-spirit is not the same thing as bowling or catching, but nor is it a third thing such that we can say that the bowler first bowls *and* then exhibits team-spirit or that a fielder is at a given moment *either* catching or displaying *esprit de corps*.

These illustrations of category-mistakes have a common feature which must be noticed. The mistakes were made by people who did not know how to wield the concepts *University*, *division* and *team-spirit*. Their puzzles arose from inability to use certain items in the English vocabulary.

The theoretically interesting category-mistakes are those made by people who are perfectly competent to apply concepts, at least in the situations with which they are familiar, but are still liable in their abstract thinking to allocate those concepts to logical types to which they do not belong. An instance of a mistake of this sort would be the following story. A student of politics has learned the main differences between the British, the French and the American Constitutions, and has learned also the differences and connections between the Cabinet, Parliament, the various Ministries, the Judicature and the Church of England. But he still becomes embarrassed when asked questions about the connections between the Church of England, the Home Office and the British Constitution. For while the Church and the Home Office are institutions the British Constitution is not another institution in the same sense of that noun. So inter-institutional relations which can be asserted or denied to hold between the Church and the Home Office cannot be asserted or denied to hold between either of them and the British Constitution. 'The British Constitution' is not a term of the same logical type as 'the Home Office' and 'the Church of England'. In a partially similar way, John Doe may be a relative, a friend, an enemy or a stranger to Richard Roe; but he cannot be any of these things to the Average Taxpayer. He knows how to talk sense in certain sorts of discussions about the Average Taxpayer, but he is baffled to say why he could not come across him in the street as he can come across Richard Roe.

It is pertinent to our main subject to notice that, so long as the student of politics continues to think of the British Constitution as a counterpart to the other institutions, he will tend to describe it as a mysteriously occult institution; and so long as John Doe continues to think of the Average Taxpayer as a fellow-citizen, he will tend to think of him as an elusive insubstantial man, a ghost who is everywhere yet nowhere.

My destructive purpose is to show that a family of radical category-mistakes is the source of the double-life theory. The representation of a person as a ghost mysteriously ensconced in a machine derives from this argument. Because, as is true, a person's thinking, feeling and purposive doing cannot be described solely in the idioms of physics, chemistry and physiology, therefore they must be described in counterpart idioms. As the human body is a complex organized unit, so the human mind must be another complex organized unit, though one made of a different sort of stuff and with a different sort of structure. Or, again, as the human body, like any other parcel of matter, is a field of causes and effects, so the mind must be another field of causes and effects, though not (Heaven be praised) mechanical causes and effects.

(3) The Origin of the Category-Mistake.

One of the chief intellectual origins of what I have yet to prove to be the Cartesian category-mistake seems to be this. When Galileo showed that his methods of scientific discovery were competent to provide a mechanical theory which should cover every occupant of space, Descartes found in himself two conflicting motives. As a man of scientific genius he could not but endorse the claims of mechanics, yet as a religious and moral man he could not accept, as Hobbes accepted, the discouraging rider to those claims, namely that human nature differs only in degree of complexity from clockwork. The mental could not be just a variety of the mechanical.

He and subsequent philosophers naturally but erroneously availed themselves of the following escape-route. Since mental conduct words are not to be construed as signifying the occurrence of mechanical processes, they must be construed as signifying the occurrence of non-mechanical processes; since mechanical laws explain movements in space as the effects of other movements in space, other laws must explain some of the non-spatial workings of minds as the effects of other non-spatial workings of minds. The difference between the human behaviours which we describe as intelligent and those which we describe as unintelligent must be a difference in their causation; so, while some movements of human tongues and limbs are the effects of mechanical causes, others must be the effects of non-mechanical causes, i.e. some issue from movements of particles of matter, others from workings of the mind.

The differences between the physical and the mental were thus represented as differences inside the common framework of the categories of 'thing', 'stuff', 'attribute', 'state', 'process', 'change', 'cause' and 'effect'. Minds are things, but different sorts of things from bodies; mental processes are causes and effects, but different sorts of causes and effects from bodily movements. And so on. Somewhat as the foreigner expected the University to be an extra edifice, rather like a college but also considerably different, so the repudiators of mechanism represented minds as extra centers of causal processes, rather like machines but also considerably different from them. Their theory was a para-mechanical hypothesis.

That this assumption was at the heart of the doctrine is shown by the fact that there was from the beginning felt to be a major theoretical difficulty in explaining how minds can influence and be influenced by bodies. How can a mental process, such as willing, cause spatial movements like the movements of the tongue? How can a physical change in the optic nerve have among its effects a mind's perception of a flash of light? This notorious crux by itself shows the logical mould into which Descartes pressed his theory of the mind. It was the self-same mould into which he and Galileo set their mechanics. Still unwittingly adhering to the grammar of mechanics, he tried to avert disaster by describing minds in what was merely an obverse vocabulary. The workings of minds had to be described by the mere negatives of the specific descriptions given to bodies; they are not in space, they are not motions, they are not modifications of matter, they are not accessible to public observation. Minds are not bits of clockwork, they are just bits of not-clockwork.

As thus represented, minds are not merely ghosts harnessed to machines, they are themselves just spectral machines. Though the human body is an engine, it it not quite an ordinary engine, since some of its workings are governed by another engine inside it—this interior governor-engine being one of a very special sort. It is invisible, inaudible and it has no size or weight. It cannot be taken to bits and the laws it obeys are not those known to ordinary engineers. Nothing is known of how it governs the bodily engine.

A second major crux points the same moral. Since, according to the doctrine, minds belong to the same category as bodies and since bodies are rigidly governed by mechanical laws, it seemed to many theorists to follow that minds must be similarly governed by rigid non-mechanical laws. The physical world is a deterministic system, so the mental world must be a deterministic system. Bodies cannot help the modifications that they undergo, so minds cannot help pursuing the careers fixed for them. *Responsibility, choice, merit* and *demerit* are therefore inapplicable concepts—unless the compromise solution is adopted of saying that the laws governing mental processes, unlike those governing physical processes, have the congenial attribute of being only rather rigid. The problem of the Freedom of the Will was the problem how to reconcile the hypothesis that minds are to be described in terms drawn from the categories of mechanics with the knowledge that higher-grade human conduct is not of a piece with the behaviour of machines.

It is an historical curiosity that it was not noticed that the entire argument was broken-backed. Theorists correctly assumed that any sane man could already recognise the differences between, say, rational and non-rational utterances or between purposive and automatic behaviour. Else there would have been nothing requiring to be salved from mechanism. Yet the explanation given presupposed that one person could in principle never recognise the difference between the rational and the irrational utterances issuing from other human bodies, since he could never get access to the postulated immaterial causes of some of their utterances. Save for the doubtful exception of himself, he could never tell the difference between a man and a Robot. It would have to be conceded, for example, that, for all that we can tell, the inner lives of persons who are classed as idiots or lunatics are as rational as those of anyone else. Perhaps only their overt behaviour is disappointing; that is to say, perhaps 'idiots' are not really idiotic, or 'lunatics' lunatic. Perhaps, too, some of those who are classed as sane are really idiots. According to the theory, external observers could never know how the overt behaviour of others is correlated with their mental powers and processes and so they could never know or even plausibly conjecture whether their applications of mental-conduct concepts to these other people were correct or incorrect. It would then be hazardous or impossible for a man to claim sanity or logical consistency even for himself, since he would be debarred from comparing his own performances with those of others. In short, our characterisations of persons and their performances as intelligent, prudent and virtuous or as stupid, hypocritical and cowardly could never have been made, so the problem of providing a special causal hypothesis to serve as the basis of such diagnoses would never have arisen. The question, 'How do persons differ from machines?' arose just because everyone already knew how to apply mental-conduct concepts before the new causal hypothesis was introduced. This causal hypothesis could not therefore be the source of the criteria used in those applications. Nor, of course, has the causal hypothesis in any degree improved our handling of those criteria. We still distinguish good from bad arithmetic, politic from impolitic conduct and fertile from infertile imaginations in the ways in which Descartes himself distinguished them before and after he speculated how the applicability of these criteria was compatible with the principle of mechanical causation.

He had mistaken the logic of his problem. Instead of asking by what criteria intelligent behaviour is actually distinguished from non-intelligent behaviour, he asked 'Given that the principle of mechanical causation does not tell us the difference, what other principle will tell it us?' He realised that the problem was not one of mechanics and assumed that it must therefore be one of some counterpart to mechanics. Not unnaturally psychology is often cast for just this role.

When two terms belong to the same category, it is proper to construct conjunctive propositions embodying them. Thus a purchaser may say that he bought a left-hand glove and a right-hand glove, but not that he bought a left-hand glove, a right-hand glove and a pair of gloves. 'She came home in a flood of tears and a sedan-chair' is a well-known joke based on the absurdity of conjoining terms of different types. It would have been equally ridiculous to construct the disjunction 'She came home either in a flood of tears or else in a sedan-chair'. Now the dogma of the Ghost in the Machine does just this. It maintains that there exist both bodies and minds; that there occur physical processes and mental processes; that there are mechanical causes of corporeal movements and mental causes of corporeal movements. I shall argue that these and other analogous conjunctions are absurd; but, it must be noticed, the argument will not show that either of the illegitimately conjoined propositions is absurd in itself. I am not, for example, denying that there occur mental processes. Doing long division is a mental process and so is making a joke. But I am saying that the phrase 'there occur mental processes' does not mean the same sort of thing as 'there occur physical processes', and, therefore, that it makes no sense to conjoin or disjoin the two.

If my argument is successful, there will follow some interesting consequences. First, the hallowed contrast between Mind and Matter will be dissipated, but dissipated not by either of the equally hallowed absorptions of Mind by Matter or of Matter by Mind, but in quite a different way. For the seeming contrast of the two will be shown to be as illegitimate as would be the contrast of 'she came home in a flood of tears' and 'she came home in a sedan-chair'. The belief that there is a polar opposition between Mind and Matter is the belief that they are terms of the same logical type.

It will also follow that both Idealism and Materialism are answers to an improper question. The 'reduction' of the material world to mental states and processes, as well as the 'reduction' of mental states and processes to physical states and processes, presuppose the legitimacy of the disjunction 'Either there exist minds or there exist bodies (but not both)'. It would be like saying, 'Either she bought a left-hand and a right-hand glove or she bought a pair of gloves (but not both)'.

It is perfectly proper to say, in one logical tone of voice, that there exist minds and to say, in another logical tone of voice, that 'there exist bodies.' But these expressions do not indicate two different species of existence, for 'existence' is not a generic word like 'coloured' or 'sexed'. They indicate two different senses of 'exist', somewhat as 'rising' has different senses in 'the tide is rising', 'hopes are rising', and 'the average age of death is rising'. A man would be thought to be making a poor joke who said that three things are now rising, namely the tide, hopes and the average age of death. It would be just as good or bad a joke to say that there exist prime numbers and Wednesdays and public opinions and navies; or that there exist both minds and bodies. In the succeeding chapters I try to prove that the official theory does rest on a batch of category-mistakes by showing that logically absurd corollaries follow from it. The exhibition of these absurdities will have the constructive effect of bringing out part of the correct logic of mental-conduct concepts.

(4) Historical Note.

It would not be true to say that the official theory derives solely from Descartes' theories, or even from a more widespread anxiety about the implications of seventeenth century mechanics. Scholastic and Reformation theology had schooled the intellects of the scientists as well as of the laymen, philosophers and clerics of that age. Stoic-Augustinian theories of the will were embedded in the Calvinist doctrines of sin and grace; Platonic and Aristotelian theories of the intellect shaped the orthodox doctrines of the immortality of the soul. Descartes was reformulating already prevalent theological doctrines of the soul in the new syntax of Galileo. The theologian's privacy of conscience became the philosopher's privacy of consciousness, and what had been the bogy of Predestination reappeared as the bogy of Determinism.

It would also not be true to say that the two-worlds myth did no theoretical good. Myths often do a lot of theoretical good, while they are still new. One benefit bestowed by the paramechanical myth was that it partly superannuated the then prevalent para-political myth. Minds and their Faculties had previously been described by analogies with political superiors and political subordinates. The idioms used were those of ruling, obeying, collaborating and rebelling. They survived and still survive in many ethical and some epistemological discussions. As, in physics, the new myth of occult Forces was a scientific improvement on the old myth of Final Causes, so, in anthropological and psychological theory, the new myth of hidden operations, impulses and agencies was an improvement on the old myth of dictations, deferences and disobediences.

DIFFICULTIES FOR ANY DUALIST THEORY

David M. Armstrong
University of Sydney

(a) *Can a Dualist account for the unity of mind and body?*

In his book *Individuals* P. F. Strawson has emphasized how natural it is to ascribe mental and physical properties to the same subject. We say 'I am thinking' and 'I am angry,' but we also say 'I am lying down' and 'I am twelve stone' and seem to have no consciousness of using the word 'I' in two different senses. ('I was lying down thinking.') Yet if a Dualist account of mind and body is correct, then in the first two cases the word 'I' refers to a spiritual substance or to a collection of non-physical items, while in the second set of cases the word refers to a certain physical object.

I do not think that this argument [against Dualism] is very strong as it stands. The Dualist can very well reply that, in ordinary speech, personal pronouns such as 'I' refer to a *compound* object 'spiritual object (or objects) related in a certain way to a certain physical object.' Consider the case of a motor-car. For certain purposes we might regard a car as a compound of two substances, the engine and the chassis. Now we say 'The *car* is back-firing' although we could speak more strictly and say 'The *engine* of the car is back-firing'. Again, we say 'The *car* is squeaking and rattling' although we could speak more strictly and say 'The *chassis* of the car is squeaking and rattling.' In the same way, the Dualist might urge, to say 'I am angry' could be put in a stricter way as 'The spiritual part of me is angry', while 'I am lying down' could be put in a stricter way as 'The physical part of me is lying down.' As the example of the car shows, we can attribute to wholes properties which are, strictly speaking, only properties of proper parts of the whole.

Such a line of defence would be greatly strengthened if Dualism were combined with Behaviorism. If the concept of mind involved *both* a spiritual substance (or spiritual events) and certain sorts of bodily behavior, then it would be easy to see why ordinary speech makes no sharp distinction between a spiritual subject and a material subject, but instead attributes both mental and physical characteristics of the same subject: the person.

Nevertheless, there is an underlying point to this objection to Dualism which is not so easy to deal with. The difficulty is this: does a Dualist theory provide for a sufficiently close connection between the spiritual and the physical components of man? We ordinarily think of the connection between the mind and the body as very close indeed. Man is a unity. Dualism is unsatisfactory because it breaks up that unity.

To develop this point. We could solve the problem by postulating, or claiming to observe, a unique and indefinable relation that holds together the spiritual and physical components of man. But if we disdain to resort to this manoeuvre, there remain only the relations of *temporal simultaneity* and *causal relationship* to tie the spiritual object or objects to the body. It is not easy to see clearly that these are the only known relations we can appeal

From D.M. Armstrong, *A Materialist Theory of the Mind* (London: Routledge & Kegan Paul, Ltd., and New Jersey: Humanities Press, Inc., 1968), pp. 24-36. Reprinted by permission of the author and the publisher.

to, because the imagination is tempted, quite illegitimately from the Dualist standpoint, to add a further relation. It is very natural to think of the mind as actually situated inside the body: as an inner realm. But this is to put the mind into physical space, and the essential point about Dualism is its denial that the mind is a spatial thing. And once we are rid of this picture of the mind as literally inside the body, there are only the relations of temporal simultaneity and causal connection to bind the mind and the body together.

In the *Sixth Meditation,* Descartes denies that his mind is in his body simply as a pilot is in his vessel. He says that the relationship of mind and body is much closer than this. The remark is a tribute to Descartes' philosophical honesty, but it is difficult to reconcile with his Dualism. For the pilot is not only causally related to his vessel, acting on it and being acted on by it, but he is also spatially inside the vessel. But without resort to completely *ad hoc* postulation of some further relation, a Dualist can only appeal to the causal relations of mind and body. So a *Dualist* ought to say that the relation of mind to body is in some ways more *distant* than that of pilot to vessel.

It might be suggested that the Dualist can provide a closer relationship in the following way. It is characteristic of our sensory field, in particular of our visual field, that *we* are in the center of it. We perceive things as nearer or further from *ourselves.* Now our body is also perceived to be in the center of our sensory field. So, in some sense, it seems that we are located in the same place as our body.

But what is the 'I' that is where my body is? I do not think it is anything more than *the body itself* as given to sense-perception. We perceive things as nearer or further from our body: it is our body that is the center of our sensory field. So as far as this point goes, all that a Dualist can say by way of linking the mind and the body more closely is that the body is a central object in our perceptual field, the central material object on which our attention is directed. The relationship between mind and body remains a remarkably distant one, and the Dualist cannot explain why we think the two are so closely connected.

The existence of bodily sensations may also be thought to point to a specially intimate relationship between a particular mind and a particular body. For bodily sensations (such as pains and itches) seem to have the two following characteristics. In the first place they are mind-dependent: there could not be a pain or itch without a mind to have it. In the second place, however, they have a bodily location: in the hand or behind the ear. So here mind and body seem to be commingled.

But does this apparent combination of mental being and physical location really assist the *Dualist's* case? It might show that there was a close link between mind and body, but to the extent that it did this, it would show that Dualism was false. For Dualism cannot locate the mind, or any part of the mind, in the body.

It is true, as has already been said, that the Dualist can claim that there is a special and unique relation, with which we are all acquainted, but which is quite distinct from causal connection, that binds together spiritual and bodily objects. And it should be emphasized that there is no logical difficulty in solving the problem in this way. But it can hardly be said to be a *plausible* solution.

(b) *How do we numerically differentiate spiritual objects?*

Another serious difficulty for any Dualist theory of mind is the question whether it can provide for the numerical difference of spiritual objects. If we consider two physical objects that exist at the same time, we can say that what makes them two, that is to say makes them numerically different, is that they are in different places. However alike they may be, their difference of place makes them distinct from each other. Difference of place *individuates* them. If they are in exactly the same place at the same time, they are not two objects but only one.

But now let us consider the possibility that there are two spiritual substances, or collections of spiritual items, which are exactly the same in nature at a certain time. What makes two such objects, or sets of objects, *two*? We cannot appeal to their spatial separation because, by hypothesis, they are not in space.

It might be replied that they can be differentiated by differences in their past history. But this reply is insufficient. For, *firstly* it is a meaningful possibility that two spiritual substances, or collections of spiritual items, should exist like two perfectly synchronized clocks, having exactly the same past spiritual history. *Secondly,* even in a case where this is not so and the spiritual histories are identical in character for a limited time, what differentiates the objects during that time? What difference is there between the case where we have two different spiritual substances, or collections of spiritual items, and the case where the two substances, or sets of items, 'coalesce' temporarily?

It might be thought that two such spiritual substances, or collections of spiritual items, can be differentiated from each other in the following way. One is connected to *this* body, while the other is connected to *that* body. For, unlike the two spiritual substances or collections of spiritual items, however much the bodies resemble, they are nevertheless made different by being in different places.

But suppose the spiritual substance, or collection of spiritual items, were disembodied? The Dualist would have to admit that this was a meaningful possibility on pain of making nonsense of his Dualism, even if he thought that such disembodied entities should not be called 'minds'. What would make the two different then? And even if the spiritual substance or collections of spiritual items, were not disembodied, reference to the bodies would not really help. For might there not be just *one* spiritual substance or collection of spiritual items, identically related to the *two* bodies? How would the Dualist differentiate between this case, and the case where two spiritual substances or collections of spiritual items, were identical in nature and each related to their own body?

The problem just considered is that of the individuation of spiritual objects that exist at the same time. In what does their difference consist? There is a parallel problem about the identity of one spiritual object or collection of objects over a stretch of time. What makes a spiritual object that exists now the very same one as a spiritual object that existed in the past? Resemblance cannot be the mark of identity, because there might be two or more spiritual objects identical in character and history. In the case of ordinary physical objects we can appeal to *spatio-temporal* continuity. My body is spatio-temporally continuous with my body yesterday, but not with my twin's body. This spatio-temporal continuity is what makes it one body. But in the case of the spiritual objects postulated by the Dualist, there can be no question of any spatial continuity. So what is the principle of continuity for spiritual objects?

It is interesting to notice that these problems troubled St. Thomas Aquinas. The problem came up for him in connection with angels. Angels are disembodied intelligences, and therefore raise the question what makes them numerically different from each other. Aquinas' solution was to say that each angel was of a separate species, a different *sort* of object from any other angel. Among angels, difference of number is simply difference of kind. (See *Summa Theologica, Pt. I,* Q. 50, Art. 4.) But Aquinas' resolution of the difficulty is clearly a makeshift. Why should not God create two identical angels? It is surely an intelligible possibility. And what would differentiate the two then?

As usual, the argument might be met by postulation. One could postulate a 'principle of individuation' of a non-spatial nature to ensure the numerical difference of spiritual objects. And, indeed, I think that the existence of such a principle of distinction is an intelligible conception. This last point has been denied by some modern philosophers. They seem to maintain that if we suppose two distinct objects that exist at the same time, then the only meaning we can give to this supposition is that the objects are in different places. If we accepted what they say, then it would seem to be a logically necessary truth that objects that are in time are also in space. But if this is so, a logically necessary truth seems to be giving us positive information about the nature of the world, viz., that whatever is temporal is also spatio-temporal, Now I do not believe that mere logic is capable of providing this information. I believe that it is *a fact* about the world that every object that is in time is also in space (indeed, I believe that it is a fact about the world that every object there is is in space and time), but I cannot think that this is a matter of logical necessity. We cannot rule out the existence of a nonspatial or even a non-temporal 'principle of individuation' *a priori.*

Nevertheless, it does seem likely that the only 'principle of individuation' with which we have any *concrete acquaintance* is that of being in different times and places. The inability of the Dualist to say anything at all about his spiritual 'principle of individuation' strongly suggests that the only way he can understand his notion is a negative way: as 'a non-spatial principle of individuation.' It seems that he is not in fact acquainted with such a principle, nor is there any reason to postulate it.

The position taken here is very similar to Immanuel Kant's view in the *Critique of Pure Reason.* For reasons that need not be discussed here, Kant speaks of space and time as the 'forms of intuition.' He recognizes, also, that it is space and time which secure the numerical difference of distinct objects. (See, *e.g. Critique,* A263/264 = B319/320.) But although space and time are the *human* forms of intuition, Kant thinks it is perfectly possible that there might be other forms of intuition, although we have no concrete acquaintance with any. (See, *e.g. Critique,* B72.) Presumably, then, he would have said that, if such other forms of intuition existed, they would differentiate objects one from the other just as space and time do.

(c) Is the Dualist account of the origin of the mind a plausible one?

Let us now consider whether Dualism is a plausible theory in the light of modern scientific knowledge, in particular, in the light of knowledge or plausible guesses about the working of the brain. We may begin by considering the question of exactly when the mind emerges in the growth of men and animals.

It seems that the Dualist must conceive of the emergence of mind in the following way. At some time after conception, when the nervous system of man and the higher animals reaches a certain level of physiological complexity, a completely new, non-spatial entity is brought into existence in a certain completely new sort of relation to the body. The emergence of this new existent could not have been predicted from laws that deal with the physical properties of physical things.

Already the account is highly implausible from the scientific point of view. It is not a particularly difficult notion that, when the nervous system reaches a certain level of complexity, it should develop new properties. Nor would there be anything particularly difficult in the notion that when the nervous system reaches a certain level of complexity it should affect something that was already in existence in a new way. But it is a quite different matter to hold that the nervous system should have the power to create something else, of a quite different nature from itself, and create it out of no materials. Admittedly, there is no *contradiction* in the notion that the nervous system should have these powers, but what we know of the workings of the world makes the hypothesis a very unlikely one.

The need for the creation of a spiritual object or objects by the nervous system would be ruled out if we assumed that the mind existed before it was embodied, and was simply brought into a special relation to the body at a certain level of physiological development. But, of course, this removes one scientific implausibility only to create another. There is very little evidence for believing that the mind preexists its body.

But whether we assume that, at a certain point, the body creates the spiritual object or objects, or whether mind and body are simply brought together at this point, there is a further difficulty for the Dualist to surmount. At what point in the development of the organism shall we say that such a momentous event occurs? The difficulty is that there seems to be nothing in the physiological development of the organism to suggest any point of sharp break. Instead we have a gradual growth from complexity to further complexity, and there is no point of which we can say 'There is such a sharp physiological change here, that this is probably the point at which the body acquires a mind.' Organisms develop by insensible gradations, and so it is natural to say the mind develops in the same way. But because the Dualist sets up so sharp a gap between the material and the mental, he must find a definite point when the mental comes into existence.

The problem we are discussing here is closely connected with one that used to be discussed (perhaps still is?) by theologians: 'When does the infant acquire a soul?' This question may appear academic or scholastic in the worst sense, but it is one that those who believe in the soul as something distinct from the body have to consider. Equally, the Dualist has to consider the question when his spiritual object or objects come into existence. To treat the question as frivolous, while still holding to a Dualist theory of mind and body, would itself be intellectual frivolity.

(d) *Do mind and body interact?*

We may now consider the dispute between the Interactionist and the Parallelist forms of Dualism, the dispute between what we called the 'thermostat' and the 'thermometer' models of the relations between mind and body.

The first thing to be said is that the Interactionist view is the natural one, and only most compelling reasons should drive anybody to accept a Parallelist account. For consider the following sequence. I am struck on the hand, I feel pain, I wring my hand. It is completely natural, and surely correct, to say that the blow *causes* me to feel pain, and the pain in turn *causes* me to wring my hand. It appears obvious that, in a case like this, body and mind interact. A bodily event causes a mental event which causes a further bodily event. There are, however, difficulties for the Dualist in accepting the interaction of body and mind.

Before considering these difficulties, however, we must be quite clear that there is no *logical* difficulty in the notion that nonphysical events may cause physical events, or vice-versa. It is a purely *empirical* question, to be decided by experience, what is capable of acting on what. As Hume says, discussing this very point:

> . . . to consider the matter *a priori,* any thing may produce any thing . . .
>
> (*Treatise*, *Vol. 1, Pt.* IV, Sect. 5, p. 247, ed. Selby-Bigge).

(Acceptance of Hume's negative point here, by the way, does not require acceptance of his notorious positive analysis of the causal relationship in terms of constant conjunction. The word 'anything,' of course, must not be understood to mean 'absolutely anything.' The number 4, for instance, cannot be a cause. It must mean 'anything of the sort that it is intelligible to speak of as a cause'—for instance, an event.) If the mind is a spiritual substance, or collection of spiritual items, there is no contradiction in supposing that it acts on the body or is acted on by the body. But, as we shall now see, there are weighty *empirical* reasons which make a Dualist theory of interaction difficult to sustain.

The difficulties arise when we try to think out an Interactionist theory in a concrete way. It seems that the mind will have to act on the body by acting on the *brain.* Now, to a physiologist, the brain is an enormously complete and highly organized material system to which physical stimuli of various sorts are applied, and which in turn has certain physical effects on the rest of the body. Inside the brain one physical event is followed by, and is the cause of, another physical event. If the Dualist is to be an Interactionist two conditions must be satisfied. In the first place, there must be last physical events in the brain which are followed by, and are the causes of, mental events. (Fulfillment of just this condition does not mark off Interactionism from Parallelism.) In the second place, there must be last mental events which are followed by, and are the causes of, events in the brain.

Let us now consider the situation where a physical stimulus of some sort, say the sounds of a human voice, brings about certain mental events, say perceptions and thoughts, which then issue in further physical action. On the 'way up' there must be a last physical event in the brain before the mental events ensue. The mental events must then bring about a first physical event in the brain on the 'way down.' So this second event will have to be an event that is not solely determined by the previous physical state of the brain and physical environment. This means that there will be, as it were, a 'gap' between the state of the brain before the mental event has had its effect and the state of the brain after the mental event has had its effect. The transition between the two states will not take place solely as a result of the physical workings of the brain and physical environment.

Now, with the gradual advance of knowledge of the operation of the brain and nervous system, physiologists are becoming increasingly unwilling to think that there is any such gap.

If the mind acts on the brain, there must be one or more *points d'appui* in the brain where the first physical effects of mental events occur. Descartes, both Dualist and Interactionist, saw that he must look for such a place and thought that he had found it in the pineal gland. He was taking his own Interactionism seriously, to his eternal intellectual credit. But later research has not backed him up about the pineal gland, nor has any other plausible candidate been found for the point or points in the brain where the first physical effects of the mental appear. This suggests that the spiritual component of man cannot act on the material one, which explains why so many Dualists have not accepted Interactionism and have turned reluctantly to Parallelism.

One modern neurophysiologist, Sir John Eccles, has accepted a Dualist Interactionism. (See his *The Neurophysiological Basis of Mind*, Clarendon Press, 1953, Ch. 8, 'The Mind-Brain Problem'.) But beyond making the suggestion that, if the mind could affect the pattern of discharge of relatively few neurones in a systematic manner, it could quite easily produce quite large alterations in the total patterns of stimulation in the brain, he does nothing in the way of producing a worked-out theory of how interaction occurs. Nevertheless, his idea that discharges might occur in neurones that could not be predicted by any physical laws, but which, occurring systematically, would bring about relatively big alterations in the state of the brain, is scientifically testable, at least in theory. But most neurophysiologists, I imagine, would be astounded to find any such non-physical interference in the workings of the brain. A puzzling feature of Eccles' view is that he says it demands a 'spatio-temporal patterning of the mind'. Apparently he regards the mind as both non-physical, yet somehow in space.

On the Parallelist view, instead of the spiritual affecting the physical, events in the brain and events in the soul are *correlated* with each other, running in double-harness with each other, or, in the language of logicians, in one-to-one correlation. Whenever there are events in the brain of a certain sort, spiritual events are brought into being 'beside' the brain events, but do not modify them. On this Parallelist view, a complete science treating of the relation of the brain to the mind would consist of a huge 'dictionary', allowing us to pass from the current existence of a certain state in the brain to a certain state of mind, and vice-versa. But the dictionary would be a dictionary of contingent truths, for it would be experience that had taught us what the correlations were.

But, of course, Parallelism escapes the arguments (or perhaps we should say, more modestly, the intuitions) of modern physiology only to fall foul of ordinary experience. If we consider the sequence (i) a blow on the hand; (ii) a pain in the hand; (iii) wringing of the hand; it seems impossible to deny that, not only is the first event the cause of the second event, but also that the second event is the cause of the third event. If this is not a causal sequence, what is? Yet the Parallelist must, quite implausibly, deny that the pain makes me (causes me to) wring my hand.

It may be objected, however, that the Parallelist can provide for the interaction of mind and body in the following way. When my hand is struck, I feel distress. Equally, when my hand is struck, certain processes occur in my brain. Whenever these processes occur, I feel distress; and whenever I feel distress, these processes occur. The next thing that happens is that I wring my hand, and the physiologist would say that the wringing was caused by the processes in the brain. But, the Parallelist may say, is it not equally correct to say that the wringing was caused by my distress? In order to assert that this was not so, we would have to find a case where the same sort of brain-process occurs, the felt distress does not, but I still wring my hand. But, on the Parallelist hypothesis, we never get such a case. Whenever we have that sort of brain-process, we feel distress.

The objection to this ingenious rejoinder is that, granted there is no 'gap' in the chain of physical causation in the brain (and it is the accepting of this consequence that leads to the unwilling acceptance of Parallelism), then we can in theory deduce the wringing of the hand given no more than the physical state of the brain, the body, the environment and the physical laws by which they operate. This implies that the existence of the spiritual object, and the correlation between brain-processes and spiritual states, has no effect on the way the physical world operates. And to assert this is to deny that mind acts on body.

There is, however, one other line that a Parallelist can take. He can argue that mind and body do seem to interact, but that this interaction is an illusion, an illusion brought about by the observed fact that wringing the hand in a certain way is regularly preceded by having a sensation of pain. The sequence is mistaken for a causal sequence, a mistake that is discovered as a result of modern neurophysiological knowledge. Ordinary speech ('the pain made me wring my hand') bears witness to the time before the mistake had been discovered.

This is a possible line of defence. But it must be realized how very extensive the 'error' turns out to be. We are constantly speaking, in all sorts of contexts, of mental events giving rise to bodily happenings ('An idea crossed my mind, *so* I said . . .'). If other evidence is sufficiently pressing, we may have to write off all these ways of expressing ourselves as embodying a mistake. But a theory that would allow for the interaction of mind and body would be preferable.

Before leaving this discussion of Interactionism and Parallelism, a further objection to Parallelism may be mentioned briefly. Everything in the physical world interacts with its environment. No material thing is purely passive: it is acted on, but it also acts. The Parallelist is maintaining that the spiritual component of man is different in this respect. Unlike everything else in the universe, the spirit is powerless. We should certainly hesitate to believe that this exception occurs.

So a Dualist Interactionism cannot be squared with physiology and a Dualist Parallelism is incompatible with ordinary experience. Yet a Dualist must either be an Interactionist or Parallelist.

There seem, then, to be serious objections to any form of Dualism. Nevertheless, . . . there is no . . . logical incoherence in Cartesian Dualism. If the Cartesian is prepared to postulate, or claim to observe, a spiritual substance; if he is prepared to postulate, or care to observe, a unique relationship that ties particular spiritual substances to particular bodies; if he is prepared to postulate, or claim to observe, a principle of numerical differentiation to secure the numerical difference of spiritual substances; if he is prepared to accept the scientific implausibilities involved in the hypothesis of the emergence of spiritual substance; and if he is prepared to accept either the scientific implausibilities involved in Interactionism, or the conflict with ordinary experience involved in Parallelism; then no actual contradiction can be shown in his position. But if we could find an account of the mind that avoids such awkward consequences, it would be preferable.

Our discussion has not merely uncovered difficulties for Dualism, but has the following positive value. It has shown us that a completely satisfactory theory of mind should meet a number of demands. (i) It should allow for the logical possibility of the disembodied existence of a mind. (ii) It should treat mental happenings as things incapable of independent existence. (iii) It should account for the unity of mind and body. (iv) It should provide a principle of numerical difference for minds. (v) It should not be scientifically implausible. (vi) It should allow for the causal interaction of mind and body. Here we have some useful touchstones with which to test the worth of different theories of mind.

PART THREE

PHILOSOPHICAL THEOLOGY

THE WATCH AND THE HUMAN EYE

William Paley

A Watch Implies a Watchmaker

In crossing a heath, suppose I pitched my foot against a *stone*, and were asked how the stone came to be there; I might possibly answer, that, for anything I knew to the contrary, it had lain there forever: nor would it perhaps be very easy to show the absurdity of this answer. But suppose I had found a *watch* upon the ground, and it should be inquired how the watch happened to be in that place: I should hardly think of the answer which I had before given, that, for anything I knew, the watch might have always been there. Yet why should not this answer serve for the watch as well as for the stone? Why is it not as admissible in the second case, as in the first? For this reason, and for no other, viz. that, when we come to inspect the watch, we perceive (what we could not discover in the stone) that its several parts are framed and put together for a purpose, e.g., that they are so formed and adjusted as to produce motion, and that motion so regulated as to point out the hour of the day; that if the different parts had been differently shaped from what they are, of a different size from what they are, or placed after any other manner, or in any other order, than that in which they are placed, either no motion at all would have been carried on in the machine, or none which would have answered the use that is now served by it.... This mechanism being observed (it requires indeed an examination of the instrument, and perhaps some previous knowledge of the subject, to perceive and understand it; but being once, as we have said, observed and understood), the inference, we think, is inevitable; that the watch must have had a maker; that there must have existed, at sometime, and at some place or other, an artificer or artificers, who formed it for the purpose which we find it actually to answer; who comprehended its construction, and designed its use.

Nor would it, I apprehend, weaken the conclusion, that we had never seen a watch made, that we had never known an artist capable of making one; that we were altogether incapable of executing such a piece of workmanship ourselves, or of understanding in what manner it was performed; all this being no more than what is true of some exquisite remains of ancient art, of some lost arts, and, to the generality of mankind, of the more curious productions of modern manufacture. Does one man in a million know how oval frames are turned? Ignorance of this kind exalts our opinion of the artist's skill, if he be unseen and unknown, but raises no doubt in our minds of the existence and agency of such an artist, at some former time, and in some place or other. Nor can I perceive that it varies at all the inference, whether the question arise concerning a human agent, or concerning an agent of a different species, or an agent possessing, in some respects, a different nature.

Neither, secondly, would it invalidate our conclusion, that the watch sometimes went wrong, or that it seldom went exactly right. The purpose of the machinery, the design and the designer, might be evident, and in the case supposed would be evident, in whatever way we

This selection comprises part of Chapters I-VI of Paley's *Evidences of the Existence and Attributes of the Deity,* first published in 1802.

accounted for the irregularity of the movement, or whether we could account for it or not. It is not necessary that a machine be perfect, in order to show with what design it was made: still less necessary, where the only question is, whether it were made with any design at all.

Nor, thirdly, would it bring any uncertainty into the argument, if there were a few parts of the watch, concerning which we could not discover, or had not yet discovered, in what manner they conduced to the general effect; or even some parts, concerning which we could not ascertain whether they conduced to that effect in any manner whatever. For, as to the first branch of the case; if by the loss, or disorder, or decay of the parts in question, the movement of the watch were found in fact to be stopped, or disturbed, or retarded, no doubt would remain in our minds as to the utility or intention of these parts, although we should be unable to investigate the manner according to which, or the connection by which, the ultimate effect depended upon their action or assistance; and the more complex is the machine, the more likely is this obscurity to arise. Then, as to the second thing supposed, namely, that there were parts which might be spared, without prejudice to the movement of the watch, and that we had proved this by experiment—these superfluous parts, even if we were completely assured that they were such, would not vacate the reasoning which we had instituted concerning other parts. The indication of contrivance remained, with respect to them, nearly as it was before.

Nor, fourthly, would any man in his senses think the existence of the watch, with its various machinery, accounted for, by being told that it was one out of possible combinations of material forms; that whatever he had found in the place where he found the watch, must have contained some internal configuration or other; and that this configuration might be the structure now exhibited, viz. of the works of a watch, as well as a different structure.

Nor, fifthly, would it yield to his inquiry more satisfaction to be answered, that there existed in things a principle of order, which had disposed the parts of the watch into their present form and situation. He never knew a watch made by the principle of order; nor can he even form to himself an idea of what is meant by a principle of order distinct from the intelligence of the watchmaker.

Sixthly, he would be surprised to hear that the mechanism of the watch was no proof of contrivance, only a motive to induce the mind to think so. . . .

Neither, lastly, would our observer be driven out of his conclusion, or from his confidence in its truth, by being told that he knew nothing at all about the matter. He knows enough for his argument. He knows the utility of the end: he knows the subserviency and adaptation of the means to the end. These points being known, his ignorance of other points, affect not the certainty of his reasoning. The consciousness of knowing little need not beget a distrust of that which he does know.

Even a "Self-Reproducing" Watch Implies a Watchmaker

Suppose, in the next place, that the person who found the watch, should, after sometime, discover, that, in addition to all the properties which he had hitherto observed in it, it possessed the unexpected property of producing, in the course of its movement, another watch like itself (the thing is conceivable), that it contained within it a mechanism, a system of parts, a mould for instance, or a complex adjustment of lathes, files, and other tools, evidently and separately calculated for this purpose; let us inquire, what effect ought such a discovery to have upon his former conclusion.

The first effect would be to increase his admiration of the contrivance, and his conviction of the consummate skill of the contriver. Whether he regarded the object of the contrivance, the distinct apparatus, the intricate, yet in many parts intelligible mechanism, by which it was carried on, he would perceive in this new observation, nothing but an additional reason for doing what he had already done,—for referring the construction of the watch to design, and to supreme art. If that construction *without* this property, or which is the same thing, before this property had been noticed, proved intention and art to have been employed about it, still more strong would the proof appear, when he came to the knowledge of this farther property, the crown and perfection of all the rest.

He would reflect, that though the watch before him were, *in some sense*, the maker of the watch which was fabricated in the course of its movements, yet it was in a very different sense from that in which a carpenter, for instance, is the maker of a chair; the author of its contrivance, the cause of the relation of its parts to their use. With respect to these, the first watch was no cause at all to the second: in no such sense as this was it the author of the constitution and order, either of the parts which the new watch contained, or of the parts by the aid and instrumentality of which it was produced. We might possibly say, but with great latitude of expression, that a stream of water ground corn; but no latitude of expression would allow us to say, no stretch of conjecture could lead us to think, that the stream of water built the mill, though it were too ancient for us to know who the builder was. What the stream of water does in the affair, is neither more nor less than this; by the application of an unintelligent impulse to a mechanism previously arranged, arranged independently of it, and arranged by intelligence, an effect is produced, viz. the corn is ground. But the effect results from the arrangement. The force of the stream cannot be said to be the cause or author of the effect, still less of the arrangement. Understanding and plan in the formation of the mill were not the less necessary, for any share which the water has in grinding the corn; yet is this share the same as that which the watch would have contributed to the production of the new watch, upon the supposition assumed in the last section. Therefore:

Though it be now no longer probable, that the individual watch which our observer had found was made immediately by the hand of an artificer, yet doth not this alteration in anywise affect the inference, that an artificer had been originally employed and concerned in the production. The argument from design remains as it was. Marks of design and contrivance are no more accounted for now than they were before. In the same thing, we may ask for the cause of different properties. We may ask for the cause of the color of a body, of its hardness, of its heat; and these causes may be all different. We are now asking for the cause of that subserviency to a case, that relation to an end, which we have remarked in the watch before us. No answer is given to this question by telling us that a preceding watch produced it. There cannot be design without a designer; contrivance, without a contriver; order, without choice; arrangement, without anything capable of arranging; subserviency and relation to a purpose, without that which could intend a purpose; means suitable to an end, and executing their office in accomplishing that end, without the end ever having been contemplated, or the means accommodated to it. Arrangement, disposition of parts, subserviency of means to an end, relation of instruments to a use, imply the presence of intelligence and mind. No one, therefore, can rationally believe, that the insensible, inanimate watch, from which the watch before us issued, was the proper cause of the mechanism we so much admire in it; could be truly said to have constructed the instrument, disposed its parts, assigned their office, determined their order, action, and mutual dependency, combined their several motions into one result, and that also a result connected with the utilities of other beings. All these properties, therefore, are as much unaccounted for as they were before.

Impossibility of an Infinite Regress

Nor is anything gained by running the difficulty farther back, i.e., by supposing the watch before us to have been produced from another watch, that from a former, and so on indefinitely. Our going back ever so far brings us no nearer to the last degree of satisfaction upon the subject. Contrivance is still unaccounted for. We still want a contriver. A deadening mind is neither supplied by this supposition, nor dispensed with. If the difficulty were diminished the farther we went back, by going back indefinitely we might exhaust it. And this is the only case to which this sort of reasoning applies. Where there is a tendency, or, as we increase the number of terms, a continual approach towards a limit, *there*, by supposing the number of terms to be what is called infinite, we may conceive the limit to be attained: but where there is no such tendency, or approach, nothing is effected by lengthening the series. There is no difference, as to the point in question (whatever there may be as to many points), between one series and another; between a series which is finite, and a series which is infinite. A chain, composed of an infinite number of links, can no more support itself, than a chain composed of a finite number of links. And of this we are assured (though we never can have tried the experiment), because, by increasing the number of links, from ten, for instance, to a hundred, from a hundred to a thousand, etc., we make not the smallest approach, we observe not the smallest tendency, towards self-support. There is no difference in this respect (yet there may be a great difference in several respects) between a chain of a greater or less length, between one chain and another, between one that is finite and one that is infinite. This very much resembles the case before us. The machine which we are inspecting demonstrates, by its construction, contrivance and design. Contrivance must have had a contriver; design, a designer; whether the machine immediately proceeded from another machine or not. That circumstance alters not the case. That other machine may, in like manner, have proceeded from a former machine: nor does that alter the case; contrivance must have had a contriver. That former one from one preceding it: no alteration still; a contriver is still necessary. No tendency is perceived, no approach towards a diminution of this necessity. It is the same with any and every succession of these machines; a succession of ten, of a hundred, of a thousand; with one series as with another; a series which is finite, as with a series which is infinite. In whatever other respects they may differ, in this they do not. In all, equally, contrivance and design are unaccounted for.

The question is not simply, How came the first watch into existence? which question, it may be pretended, is done away by supposing the series of watches thus produced from one another to have been infinite, and consequently to have had no such *first*, for which it was necessary to provide a cause. This, perhaps, would have been nearly the state of the question, if nothing had been before us but an unorganized, unmechanized substance, without mark or indication of contrivance. It might be difficult to show that such substance could not have existed from eternity, either in succession (if it were possible, which I think it is not, for unorganized bodies to spring from one another) or by individual perpetuity. But that is not the question now. To suppose it to be so, is to suppose that it made no difference whether we had found a watch or a stone. As it is, the metaphysics of that question have no place; for, in the watch which we are examining, are seen contrivance, design; an end, a purpose; means for the end, adaptation to the purpose. And the question which irresistibly presses upon our thoughts, is, whence this contrivance and design? The thing required is the intending mind, the adapting hand, the intelligence by which the hand was directed. This question, this demand, is not shaken off, by increasing a number or succession of substances, destitute of these properties; nor the more, by increasing that number to infinity. If it be said, that upon the supposition of one watch being produced from another in the course of that other's movements, and by means of the mechanism within it, we have a cause for the watch in my hand, viz. the watch from which it proceeded: I deny, that for the design, the contrivance, the suitableness of means to an end, the adaptation of instruments to a use (all means which we discover in a watch), we have any cause whatever. It is in vain, therefore, to assign a series of such causes, or to allege that a series may be carried back to infinity; for I do not admit that we have yet any cause at all of the phenomena, still less any series of causes either finite or infinite. Here is contrivance, but no contriver: proofs of design, but no designer.

Our observer would farther also reflect, that the maker of the watch before him, was, in truth and reality, the maker of every watch produced from it; there being no difference (except that the latter manifests a more exquisite skill) between the making of another watch with his own hands, by the mediation of files, lathes, chisels, etc., and the disposing, fixing, and inserting of these instruments, or of others equivalent to them, in the body of the watch already made, in such a manner as to form a new watch in the course of the movements which he had given to the old one. It is only working by one set of tools instead of another.

The conclusion which the *first* examination of the watch, of its works, construction, and movement, suggested, was, that it must have had, for the cause and author of that construction, an artificer, who understood its mechanism, and designed its use. This conclusion is invincible. A *second* examination presents us with a new discovery. The watch is found, in the course of its movement, to produce another watch, similar to itself: and not only so, but we perceive in it a system or organization, separately calculated for that purpose. What effect would this discovery have or ought it to have, upon our former inference? What, as hath already been said, but to increase, beyond measure, our admiration of the skill which had been employed in the formation of such a machine! Or shall it, instead of this, all at once turn us round to an opposite conclusion, viz. that no art or skill whatever has been concerned in the business, although all other evidences of art and skill remain as they were, and this last and supreme piece of art be now added to the rest? Can this be maintained without absurdity? Yet this is atheism.

This is atheism: for every indication of contrivance, every manifestation of design, which existed in the watch, exists in the works of nature; with the difference, on the side of nature, of being greater and more, and that in a degree which exceeds all computation. I mean, that the contrivances of nature surpass the contrivances of art, in the complexity, subtlety, and curiosity of the mechanism; and still more, if possible, do they go beyond them in number and variety: yet, in a multitude of cases, are not less evidently mechanical, not less evidently contrivances, not less evidently accommodated to their end, or suited to their office, than are the most perfect productions of human ingenuity.

The Eye and the Telescope

I know no better method of introducing so large a subject, than that of comparing a single thing with a single thing; an eye, for example, with a telescope. As far as the examination of the instrument goes, there is precisely the same proof that the eye was made for vision, as there is that the telescope was made for assisting it. They are made upon the same principles; both being adjusted to the laws by which the transmission and reflection of rays of light are regulated. I speak not of the origin of the laws themselves; but such laws being fixed, the construction in both cases, is adapted to them. For instance; these laws require, in order to produce the same effect, that the rays of light, in passing from water into the eye, should be refracted by a more convex surface than when it passes out of air into the eye. Accordingly we find, that the eye of a fish, in that part of it called the crystalline lens, is much rounder than the eye of terrestrial animals. What plainer manifestation of design can there be than this difference? What could a mathematical instrument-maker have done more, to show his knowledge of his principle, his application of that knowledge, his suiting of his means to his end; I will not say to display the compass or excellence of his skill and art, for in these all comparison is indecorous, but to testify counsel, choice, consideration, purpose?

To some it may appear a difference sufficient to destroy all similitude between the eye and the telescope, that the one is a perceiving organ, the other an unperceiving instrument. The fact is, that they are both instruments. And as to the mechanism, at least as to mechanism being employed, and even as to the kind of it, this circumstance varies not the analogy at all.... The lenses of the telescope, and the humours of the eye, bear a complete resemblance to one another, in their figure, their position, and in their power over the rays of light, viz. in bringing each pencil to a point at the right distance from the lens; namely in the eye, at the exact place where the membrane is spread to receive it. How is it possible, under circumstances of such close affinity, and under the operation of equal evidence, to exclude contrivance from the one, yet to acknowledge the proof of contrivance having been employed, as the plainest and clearest of all propositions, in the other?

The resemblance between the two cases is still more accurate, and obtains in more points than we have yet represented, or than we are, on the first view of the subject, aware of. In dioptric telescopes there is an imperfection of this nature. Pencils of light, in passing through glass lenses, are separated into different colors, thereby tinging the object, especially the edges of it, as if it were viewed through a prism. To correct this inconvenience had been long a desideratum in the art. At last it came into the mind of a sagacious optician, to inquire how this matter was managed in the eye; in which there was exactly the same difficulty to contend with as in the telescope. His observation taught him, that, in the eye, the evil was cured by combining lenses composed of different substances, i.e. of substances which possessed different refracting powers. Our artist borrowed thence his hint; and produced a correction of the defect by imitating, in glasses made from different materials, the effects of the different humours through which the rays of light pass before they reach the bottom of the eye. Could this be in the eye without purpose, which suggested to the optician the only effectual means of attaining that purpose?

But farther; there are other points, not so much perhaps of strict resemblance between the two, as of superiority of the eye over the telescope, which being found in the laws that regulate both, may furnish topics of fair and just comparison. . . .

Further Evidence of Design in the Eye

In considering vision as achieved by the means of an image formed at the bottom of the eye, we can never reflect without wonder upon the smallness, yet correctness, of the picture, the subtility of the touch, the fineness of the lines. A landscape of five or six square leagues is brought into a space of half an inch diameter; yet the multitude of objects which it contains, are all preserved; are all discriminated in their magnitudes, positions, figures, colors. The prospect from Hampstead-hill is compressed into the compass of a sixpence, yet circumstantially represented. A stagecoach, travelling at its ordinary speed for half an hour, passes, in the eye, only over one-twelfth of an inch, yet is this change of place in the image distinctly perceived throughout its whole progress; for it is only by means of that perception that the motion of the coach itself is made sensible to the eye. If anything can abate our admiration of the smallness of the visual tablet compared with the extent of vision, it is a reflection, which the view of nature leads us, every hour, to make, viz. that in the hands of the Creator, great and little are nothing.

Sturmius held, that the examination of the eye was a cure for atheism. Besides that conformity to optical principles which its internal constitution displays, and which alone amounts to a manifestation of intelligence having been exerted in the structure; besides this, which forms no doubt, the leading character of the organ, there is to be seen, in everything belonging to it and about it, an extraordinary degree of care, and amenity for its preservation, due, if we may so speak, to its value and its tenderness. It is lodged in a strong, deep, bony socket, composed by the junction of seven different bones, hollowed out at their edges. In some few species, as that of the coatimondi, the orbit is not bony throughout; but whenever this is the case, the upper, which is the deficient part, is supplied by a cartilaginous ligament; a substitution which shows the same care. Within this socket it is embedded in fat, of all animal substances the best adapted both to its repose and motion. It is sheltered by the eyebrows; an arch of hair, which like a thatched penthouse, prevents the sweat and moisture of the forehead from running down into it.

But it is still better protected by its lid. Of the superficial parts of the animal frame, I know none which, in its office and structure, is more deserving of attention than the eyelid. It defends the eye; it wipes it; it closes it in sleep. Are there, in any work of art whatever, purposes more evident than those which this organ fulfills? or an apparatus for executing those purposes more intelligible, more appropriate, or more mechanical? If it be overlooked by the observer of nature, it can only be because it is obvious and familiar. This is a tendency to be guarded against. We pass by the plainest instances, whilst we are exploring those which are rare and curious; by which conduct of the understanding, we sometimes neglect the strongest observations, being taken up with others, which though more recondite and scientific, are, as solid arguments, entitled to much less consideration.

In order to keep the eye moist and clean (which qualities are necessary to its brightness and its use), a wash is constantly supplied by a secretion for the purpose; and the superfluous brine is conveyed to the nose through a perforation in the bone as large as a goose-quill. When once the fluid has entered the nose, it spreads itself upon the inside of the nostril, and is evaporated by the current of warm air, which, in the course of respiration, is continually passing over it. Can any pipe or outlet for carrying off the waste liquor from a dye-house or a distillery, be more mechanical than this is? It is easily perceived, that the eye must want moisture: but could the want of the eye generate the gland which produces the tear, or bore the hole by which it is discharged,—a hole through a bone? . . .

Some Objections Answered

Every observation which was made concerning the watch, may be repeated with strict propriety concerning the eye; concerning animals; concerning plants; concerning, indeed, all the organized parts of the works of nature:

1. Imperfections in the Mechanism

When we are inquiring simply after the existence of an intelligent Creator, imperfection, inaccuracy, liability to disorder, occasional irregularities, may subsist in a considerable degree, without inducing any doubt into the question; just as a watch may frequently go wrong, seldom perhaps exactly right, may be faulty in some parts, defective in some, without the smallest ground of suspicion from thence arising that it was not a watch; not made; or not made for the purpose ascribed to it. When faults are pointed out, and when a question is started concerning the skill of the artist, or the dexterity with which the work is executed, then, indeed, in order to defend these qualities from accusation, we must be able, either to expose some intractableness and imperfection in the materials, or point out some invincible difficulty in the execution, into which imperfection and difficulty the matter of complaint may be resolved; or if we cannot do this, we must adduce such specimens of consummate art and contrivance, proceeding from the same hand, as may convince the inquirer of the existence, in the case before him, of impediments like those which we have mentioned, although, what from the nature of the case is very likely to happen, they be unknown and unperceived by him. This we must do in order to vindicate the artist's skill, or, at least, the perfection of it; as we must also judge of his intention, and of the provision employed in fulfilling that intention, not from an instance in which they fail, but from the great plurality of instances in which they succeed. But, after all, these are different questions from the question of the artist's existence; or, which is the same, whether the thing before us be a work of art or not: and the question ought always to be kept separate in the mind. So likewise it is in the works of nature. Irregularities and imperfections are of little or no weight in the consideration, when that consideration relates simply to the existence of a Creator. When the argument respects his attributes, they are of weight; but are then to be taken in conjunction (the attention is not to rest upon them, but they are to be taken in conjunction) with the unexceptionable evidences which we possess, of skill, power, and benevolence, displayed in other instances; which evidences may, in strength, number, and variety, be such, and may so overpower apparent blemishes, as to induce us, upon the most reasonable ground, to believe, that these last ought to be referred to some cause, though we be ignorant of it, other than defect of knowledge or of benevolence in the author.

2. Apparently Useless Parts

There may be also parts of plants and animals, as there were supposed to be of the watch, of which, in some instances, the operation, in others, the use, is unknown. These form different causes; for the operation may be unknown, yet the use be certain. Thus it is with the lungs of animals. It does not, I think, appear, that we are acquainted with the action of the air upon the blood, or in what manner that action is communicated by the lungs; yet we find that a very short suspension of their office destroys the life of the animal. In this case, therefore, we may be said to know the use, nay we experience the necessity, of the organ, though we are ignorant of its operation. Nearly the same thing may be observed of what is called the lymphatic system. We suffer grievous inconveniences from its disorder, without being informed of the office which it sustains in the economy of our bodies. There may possibly also be some few examples of the second class, in which not only the operation is unknown, but in which experiments may seem to prove that the part is not necessary; or may leave a doubt, how far it is even useful to the plant or animal in which it is found. This is said to be the case with the spleen; which has been extracted from dogs, without any sensible injury to their vital function. Instances of the former kind, namely, in which we cannot explain the operation, may be numerous; for they will be so in proportion to our ignorance. They will be more or fewer to different persons, and in different stages of science. Every improvement of knowledge diminishes their number. There is hardly, perhaps, a year passes that does not, in the works of nature, bring some operation, or some mode of operation, to light, which was before undiscovered,—probably unsuspected. Instances of the second kind, namely, where the part appears to be totally useless, I believe to be extremely rare; compared with the number of those of which the use is evident, they are beneath any assignable proportion; and, perhaps, have never been submitted to a trial and examination sufficiently accurate, long enough continued, or often enough repeated. No accounts which I have seen are satisfactory. The mutilated animal may live and grow fat, (as was the case of the dog deprived of its spleen,) yet may be defective in some other of its functions; which, whether they can all, or in what degree of vigor and perfection, be performed, or how long preserved, without the extirpated organ, does not seem to be ascertained by experiment. But to this case, even were it fully made out, may be applied the consideration which we suggested concerning the watch, viz. that these superfluous parts do not negative the reasoning which we instituted concerning those parts which are useful, and of which we know the use. The indication of contrivance, with respect to them, remains as it was before.

3. The Possible Role of Chance

One atheistic way of replying to our observations upon the works of nature, and to the proofs of a Deity which we think that we perceive in them, is to tell us, that all which we see must necessarily have had some form, and that it might as well be its present form as any other. Let us now apply this answer to the eye, as we did before to the watch. Something or other must have occupied that place in the animal's head; must have filled up, we will say, that socket: we will say also, that it must have been of that sort of substance which we call animal substance, as flesh, bone, membrane, cartilage, etc. But that it should have been an eye, knowing as we do, what an eye comprehends—viz. that it should have consisted, first, of a series of transparent lenses (very different, by the by, even in their substance, from the opaque materials of which the rest of the body is, in general at least, composed; and with which the whole of its surface, this single portion of it excepted, is covered); secondly, of a black cloth or canvas (the only membrane of the body which is black) spread out behind these lenses, so as to receive the image formed by pencils of light transmitted through them; and placed at the precise geometrical distance at which, and at which alone, a distinct image could be formed, namely, at the concourse of the refracted rays; thirdly, of a large nerve communicating between this membrane and the brain; without which, the action of light upon the membrane; however modified by the organ, would be lost to the purposes of sensation: that this fortunate conformation of parts should have been the lot, not of one individual out of many thousand individuals, like the great prize in a lottery, or like some singularity in nature, but the happy chance of a whole species; nor of one species out of many thousand species, with which we are acquainted, but of by far the greatest number of all that exist; and that under varieties, not casual or capricious, but bearing marks of being suited to their respective exigencies—that all this should have taken place, merely because something must have occupied those points in every animal's forehead—or, that all this should be thought to be accounted for, by the short answer, "that whatever was there, must have had some form or other," is too absurd to be made more so by any augmentation. We are not contented with this answer; we find no satisfaction in it, by way of accounting for appearances of organization far short of those of the eye, such as we observe in fossil shells, petrified bones, or other substances which bear the vestiges of animal or vegetable referents, but which, either in respect of utility, or of the situation in which they are discovered, may seem accidental enough. It is no way of accounting even for these things, to say that the stone, for instance, which is shown to us, (supposing the question to be concerning a petrification,) must have contained some internal conformation or other. Nor does it mend the answer to add, with respect to the singularity of the conformation, that, after the event, it is no longer to be computed what the chances were against it. This is always to be computed, when the question is, whether a useful or imitative conformation be the produce of chance, or not: I desire no greater certainty in reasoning, than that by which chance is excluded from the present disposition of the natural world. Universal experience is against it. What does chance ever do for us? In the human body, for instance, chance, i.e., the operation of causes without design, may produce a wen, a wart, a mole, a pimple, but never an eye. Amongst inanimate substances, a clod, a pebble, a liquid drop might be; but never was a watch, a telescope, an organized body of any kind; answering a valuable purpose by a complicated mechanism, the effect of chance. In no assignable instance hath such a thing existed without intention somewhere.

4. The Theory of the Elimination of the Unfit

There is another answer, which has the same effect as the resolving of things into chance; which answer would persuade us to believe, that the eye, the animal to which it belongs, every other animal, every plant, indeed every organized body which we see, are only so many out of the possible varieties and combinations of being which the lapse of infinite ages has brought into existence: that the present world is the relic of that variety; millions of other bodily forms and other species having perished, being by the defect of their constitutions incapable of preservation, or of continuance by generation. Now there is no foundation whatever for this conjecture in anything which we observe in the works of nature; no such experiments are going on at present; no such energy operates, as that which is here supposed, and which should be constantly pushing into existence new varieties of beings: Nor are there any appearances to support an opinion, that every possible combination of vegetable or animal structure has formerly been tried. Multitudes of conformations, both of vegetables and animals, may be conceived capable of existence and succession, which yet do not exist. Perhaps almost as many forms of plants might have been found in the fields, as figures of plants can be delineated upon paper. A countless variety of animals might have existed, which do not exist. Upon the supposition here stated, we should see unicorns and mermaids, sylphs and centaurs, the fancies of painters, and the fables of poets, realized by examples. Or, if it be alleged that these may transgress the limits of possible life and propagation, we might, at least, have nations of human beings without nails upon their fingers, with more or fewer fingers and toes than ten; some with one eye, others with one ear, with one nostril, or without the sense of smelling at all. All these, and a thousand other imaginable varieties, might live and propagate. We may modify any one species many different ways, all consistent with life, and with the actions necessary to preservation, although affording different degrees of convenience and enjoyment to the animal. And if we carry these modifications through the different species which are known to subsist, their number would be incalculable. No reason can be given why, if these deperdits ever existed, they have now disappeared. Yet, if all possible existences have been tried, they must have formed part of the catalogues.

But, moreover, the division of organized substances into animals and vegetables, and the distribution and sub-distribution of each into genera and species, which distribution is not an arbitrary act of the mind, but founded in the order which prevails in external nature, appear to me to contradict the supposition of the present world being the remains of an indefinite variety of existences; of a variety which rejects all plan. The hypothesis teaches, that every possible variety of being hath, at one time or other, found its way into existence (by what cause or in what manner is not said), and that those which were badly formed, perished; but how or why those which survived should be cast, as we see that plants and animals are cast, into regular classes, the hypothesis does not explain; or rather, the hypothesis is inconsistent with this phenomenon.

The hypothesis, indeed, is hardly deserving of the consideration which we have given to it. What should we think of a man who, because we had never ourselves seen watches, telescopes, stocking mills, steam engines, etc., made, knew not how they were made, or by whom,—would have us believe that these machines, instead of deriving their curious structures from the thought and design of their inventors and contrivers, in truth derive them from no other origin than this, viz. that a mass of metals and other materials having run when melted into all possible figures, and combined themselves in all possible forms and shapes, and proportions, these things which we see, are what were left from the accident, as best worth preserving: and, as such, are become the remaining stock of a magazine, which, at one time or other, has by this means, contained every mechanism, useful and useless, convenient and inconvenient, into which such like materials could be thrown? I cannot distinguish the hypothesis as applied to the works of nature, from this solution, which no one would accept as applied to a collection of machines....

Our Ignorance of Many Points Need Not Suspend Our Assurance of a Few

The confidence which we place in our observations upon the works of nature, in the marks which we discover of contrivance, choice, and design, and in our reasoning upon the proofs afforded us, ought not to be shaken, as it is sometimes attempted to be done, by bringing forward to our view our own ignorance, or rather the general imperfection of our knowledge of nature. Nor, in many cases, ought this consideration to affect us, even when it respects some parts of the subject immediately under our notice. True fortitude of understanding consists in not suffering what we know to be disturbed by what we do not know. If we perceive a useful end, and means adapted to that end, we perceive enough for our conclusion. If these things be clear, no matter what is obscure. The argument is finished. For instance; if the utility of vision to the animal which enjoys it, and the adaptation of the eye to this office, be evident and certain (and I can mention nothing which is more so), ought it to prejudice the inference which we draw from these premises, that we cannot explain the use of the spleen? Nay, more; if there be parts of the eye, viz. the cornea, the crystalline, the retina, in their substance, figure, and position, manifestly suited to the formation of an image by the refraction of rays of light, at least, as manifestly as the glasses and tubes of a dioptric telescope are suited to that purpose; it concerns not the proof which these afford of design, and of a designer, that there may perhaps be other parts, certain muscles, for instance, or nerves in the same eye, of the agency or effect of which we can give no account; any more than we should be inclined to doubt, or ought to doubt, about the construction of a telescope, viz. for what purpose it was constructed, or whether it were constructed at all, because there belonged to it certain screws and pins, the use or action of which we did not comprehend. I take it to be a general way of infusing doubts and scruples into the mind to recur to its own ignorance, its own imbecility; to tell us that upon these subjects we know little; that little imperfectly; or rather, that we know nothing properly about the matter. These suggestions so fall in with our consciousness, as sometimes to produce a general distrust of our faculties and our conclusions. But this is an unfounded jealousy. The uncertainty of one thing, does not necessarily affect the certainty of another thing. Our ignorance of many points need not suspend our assurance of a few. Before we yield, in any particular instance, to the skepticism which this sort of insinuation would induce, we ought accurately to ascertain, whether our ignorance or doubt concern those precise points upon which our conclusion rests. Other points are nothing. Our ignorance of other points may be of no consequence to these, though they be points, in various respects, of great importance. A just reasoner removes from his consideration, not only what he knows, but what he does not know, touching matters not strictly connected with his argument, i.e., not forming the very steps of his deduction; beyond these, his knowledge and his ignorance are alike relative.

Were there no example in the world of contrivance except that of the eye, it would be alone sufficient to suppose the conclusion which we draw from it, as to the necessity of an intelligent Creator. It could never be got rid of because it could not be accounted for by any other supposition, which did not contradict all the principles we possess of knowledge: the principles, according to which things do, as often as they can be brought to the test of experience, turn out to be true or false.... If other parts of nature were inaccessible to our inquiries, or even if other parts of nature presented nothing to our examination but disorder and confusion, the validity of this example would remain the same. If there were but one watch in the world, it would not be less certain that it had a maker. If we had never in our lives seen any but one single kind of hydraulic machine, yet, if of that one kind we understood the mechanism and use, we should be as perfectly assured that it proceeded from the hand, and thought, and skill of a workman, as if we visited a museum of the arts, and saw collected there twenty different kinds of machines for drawing water, or a thousand different kinds for other purposes. Of this point, each machine is a proof, independently of all the rest. So it is with the evidences of a divine agency. The proof is not a conclusion which lies at the end of a chain of reasoning, of which chain each instance of contrivance is only a link, and of which, if one link fail, the whole fails; but is an argument separately supplied by every separate example. An error in stating an example affects only that example. The argument is cumulative, in the fullest sense of that term. The eye proves it without the ear; the ear without the eye. The proof in each example is complete; for when the design of the part, and the conduciveness of its structure to that design is shown, the mind may set itself at rest; no future consideration can detract anything from the force of the example.

V.H

THE FIVE WAYS

St. Thomas Aquinas

We proceed thus to the Third Article:—

Objection 1 It seems that God does not exist; because if one of two contraries be infinite, the other would be altogether destroyed. But the name *God* means that He is infinite goodness. If, therefore, God existed, there would be no evil discoverable; but there is evil in the world. Therefore God does not exist.

Objection 2 Further, it is superfluous to suppose that what can be accounted for by a few principles has been produced by many. But it seems that everything we see in the world can be accounted for by other principles, supposing God did not exist. For all natural things can be reduced to one principle, which is nature; and all voluntary things can be reduced to one principle, which is human reason, or will. Therefore there is no need to suppose God's existence.

On the contrary, It is said in the person of God: *I am Who am* (*Exod.* iii. 14)

I answer that, The existence of God can be proved in five *ways.*

The first and more manifest way is the argument from motion. It is certain, and evident to our senses, that in the world some things are in motion. Now whatever is moved is moved by another, for nothing can be moved except it is in potentiality to that towards which it is moved; whereas a thing moves inasmuch as it is in act. For motion is nothing else than the reduction of something from potentiality to actuality. But nothing can be reduced from potentiality to actuality, except by something in a state of actuality. Thus that which is actually hot, as fire, makes wood, which is potentially hot, to be actually hot, and thereby moves and changes it. Now it is not possible that the same thing should be at once in actuality and potentiality in the same respect, but only in different respects. For what is actually hot cannot simultaneously be potentially hot; but it is simultaneously potentially cold. It is therefore impossible that in the same respect and in the same way a thing should be both mover and moved, *i.e.*, that it should move itself. Therefore, whatever is moved must be moved by another. If that by which it is moved be itself moved, then this also must needs be moved by another, and that by another again. But this cannot go on to infinity, because then there would be no first mover, and, consequently, no other mover, seeing that subsequent movers move only inasmuch as they are moved by the first mover; as the staff moves only because it is moved by the hand. Therefore it is necessary to arrive at a first mover, moved by no other; and this everyone understands to be God.

The second way is from the nature of efficient cause. In the world of sensible things we find there is an order of efficient causes. There is no case known (neither is it, indeed, possible) in which a thing is found to be the efficient cause of itself; for so it would be prior to itself, which is impossible. Now in efficient causes it is not possible to go on to infinity, because in all efficient causes following in order, the first is the cause of the intermediate cause, and the intermediate is the cause of the ultimate cause, whether the intermediate cause be several, or one only. Now to take away the cause is to take away the effect. Therefore, if there be no first cause among efficient causes, there will be no ultimate, nor any intermediate, cause. But if in efficient causes it is possible to go on to infinity, there will be no first efficient cause, neither will there be an ultimate effect, nor any intermediate efficient causes; all of which is plainly false. Therefore it is necessary to admit a first efficient cause, to which everyone gives the name of God.

The third way is taken from possibility and necessity, and runs thus. We find in nature things that are possible to be and not to be, since they are found to be generated, and to be corrupted, and consequently, it is possible for them to be and not to be. But it is impossible for these always to exist, for that which can not-be at some time is not. Therefore, if everything can not-be, then at one time there was nothing in existence. Now if this were true, even now there would be nothing in existence, because that which does not exist begins to exist only through something already existing. Therefore, if at one time nothing was in existence, it would have been impossible for anything to have begun to exist; and thus even now nothing would be in existence—which is absurd. Therefore, not all beings are merely possible, but here must exist something the existence of which is necessary. But every necessary thing either has its necessity caused by another, or not. Now it is impossible to go on to infinity in necessary things which have their necessity caused by another, as has been already proved in regard to efficient causes. Therefore we cannot but admit the existence of some being having of itself its own necessity, and not receiving it from another, but rather causing in others their necessity. This all men speak of as God.

The fourth way is taken from the gradation to be found in things. Among beings there are some *more* and some *less* good, true, noble, and the like. But more and less are predicated of different things according as they resemble in their different ways something which is the maximum, as a thing is said to be hotter according as it more nearly resembles that which is hottest; so that there is something which is truest, something best, something noblest, and, consequently, something which is most being, for those things that are greatest in truth are greatest in being. . . . Now the maximum in any genus is the cause of all in that genus, as fire, which is the maximum of heat, is the cause of all hot things. . . . Therefore there must also be something which is to all beings the cause of their being, goodness, and every other perfection; and this we call God.

The fifth way is taken from the governance of the world. We see that things which lack knowledge, such as natural bodies, act for an end, and this is evident from their acting always, or nearly always, in the same way, so as to obtain the best result. Hence it is plain that they achieve their end, not fortuitously but designedly. Now whatever lacks knowledge cannot move towards an end, unless it be directed by some being endowed with knowledge and intelligence; as the arrow is directed by the archer. Therefore some intelligent being exists by whom all natural things are directed to their end; and this being we call God.

Reply Objection 1 As Augustine says: *Since God is the highest good, He would not allow any evil to exist in His works, unless His omnipotence and goodness were such as to bring good even out of evil.* This is part of the infinite goodness of God, that He should allow evil to exist, and out of it produce good.

Reply Objection 2 Since nature works for a determinate end under the direction of a higher agent, whatever is done by nature must be traced back to God as to its first cause. So likewise whatever is done voluntarily must be traced back to some higher cause other than human reason and will, since these can change and fail; for all things that are changeable and capable of defect must be traced back to an immovable and self-necessary first principle, as has been shown.

ON THE ULTIMATE ORIGINATION OF THE UNIVERSE

Gottfried Wilhelm von Leibniz

November 23, 1697

Besides the World, that is, besides the aggregate of finite things, there is some dominant unit, not only as my soul is in myself, or rather as my ego itself is in my body, but manifesting a much higher reason. For the one being which dominates the universe not only rules the world, it also makes or creates it. It is superior to the world and, so to speak, beyond the world, and is therefore the ultimate reason of things. Neither in any single thing, nor in the total aggregate and series of things, can the sufficient reason for their existence be discovered. Let us suppose a book entitled *The Elements of Geometry* to have existed eternally, one edition having always been copied from the preceding: it is evident then that, although you can account for the present copy by a reference to the past copy which it reproduces, yet, however far back you go in this series of reproductions, you can never arrive at a complete examination since you always will have to ask why at all times these books have existed, that is, why there have been any books at all and why this book in particular. What is true concerning these books is equally true concerning the diverse states of the world, for here too the following state is in some way a copy of the preceding one (although changed according to certain laws). However far you turn back to antecedent states, you will never discover in any or all of these states the full reason why there is a world rather than nothing, nor why it is such as it is.

You may well suppose the world to be eternal; yet what you thus posit is nothing but the succession of its states, and you will not find the sufficient reason in any one of them, nor will you get any nearer to accounting rationally for the world by taking any number of them together: the reason must therefore be sought elsewhere. Things eternal may have no cause of existence, yet a reason for their existence must be conceived. Such a reason is, for immutable things, their very necessity or essence; while in the series of changing things, even though this series itself may be supposed a priori to be eternal,[2] this reason would consist in the very prevailing of inclinations, as will become clear soon. For in this case reasons do not necessitate (that is, operate with absolute or metaphysical necessity, so that the contrary would imply contradiction), but only incline. Hence it is evident that even by supposing the world to be eternal, the recourse to an ultimate cause of the universe beyond this world, that is, to God, cannot be avoided.

The reasons for the world are therefore concealed in some entity outside the world, which is different from the chain or series of things, the aggregate of which constitutes the world. Thus we must pass from the physical or hypothetical necessity, which determines the later states of the world by the earlier, to something endowed with absolute or metaphysical necessity, for which no reason can be given. For the actually existing world is necessary only physically or hypothetically, but not absolutely or metaphysically. Suppose the world to be indeed in a determinate state now; then other determinate states will be necessarily engendered by it. Since therefore the ultimate root of the world must be in something which exists of metaphysical necessity, and since furthermore the reason for any existent can be only another existence, it follows that a unique entity must exist of metaphysical necessity, that is, that there is a being whose essence implies existence. Hence there exists a being which is different from the plurality of beings, that is, from the world; for it has been granted and proved that the world does not exist of metaphysical necessity.

But let us explain somewhat more distinctly how, from the eternal or essential—that is, metaphysical—truths, the temporal or contingent—that is, physical—truths are derived. First we must recognize this: from the fact that something rather than nothing exists, it follows that in possible things, or in their possibility or essence itself, there is a certain demand or (so to speak) a claim for existence; in short, that essence tends by itself toward existence. From this it follows, furthermore, that everything possible, that is, all that expresses a possible essence or reality, tends with equal right toward existence, the degree of this tendency being proportionate to the quantity of essence or reality, that is, to the degree of perfection of the possible involved. Perfection, indeed, is nothing else but the quantity of essence.

From this it must be concluded that, out of the infinite number of combinations and series of possibilities, one exists through which a maximum of essence of possibilities is produced into existence. For in all things there is a principle of determination which must be drawn from the consideration of maxima or minima, namely, that the maximum effect must be attained with a minimum of expenditure. In this respect, time and space—in short, the receptivity or capacity of the world—may be regarded as the expenditure or the area allotted for the erection of the most advantageous construction; while the variety of forms in the world represents the comfort of the building and the multitude and beauty of its rooms. The problem is analogous to that arising in certain games, in which all the squares of a board have to be filled according to given rules: if you do not use a certain skill, you eventually will find yourself excluded from certain squares and forced to leave more spaces empty than you could and should have. There is, however, a method by which a maximum number of squares can be filled with ease and certainty.[3] Or suppose, for instance, that it is decreed that a triangle be constructed, without any further determining condition being added: consequently, an equilateral triangle will be produced. [4] Or suppose that from one given point a second point has to be reached, without any further condition to determine the path: the easiest or the shortest way will be taken. So also, once it be established that being prevails over nonbeing, that is, that there is a reason why there exists something rather than nothing, or (which comes to the same) that mere possibility has to pass into actuality—this established, without any further determinations being offered: it follows that the maximum compatible with the capacity of time and place (that is, with the order of possible existence) does exist. The procedure is the same as in the game mentioned a while ago, where the greatest possible number of pieces have to be placed in a given area.

It will become admirably clear from this how, in the very origination of the universe, a sort of Divine Mathematics or a Metaphysical Mechanism is used, and how determination through the idea of a maximum takes place. Examples of this kind of determination occur in geometry where the right angle is the most determinate among all others;[5] or in physics, when one liquid put into another heterogeneous one takes the shape of the maximum volume, namely of the sphere; or in ordinary mechanics itself, when the action of several competing heavy bodies tending downward eventually results in the motion producing the maximum descent.[6] For just as all possibilities tend toward existence with the same right, but in proportion to their reality, so all weights tend toward falling downward with the same right, but in proportion to their gravity. And just as, in the case of the weights, that motion results which produces the greatest possible descent of weight, so also, in the case of the possible, that world emerges through which the maximum of possibilities is produced into actuality.

Thus, we have already derived physical from metaphysical necessity: for though the world is not necessary, metaphysically speaking, so that the contrary would imply contradiction or logical absurdity, yet it is physically necessary, or determined in such a manner that the contrary would imply imperfection or moral absurdity. And just as possibility is the principle of essence, so perfection or degree of essence (through which the greatest number is made impossible) is the principle of existence. At the same time, this makes it evident that freedom must be attributed to the Author of the World, though he does everything in a manner which is determined: he acts according to the principle of wisdom, that is, perfection. Indifference, indeed, originates in ignorance, and the wiser anyone is, the more he is determined to choose the most perfect.

This comparison of some determinant metaphysical mechanism with the physical mechanism of heavy bodies—thus you may object—may appear ingenious. Yet it is inadequate in that the downward-tending heavy bodies really exist, while the possibles or essences are imaginary or fictitious before, or independently of, existence; therefore no reason for existence can be drawn from them. To this I answer that neither those essences nor the so-called eternal truths about them are fictitious, but that they do exist, so to speak, in some region of ideas, namely in God himself, who is the source of all essences and of the existence of all that exists outside himself. This is not to be considered a groundless affirmation: it is confirmed by the actual existence of the series of states of the world. For it has been proved above that the reason for existence cannot be found in this series, but has to be looked for in metaphysical necessities or eternal truths; it has also been pointed out that existence can derive only from existence: hence the eternal truths must have existence in some absolutely, that is, metaphysically, necessary subject, namely in God by whom the possibilities which otherwise would be imaginary are realized (if I may use a barbaric but significant expression).[7]

We observe, indeed, that everything that happens in the world follows the laws of the eternal truths, which belong not only to geometry, but equally to metaphysics. This means that whatever happens does so not only according to material necessities, but also according to formal reasons. This is true not only in general, when it is a question of explaining, as we have just done, why a world exists rather than no world, and why it is as it is and not different—a reason which certainly must be drawn from the tendency of all possibilities toward annuality; it is equally true when we now step down to special cases. We shall then understand that everywhere in nature the metaphysical laws of cause, potency, and action apply in an admirable way and that they even prevail over the very laws of pure geometry which determine material processes. This I understood with great admiration when I tried to account for the laws of movement. Finally I was forced by this discovery to abandon the law of the geometrical composition of forces, which I had myself defended in my youth, when I thought more materialistically. But this I have explained in greater detail elsewhere.[8]

Thus we have found the ultimate reason for the reality of the essences as well as of the existences in a unique being, which is necessarily and incontestably greater than, superior to, and anterior to, the world, since to Him not only all existing things comprehended in the world but also the possibilities owe their reality. This reality can emanate only from a single source, in view of the interconnection of all these possibilities and existences. It is evident that the existing things continually emanate from this source, that they are being and have been produced by it, since there is no reason why any one state of the world rather than another, why yesterday's rather than today's, should flow from it. It becomes clear also how God acts according to laws of physics, yet freely; how he can be not only the efficient but also the final cause of the world; and how he not only manifests his greatness or power in the machine of the universe which is already working, but manifests also his goodness and wisdom in its construction.

Some might believe that I am here confounding moral perfection, that is, goodness, with metaphysical perfection, that is, greatness, and might concede the latter but deny the former. To avoid such a misinterpretation, the consequences of what has been proved must be kept in mind. Namely, not only that the world is physically or (if you prefer) metaphysically perfect—that is, that the series of things which has been produced offers the greatest possible sum total of actual reality—but that this world is also morally the most perfect, because moral perfection is indeed the natural perfection of minds. Hence the world is not only the most admirable machine, but in so far as it consists of minds, it is also the best Republic, that in which the minds are granted the greatest possible happiness and joy; for in this consists their natural perfection.

But experience in this world, you may object, shows us the contrary. For the best people often have the worst lives; innocents—not only beasts but also men—are cruelly afflicted with evils and even put to death; and finally, the world, particularly if we consider the government of the human race, looks like a confused chaos rather than like the well-ordered work of supreme wisdom. That *prima facie* this may be the impression you gain, I do not deny. But on closer inspection, the contrary must be stated. It is certain a priori, by the very reasons we have adduced, that all things, and especially minds, obtain the greatest possible perfection.

It is unjust indeed, as the jurists are wont to say, to judge before having studied the entire law. We know only an infinitesimally small part of the eternity which stretches out beyond measure, and the memory of a few thousand years which history preserves for us is of very little avail here. Yet from such small experience we cast judgment with temerity on the immense and eternal, behaving in this respect like men born and brought up in prison, or, if you prefer, in the underground salt mines of Sarmatia, who would believe that there is no other light in the world than that miserable lamp which hardly suffices to direct their steps. Let us view a very beautiful picture and then cover it up, leaving visible only a tiny particle of its surface. What else will then appear to us, even if we inspect it from very near—indeed, the more so the nearer we get to it—what else will we see, but confused patches of colors without meaning and art? Yet, once you have removed the cover and contemplated the whole picture from a suitable distance, you will understand that what looked like color patches made at random has been created with art by the author of the work. What the eyes apprehend in a painting is apprehended by the ears in music. The greatest composers, indeed, are accustomed to mixing frequent dissonances among the consonances, in order to excite and to shock, so to speak, the auditor, who becomes anxious about what is going to happen; when after a short while all returns to order again, his pleasure will be so much more intense. Similarly, we enjoy insignificant dangers and painful experiences, because they give us the proud consciousness of our power and our happiness. Similarly also, when we see tight-rope walkers or sword dancers performing, we draw pleasure from our very shivers of fear. And frequently when playing with children, we laughingly pretend to throw and almost drop them. So it was that a female monkey once seized King Christian of Denmark, then still an infant in swaddling bands, and carried him to the top of the roof; then amid general anxiety the monkey—apparently enjoying the joke—carried him back, safe and sound, to his cradle. For the same reason one becomes tired of eating nothing but sweets; acrid, sour, even bitter ingredients have to be added to stimulate the taste. Who has not tasted bitter food does not deserve sweets and will not even appreciate them. This is the very law of pleasure, that uniformity does not allow it to continue with the same intensity, but produces satiety and dullness instead of enjoyment.

What we have just pointed out concerning disorder in certain parts, which may well be consistent with the harmony of the whole, should not be understood to mean that the parts were not taken into consideration at all, as though it sufficed that the world as a whole be perfect; for if this were so, the entire human race might be miserable. Nor does it mean that no care has been taken to safeguard justice or to protect our own interests. This, indeed, has been the opinion of certain authors whose judgment about the totality of things has not been sufficiently thought through. For it must be realized that in the best constituted republic care is taken to grant everyone the greatest possible good, and that, analogously, the universe would not be sufficiently perfect unless the interest of everyone were taken into consideration, without prejudice, of course, to the harmony. There is no better verification of this than the very law of justice which ordains that each one should have his share in the perfection of the universe, and that his happiness should be proportionate to his virtue and to his voluntary contribution to the common good; this is what we call charity and love of God, and in this alone consists also the essence and power of the Christian religion, according to the judgments of learned theologians. Nor should one be surprised that in the universe spirits are the objects of so much solicitude, since they most faithfully reflect the image of the Supreme Creator, and since their relation to him is not so much that of a machine to its artificer (as is the case with all other created things), as it is that of a citizen to his prince. Moreover, the spirits will last as long as the universe itself, and in a certain way they express the whole and concentrate it in themselves, so that we may well call them total parts.

With regard to the afflictions of good people, in particular, it may be considered certain that these will turn to their greater advantage. This is true not only theologically but also physically, as evidenced by the grain of wheat fallen into the ground, which must die before it can bring forth fruit.[9] In general it may be affirmed that affections are temporary evils leading to good effects, since they are shortcuts to greater perfection. Just so, in physics, liquids with slow fermentation also clarify more slowly, while those in which the disturbance is more violent eliminate certain particles with greater force and are thus clarified more promptly. It might be said of these evils that one steps back, the better to jump forward. What I have just said is not simply pleasing and comforting; it is truth itself. And in general, I believe that nothing is truer than happiness, nor anything pleasanter and happier than the truth.

As the climax of the universal beauty and perfection of God's works, it must also be recognized that the total universe is engaged in a perpetual and spontaneous progress, so that it always advances toward greater culture. Thus a large part of our earth is now cultivated, and this part will receive ever-growing extension. Though it is true that meanwhile certain parts may return to the state of wilderness or be again destroyed or deteriorated, this must be interpreted in the same manner which we proposed a while ago, concerning the affections of good people: namely, that this very destruction and deterioration promotes the future conquest of a greater good, so that the very damage turns, in a way, into profit.

To the possible objection that thus the world would of necessity have long ago turned into a paradise, it is easy to reply: Many substances already may have attained great perfection; yet, the continuum being infinitely divisible, there will always remain in the unfathomable depth of the universe some somnolent elements which are still to be awakened, developed, and improved—in a word, promoted to higher culture. This is why the end of progress can never be attained.

NOTES

1. The word originatio in this title has sometimes been translated "origin." Leibniz would certainly not have written *originatio* - a term which is used by Quintillian and later authors in the sense of etymology if he had wished to say *origo.* Moreover, the word origination seems to express better the active and "dynamic" character of the process by which, according to Leibniz, the possibles pass into actual existence.

2. The Latin text as it appears in Erdmann and in Gerhardt is corrupted here. The correction after the Hanover manuscript follows: Gerhardt *Philosophische Schriften,* VII, 302: line 21, for *debet* read *deberet;* line 22, for *a priore* read *a priori;* line 23, for *intelligetur* read *intelligeretur*.

3. Leibniz was very much interested in the application of mathematics, particularly of the method of maxima and minima, to the theory of games. See the references in Couturat, *La logique de Leibniz (The Logic of Leibniz),* pp.242-243. See also the discussion of the *ludus aggerum* in Leibniz' correspondence with Jakob Bernoulli *(Mathematische Schriften,* Gerhardt edn.,III, 94).

4. Leibniz seems to have forgotten here to set the condition: "a triangle of a given perimeter." In that case, the equilateral triangle is in fact the one which has the greatest surface. Compare *Tentamen anagogicum (Anagogical Essay) (Philosophische Schriften,* Gerhardt edn., VII, 278): "Suppose that nature had been obliged to construct a triangle, and that for this result only the perimeter, or the sum of the sides, had been given, nothing more; she would construct an equilateral triangle." It is quite possible that in our text, Leibniz wished to present an example not of determination by a maximum, but of a maximum of determination. In the Tentamen *anagogicum—* which is the most important and the most explicit text on the principle which was to give birth to the *principle of least action—*he completes the principle of determination by a maximum or minimum by that other, "that instead of the least, it is necessary to adhere to the *most determined,* which can be the *simplest,* even when it is the greatest" (p. 274). The equilateral triangle is a case of the most determined effect, since there are an infinity of different triangles of unequal sides, but only one equilateral triangle.

5. The right angle is again an example of a maximum of determination: there is only one right angle, and there is an infinity of oblique angles.

6. It must be remembered that the lowest point of the common center of gravity of a system of bodies lies between them (for example, that of a chain fixed at both ends). This principle had been established by Torricelli, *De motu gravium natualiter descendentium (Opera geometrica,* Florence, 1644).

7. In Latin, the word *realizare* is, in fact, a barbaric neologism.

8. See the *Specimen dynamicum pro admirandis naturae legibus circa corporum vires et mutuas actiones detegendis et ad suas causas revocandis (A Dynamic Model for Discovering and Referring Back to Their Causes the Admirable Laws of Nature Governing the Forces and Mutual Actions of Bodies)* (*Mathematische Schriftcn,* Gerhardt edn., VI, 234) and the *Critical Remarks Concerning the General part of Descartes' Principles,* Part II, article 64.

9. John 12:24.

THE PROSLOGIUM:
DISCOURSE ON THE EXISTENCE OF GOD

Saint Anselm

PREFACE

In this brief work the author aims at proving in a single argument the existence of God, and whatsoever we believe of God.—The difficulty of the task.—The author writes in the person of one who contemplates God, and seeks to understand what he believes. To this work he had given this title: Faith Seeking Understanding. He finally named it Proslogium,—that is, A Discourse.

AFTER I had published, at the solicitous entreaties of certain brethren, a brief work (the *Monologium)* as an example of meditation on the grounds of faith, in the person of one who investigates, in a course of silent reasoning with himself, matters of which he is ignorant; considering that this book was knit together by the linking of many arguments, I began to ask myself whether there might be found a single argument which would require no other for its proof than itself alone; and alone would suffice to demonstrate that God truly exists, and that there is a supreme good requiring nothing else, which all other things require for their existence and well-being; and whatever we believe regarding the divine Being.

Although I often and earnestly directed my thought to this end, and at some times that which I sought seemed to be just within my reach, while again it wholly evaded my mental vision, at last in despair I was about to cease, as if from the search for a thing which could not be found. But when I wished to exclude this thought altogether, lest, by busying my mind to no purpose, it should keep me from other thoughts, in which I might be successful; then more and more, though I was unwilling and shunned it, it began to force itself upon me, with a kind of importunity. So, one day, when I was exceedingly wearied with resisting its importunity, in the very conflict of my thoughts, the proof of which I had despaired offered itself, so that I eagerly embraced the thoughts which I was strenuously repelling.

Thinking, therefore, that what I rejoiced to have found, would, if put in writing, be welcome to some readers, of this very matter, and of some others, I have written the following treatise, in the person of one who strives to lift his mind to the contemplation of God, and seeks to understand what he believes. In my judgment, neither this work nor the other, which I mentioned above, deserved to be called a book, or to bear the name of an author; and yet I thought they ought not to be sent forth without some title by which they might, in some sort, invite one into whose hands they fell to their perusal. I accordingly gave each a title, that the first might be known as, An Example of Meditation

Reprinted from *Saint Anselm: Basic Writings*, translated by S.N. Deane by permission of Open Court Publishing Company, La Salle, Illinois.

on the Grounds of Faith, and its sequel as, Faith Seeking Understanding. But, after both had been copied by many under these titles, many urged me, and especially Hugo, the reverend Archbishop of Lyons, who discharges the apostolic office in Gaul, who instructed me to this effect on his apostolic authority—to prefix my name to these writings. And that this might be done more fitly, I named the first, *Monologium,* that is, A Soliloquy; but the second, *Proslogium,* that is, A Discourse.

CHAPTER I.

Exhortation of the mind to the contemplation of God.—It casts aside cares, and excludes all thoughts save that of God, that it may seek Him. Man was created to see God. Man by sin lost the blessedness for which he was made, and found the misery for which he was not made. He did not keep this good when he could keep it easily. Without God it is ill with us. Our labors and attempts are in vain without God. Man cannot seek God, unless God himself teaches him; nor find him, unless he reveals himself. God created man in his image, that he might be mindful of him, think of him, and love him. The believer does not seek to understand, that he may believe, but he believes that he may understand: for unless he believed he would not understand.

UP NOW, slight man! flee, for a little while, thy occupations; hide thyself, for a time, from thy disturbing thoughts. Cast aside, now, thy burdensome cares, and put away thy toilsome business. Yield room for some little time to God; and rest for a little time in him. Enter the inner chamber of thy mind; shut out all thoughts save that of God, and such as can aid thee in seeking him; close thy door and seek him. Speak now, my whole heart! speak now to God, saying, I seek thy face; thy face, Lord, will I seek (Psalms xxvii. 8). And come thou now, O Lord my God, teach my heart where and how it may seek thee, where and how it may find thee.

Lord, if thou art not here, where shall I seek thee, being absent? But if thou art everywhere, why do I not see thee present? Truly thou dwellest in unapproachable light. But where is unapproachable light, or how shall I come to it? Or who shall lead me to that light and into it, that I may see thee in it? Again, by what marks, under what form, shall I seek thee? I have never seen thee, O Lord, my God; I do not know thy form. What, O most high Lord, shall this man do, an exile far from thee? What shall thy servant do, anxious in his love of thee, and cast out afar from thy face? He pants to see thee, and thy face is too far from him. He longs to come to thee, and thy dwelling-place is inaccessible. He is eager to find thee, and knows not thy place. He desires to seek thee, and does not know thy face. Lord, thou art my God, and thou art my Lord, and never have I seen thee. It is thou that hast made me, and hast made me anew, and hast bestowed upon me all the blessings I enjoy; and not yet do I know thee. Finally, I was created to see thee, and not yet have I done that for which I was made.

O wretched lot of man, when he hath lost that for which he was made! O hard and terrible fate! Alas, what has he lost, and what has he found? What has departed, and what remains? He has lost the blessedness for which he was made, and has found the misery for which he was not made. That has departed without which nothing is happy, and that remains which, in itself, is only miserable. Man once did eat the bread of angels, for which he hungers now; he eateth now the bread of sorrows, of which he knew not then. Alas! for the mourning of all mankind, for the universal lamentation of the sons of Hades! He choked with satiety, we sigh with hunger. He abounded, we beg. He possessed in happiness, and miserably forsook his possession; we suffer want in unhappiness, and feel a miserable longing, and alas! we remain empty.

Why did he not keep for us, when he could so easily, that whose lack we should feel so heavily? Why did he shut us away from the light, and cover us over with darkness? With what purpose did he rob us of life, and inflict death upon us? Wretches that we are, whence have we been driven out; whither are we driven on? Whence hurled? Whither consigned to ruin? From a native country into exile, from the vision of God into our present blindness, from the joy of immortality into the bitterness and horror of death. Miserable exchange of how great a good, for how great an evil! Heavy loss, heavy grief, heavy all our fate!

But alas! wretched that I am, one of the sons of Eve, far removed from God! What have I undertaken? What have I accomplished? Whither was I striving? How far have I come? To what did I aspire? Amid what thoughts am I sighing? I sought blessings, and lo! confusion. I strove toward God, and I stumbled on myself. I sought calm in privacy, and I found tribulation and grief, in my inmost thoughts. I wished to smile in the joy of my mind, and I am compelled to frown by the sorrow of my heart. Gladness was hoped for, and lo! a source of frequent sighs!

And thou too, O Lord, how long? How long, O Lord, dost thou forget us; how long dost thou turn thy face from us? When wilt thou look upon us, and hear us? When wilt thou enlighten our eyes, and show us thy face? When wilt thou restore thyself to us? Look upon us, Lord; hear us, enlighten us, reveal thyself to us. Restore thyself to us, that it may be well with us,—thyself, without whom it is so ill with us. Pity our toilings and strivings toward thee, since we can do nothing without thee. Thou dost invite us; do thou help us. I beseech thee, O Lord, that I may not lose hope in sighs, but may breathe anew in hope. Lord, my heart is made bitter by its desolation; sweeten thou it, I beseech thee, with thy consolation. Lord, in hunger I began to seek thee; I beseech thee that I may not cease to hunger for thee. In hunger I have come to thee; let me not go unfed. I have come in poverty to the Rich, in misery to the Compassionate; let me not return empty and despised. And if, before I eat, I sigh, grant, even after sighs, that which I may eat. Lord, I am bowed down and can only look downward; raise me up that I may look upward. My iniquities have gone over my head; they overwhelm me; and, like a heavy load, they weigh me down. Free me from them; unburden me, that the pit of iniquities may not close over me.

Be it mine to look up to thy light, even from afar, even from the depths. Teach me to seek thee, and reveal thyself to me, when I seek thee, for I cannot seek thee, except thou teach me, nor find thee, except thou reveal thyself. Let me seek thee in longing, let me long for thee in seeking; let me find thee in love, and love thee in finding. Lord, I acknowledge and I thank thee that thou hast created me in this thine image, in order that I may be mindful of thee, may conceive of thee, and love thee; but that image has been so consumed and wasted away by vices, and obscured by the smoke of wrong-doing, that it cannot achieve that for which it was made, except thou renew it, and create it anew. I do not endeavor, O Lord, to penetrate thy sublimity, for in no wise do I compare my understanding with that; but I long to understand in some degree thy truth, which my heart believes and loves. For I do not seek to understand that I may believe, but I believe in order to understand. For this also I believe,—that unless I believed, I should not understand.

CHAPTER II.

Truly there is a God, although the fool hath said in his heart, There is no God.

AND SO, Lord, do thou, who dost give understanding to faith, give me, so far as thou knowest it to be profitable, to understand that thou art as we believe; and that thou art that which we believe. And, indeed, we believe that thou art a being than which nothing greater can be conceived. Or is there no such nature, since the fool hath said in his heart, there is no God? (Psalms xiv. I) But, at any rate, this very fool, when he hears of this being of which I speak—a being than which nothing greater can be conceived—understands what he hears, and what he understands is in his understanding; although he does not understand it to exist.

For, it is one thing for an object to be in the understanding, and another to understand that the object exists. When a painter first conceives of what he will afterwards perform, he has it in his understanding, but he does not yet understand it to be, because he has not yet performed it. But after he has made the painting, he both has it in his understanding, and he understands that it exists, because he has made it.

Hence, even the fool is convinced that something exists in the understanding, at least, than which nothing greater can be conceived. For, when he hears of this, he understands it. And whatever is understood, exists in the understanding. And assuredly that, than which nothing greater can be conceived, cannot exist in the understanding alone. For, suppose it exists in the understanding alone: then it can be conceived to exist in reality; which is greater.

Therefore, if that, than which nothing greater can be conceived, exists in the understanding alone, the very being, than which nothing greater can be conceived, is one, than which a greater can be conceived. But obviously this is impossible. Hence, there is no doubt that there exists a being, than which nothing greater can be conceived, and it exists both in the understanding and in reality.

CHAPTER III.

God cannot be conceived not to exist.—God is that, than which nothing greater can be conceived.—That which can be conceived not to exist is not God.

AND it assuredly exists so truly, that it cannot be conceived not to exist. For, it is possible to conceive of a being which cannot be conceived not to exist; and this is greater than one which can be conceived not to exist. Hence, if that, than which nothing greater can be conceived, can be conceived not to exist, it is not that, than which nothing greater can be conceived. But this is an irreconcilable contradiction. There is, then, so truly a being than which nothing greater can be conceived to exist, that it cannot even be conceived not to exist; and this being thou art, O Lord, our God.

So truly, therefore, dost thou exist, O Lord, my God, that thou canst not be conceived not to exist; and rightly. For, if a mind could conceive of a being better than thee, the creature would rise above the Creator; and this is most absurd. And, indeed, whatever else there is, except thee alone, can be conceived not to exist. To thee alone, therefore, it belongs to exist more truly than all other beings, and hence in a higher degree than all others. For, whatever else exists does not exist so truly, and hence in a less degree it belongs to it to exist. Why, then, has the fool said in his heart, there is no God (Psalms xiv. I), since it is so evident, to a rational mind, that thou dost exist in the highest degree of all? Why, except that he is dull and a fool?

CHAPTER IV.

How the fool has said in his heart what cannot be conceived.—A thing may be conceived in two ways: (I) when the word signifying it is conceived; (2) when the thing itself is understood As far as the word goes, God can be conceived not to exist; in reality he cannot.

BUT how has the fool said in his heart what he could not conceive; or how is it that he could not conceive what he said in his heart? since it is the same to say in the heart, and to conceive.

But, if really, nay, since really, he both conceived, because he said in his heart; and did not say in his heart, because he could not conceive; there is more than one way in which a thing is said in the heart or conceived. For, in one sense, an object is conceived, when the word signifying it is conceived; and in another, when the very entity, which the object is, is understood.

In the former sense, then, God can be conceived not to exist; but in the latter, not at all. For no one who understands what fire and water are can conceive fire to be water, in accordance with the nature of the facts themselves, although this is possible according to the words. So, then, no one who understands what God is can conceive that God does not exist; although he says these words in his heart, either without any. or with some foreign, signification. For, God is that than which a greater cannot be conceived. And he who thoroughly understands this, assuredly understands that this being so truly exists, that not even in concept can it be non-existent. Therefore, he who understands that God so exists, cannot conceive that he does not exist.

I thank thee, gracious Lord, I thank thee; because what I formerly believed by thy bounty, I now so understand by thine illumination, that if I were unwilling to believe that thou dost exist, I should not be able not to understand this to be true.

CHAPTER V.

God is whatever it is better to be than not to be; and he, as the only self-existent being, creates all things from nothing.

WHAT art thou, then, Lord God, than whom nothing greater can be conceived? But what art thou, except that which, as the highest of all beings, alone exists through itself, and creates all other things from nothing? For, whatever is not this is less than a thing which can be conceived of. But this cannot be conceived of thee. What good, therefore, does the supreme Good lack, through which every good is? Therefore, thou art just, truthful, blessed, and whatever it is better to be than not to be. For it is better to be just than not just; better to be blessed than not blessed.

CHAPTER VI.

How God is sensible *(sensibilis)* although he is not a body.—God is sensible, omnipotent, compassionate, passionless; for it is better to be these than not be. He who in any way knows, is not improperly said in some sort to feel.

BUT, although it is better for thee to be sensible, omnipotent, compassionate, passionless, than not to be these things; how art thou sensible, if thou art not a body; or omnipotent, if thou hast not all powers; or at once compassionate and passionless? For, if only corporeal things are sensible, since the senses encompass a body and are in a body, how art thou sensible, although thou art not a body, but a supreme Spirit, who is superior to body? But, if feeling is only cognition, or for the sake of cognition,—for he who feels obtains knowledge in accordance with the proper functions of his senses; as through sight, of colors; through taste, of flavors,—whatever in any way cognises is not inappropriately said, in some sort, to feel.

Therefore, O Lord, although thou art not a body, yet thou art truly sensible in the highest degree in respect of this, that thou dost cognise all things in the highest degree; and not as an animal cognises, through a corporeal sense.

APPENDIX.
IN BEHALF OF THE FOOL.

AN ANSWER TO THE ARGUMENT OF ANSELM IN THE PROSLOGIUM.
BY GAUNILON, A MONK OF MARMOUTIER.

1. IF one doubts or denies the existence of a being of such a nature that nothing greater than it can be conceived, he receives this answer:

The existence of this being is proved, in the first place, by the fact that he himself, in his doubt or denial regarding this being, already has it in his understanding; for in hearing it spoken of he understands what is spoken of. It is proved, therefore, by the fact that what he understands must exist not only in his understanding, but in reality also.

And the proof of this is as follows.—It is a greater thing to exist both in the understanding and in reality than to be in the understanding alone. And if this being is in the understanding alone, whatever has even in the past existed in reality will be greater than this being. And so that which was greater than all beings will be less than some being, and will not be greater than all: which is a manifest contradiction.

And hence, that which is greater than all, already proved to be in the understanding, must exist not only in the understanding, but also in reality: for otherwise it will not be greater than all other beings.

2. The fool might make this reply:

This being is said to be in my understanding already, only because I understand what is said. Now could it not with equal justice be said that I have in my understanding all manner of unreal objects, having absolutely no existence in themselves, because I understand these things if one speaks of them, whatever they may be?

Unless indeed it is shown that this being is of such a character that it cannot be held in concept like all unreal objects, or objects whose existence is uncertain: and hence I am not able to conceive of it when I hear of it, or to hold it in concept; but I must understand it and have it in my understanding; because, it seems, I cannot conceive of it in any other way than by understanding it, that is, by comprehending in my knowledge its existence in reality.

But if this is the case, in the first place there will be no distinction between what has precedence in time—namely, the having of an object in the understanding—and what is subsequent in time—namely, the understanding that an object exists; as in the example of the picture, which exists first in the mind of the painter, and afterwards in his work.

Moreover, the following assertion can hardly be accepted: that this being, when it is spoken of and heard of, cannot be conceived not to exist in the way in which even God can be conceived not to exist. For if this is impossible, what was the object of this argument against one who doubts or denies the existence of such a being?

Finally, that this being so exists that it cannot be perceived by an understanding convinced of its own indubitable existence, unless this being is afterwards conceived of—this should be proved to me by an indisputable argument, but not by that which you have advanced: namely, that what I understand, when I hear it, already is in my understanding. For thus in my understanding, as I still think, could be all sorts of things whose existence is uncertain, or which do not exist at all, if some one whose words I should understand mentioned them. And so much the more if I should be deceived, as often happens, and believe in them: though I do not yet believe in the being whose existence you would prove.

3. Hence, your example of the painter who already has in his understanding what he is to paint cannot agree with this argument. For the picture, before it is made, is contained in the artificer's art itself; and any such thing, existing in the art of an artificer, is nothing but a part of his understanding itself. A joiner, St. Augustine says, when he is about to make a box in fact, first has it in his art. The box which is made in fact is not life; but the box which exists in his art is life. For the artificer's soul lives, in which all these things are, before they are produced. Why, then, are these things life in the living soul of the artificer, unless because they are nothing else than the knowledge or understanding of the soul itself ?

With the exception, however, of those facts which are known to pertain to the mental nature, whatever, on being heard and thought out by the understanding, is perceived to be real, undoubtedly that real object is one thing, and the understanding itself, by which the object is grasped, is another. Hence, even if it were true that there is a being than which a greater is inconceivable: yet to this being, when heard of and understood, the not yet created picture in the mind of the painter is not analogous.

4. Let us notice also the point touched on above, with regard to this being which is greater than all which can be conceived, and which, it is said, can be none other than God himself. I, so far as actual knowledge of the object, either from its special or general character, is concerned, am as little able to conceive of this being when I hear of it, or to have it in my understanding, as I am to conceive of or understand God himself: whom, indeed, for this very reason I can conceive not to exist. For I do not know that reality itself which God is, nor can I form a conjecture of that reality from some other like reality. For you yourself assert that that reality is such that there can be nothing else like it.

For, suppose that I should hear something said of a man absolutely unknown to me, of whose very existence I was unaware. Through that special or general knowledge by which I know what man is, or what men are, I could conceive of him also, according to the reality itself, which man is. And yet it would be possible, if the person who told me of him deceived me, that the man himself, of whom

I conceived, did not exist; since that reality according to which I conceived of him, though a no less indisputable fact, was not that man, but any man.

Hence, I am not able, in the way in which I should have this unreal being in concept or in understanding, to have that being of which you speak in concept or in understanding, when I hear the word God or the words, *a being greater than all other beings*. For I can conceive of the man according to a fact that is real and familiar to me: but of God, or a being greater than all others, I could not conceive at all, except merely according to the word. And an object can hardly or never be conceived according to the word alone.

For when it is so conceived, it is not so much the word itself (which is, indeed, a real thing—that is, the sound of the letters and syllables) as the signification of the word, when heard, that is conceived. But it is not conceived as by one who knows what is generally signified by the word; by whom, that is, it is conceived according to a reality and in true conception alone. It is conceived as by a man who does not know the object, and conceives of it only in accordance with the movement of his mind produced by hearing the word, the mind attempting to image for itself the signification of the word that is heard. And it would be surprising if in the reality of fact it could ever attain to this.

Thus, it appears, and in no other way, this being is also in my understanding, when I hear and understand a person who says that there is a being greater than all conceivable beings. So much for the assertion that this supreme nature already is in my understanding.

5. But that this being must exist, not only in the understanding but also in reality, is thus proved to me:

If it did not so exist, whatever exists in reality would be greater than it. And so the being which has been already proved to exist in my understanding, will not be greater than all other beings.

I still answer: if it should be said that a being which cannot be even conceived in terms of any fact, is in the understanding, I do not deny that this being is, accordingly, in my understanding. But since through this fact it can in no wise attain to real existence also, I do not yet concede to it that existence at all, until some certain proof of it shall be given.

For he who says that this being exists, because otherwise the being which is greater than all will not be greater than all, does not attend strictly enough to what he is saying. For I do not yet say, no, I even deny or doubt that this being is greater than any real object. Nor do I concede to it any other existence than this (if it should be called existence) which it has when the mind, according to a word merely heard, tries to form the image of an object absolutely unknown to it.

How, then, is the veritable existence of that being proved to me from the assumption, by hypothesis, that it is greater than all other beings? For I should still deny this, or doubt your demonstration of it, to this extent, that I should not admit that this being is in my understanding and concept even in the way in which many objects whose real existence is uncertain and doubtful, are in my understanding and concept. For it should be proved first that this being itself really exists somewhere; and then, from the fact that it is greater than all, we shall not hesitate to infer that it also subsists in itself.

6. For example: it is said that somewhere in the ocean is an island, which, because of the difficulty, or rather the impossibility, of discovering what does not exist, is called the lost island. And they say that this island has an inestimable wealth of all manner of riches and delicacies in greater abundance than is told of the Islands of the Blest; and that having no owner or inhabitant, it is more excellent than all other countries, which are inhabited by mankind, in the abundance with which it is stored.

Now if some one should tell me that there is such an island, I should easily understand his words, in which there is no difficulty. But suppose that he went on to say, as if by a logical inference: "You can no longer doubt that this island which is more excellent than all lands exists somewhere, since you have no doubt that it is in your understanding. And since it is more excellent not to be in the understanding alone, but to exist both in the understanding and in reality, for this reason it must exist. For if it does not exist, any land which really exists will be more excellent than it; and so the island already understood by you to be more excellent will not be more excellent."

If a man should try to prove to me by such reasoning that this island truly exists, and that its existence should no longer be doubted, either I should believe that he was jesting, or I know not which I ought to regard as the greater fool: myself, supposing that I should allow this proof; or him, if he should suppose that he had established with any certainty the existence of this island. For he ought to show first that the hypothetical excellence of this island exists as a real and indubitable fact, and in no wise as any unreal object, or one whose existence is uncertain, in my understanding.

7. This, in the mean time, is the answer the fool could make to the arguments urged against him. When he is assured in the first place that this being is so great that its non-existence is not even conceivable, and that this in turn is proved on no other ground than the fact that otherwise it will not be greater than all things, the fool may make the same answer, and say:

When did I say that any such being exists in reality, that is, a being greater than all others?—that on this ground it should be proved to me that it also exists in reality to such a degree that it cannot even be conceived not to exist? Whereas in the first place it should be in some way proved that a nature which is higher, that is, greater and better, than all other natures, exists; in order that from this we may then be able to prove all attributes which necessarily the being that is greater and better than all possesses.

Moreover, it is said that the non-existence of this being is inconceivable. It might better be said, perhaps, that its non-existence, or the possibility of its non-existence, is unintelligible. For according to the true meaning of the word, unreal objects are unintelligible. Yet their existence is conceivable in the way in which the fool conceived of the non-existence of God. I am most certainly aware of my own existence; but I know, nevertheless, that my non-existence is possible. As to that supreme being, moreover, which God is, I understand without any doubt both his existence, and the impossibility of his non-existence. Whether, however, so long as I am most positively aware of my existence, I can conceive of my non-existence, I am not sure. But if I can, why can I not conceive of the non-existence of whatever else I know with the same certainty? If, however, I cannot, God will not be the only being of which it can be said, it is impossible to conceive of his non-existence.

8. The other parts of this book are argued with such truth, such brilliancy, such grandeur; and are so replete with usefulness, so fragrant with a certain perfume of devout and holy feeling, that though there are matters in the beginning which, however rightly sensed, are weakly presented, the rest of the work should not be rejected on this account. The rather ought these earlier matters to be reasoned more cogently, and the whole to be received with great respect and honor.

EVIL AND OMNIPOTENCE

J. L. Mackie
University College, Oxford

The traditional arguments for the existence of God have been fairly thoroughly criticized by philosophers. But the theologian can, if he wishes, accept this criticism. He can admit that no rational proof of God's existence is possible. And he can still retain all that is essential to his position, by holding that God's existence is known in some other, nonrational way. I think, however, that a more telling criticism can be made by way of the traditional problem of evil. Here it can be shown, not that religious beliefs lack rational support, but that they are positively irrational, that the several parts of the essential theological doctrine are inconsistent with one another, so that the theologian can maintain his position as a whole only by a much more extreme rejection of reason than in the former case. He must now be prepared to believe, not merely what cannot be proved, but what can be disproved from other beliefs that he also holds.

The problem of evil, in the sense in which I shall be using the phrase, is a problem only for someone who believes that there is a God who is both omnipotent and wholly good. And it is a logical problem, the problem of clarifying and reconciling a number of beliefs: it is not a scientific problem that might be solved by further observations, or a practical problem that might be solved by a decision or an action. These points are obvious; I mention them only because they are sometimes ignored by theologians, who sometimes parry a statement of the problem with such remarks as "Well, can you solve the problem yourself?" or "This is a mystery which may be revealed to us later" or "Evil is something to be faced and overcome, not to be merely discussed."

In its simplest form the problem is this: God is omnipotent; God is wholly good; and yet evil exists. There seems to be some contradiction between these three propositions, so that if any two of them were true the third would be false. But at the same time all three are essential parts of most theological positions: the theologian, it seems, at once must adhere and cannot consistently adhere to all three. (The problem does not arise only for theists, but I shall discuss it in the form in which it presents itself for ordinary theism.)

However, the contradiction does not arise immediately; to show it we need some additional premises, or perhaps some quasi-logical rules connecting the terms "good," "evil," and "omnipotent." These additional principles are that good is opposed to evil, in such a way that a good thing always eliminates evil as far as it can, and that there are no limits to what an omnipotent thing can do. From these it follows that a good omnipotent thing eliminates evil completely, and then the propositions that a good omnipotent thing exists and that evil exists, are incompatible.

From *Mind*, Vol LXIV, no. 254 (1955). Reprinted by permission of Oxford University Press.

Adequate Solutions

Now once the problem is fully stated it is clear that it can be solved, in the sense that the problem will not arise if one gives up at least one of the propositions that constitute it. If you are prepared to say that God is not wholly good, or not quite omnipotent, or that evil does not exist, or that good is not opposed to the kind of evil that exists, or that there are limits to what an omnipotent thing can do, then the problem of evil will not arise for you.

There are, then, quite a number of adequate solutions of the problem of evil, and some of these have been adopted, or almost adopted, by various thinkers. For example, a few have been prepared to deny God's omnipotence, and rather more have been prepared to keep the term "omnipotence" but severely to restrict its meaning, recording quite a number of things that an omnipotent being cannot do. Some have said that evil is an illusion, perhaps because they held that the whole world of temporal, changing things is an illusion, and that what we call evil belongs only to this world, or perhaps because they held that although temporal things are much as we see them, those that we call evil are not really evil. Some have said that what we call evil is merely the privation of good, that evil in a positive sense, evil that would really be opposed to good, does not exist. Many have agreed with Pope that disorder is harmony not understood, and that partial evil is universal good. Whether any of these views is true is, of course, another question. But each of them gives an adequate solution of the problems of evil in the sense that if you accept it this problem does not arise for you, though you may, of course, have other problems to face.

But often enough these adequate solutions are only almost adopted. The thinkers who restrict God's power, but keep the term "omnipotence," may reasonably be suspected of thinking, in other contexts, that his power is really unlimited. Those who say that evil is an illusion may also be thinking, inconsistently, that this illusion is itself an evil. Those who say that "evil" is merely privation of good may also be thinking, inconsistently, that privation of good is an evil. . . If Pope meant what he said in the first line of his couplet, that "disorder" is only harmony not understood, the "partial evil" of the second line must, for consistence, mean "that which, taken in isolation, falsely appears to be evil," but it would more naturally mean "that which, in isolation, really is evil." The second line, in fact, hesitates between two views, that "partial evil" isn't really evil, since only the universal quality is real, and that "partial evil" is really an evil, but only a little one.

In addition, therefore, to adequate solutions, we must recognize unsatisfactory inconsistent solutions, in which there is only a half-hearted or temporary rejection of one of the propositions which together constitute the problem. In these, one of the constituent propositions is explicitly rejected, but it is covertly reasserted or assumed elsewhere in the system.

Fallacious Solutions

Besides these half-hearted solutions, which explicitly reject but implicitly assert one of the constituent propositions, there are definitely fallacious solutions which explicitly maintain all the constituent propositions, but implicitly reject at least one of them in the course of the argument that explains away the problem of evil.

There are, in fact, many so-called solutions which purport to remove the contradictions without abandoning any of its constituent propositions. These must be fallacious, as we can see from the very statement of the problem, but it is not so easy to see in each case precisely where the fallacy lies. I suggest that in all cases that fallacy has the general form suggested above: in order to solve the problem one (or perhaps more) of its constituent propositions is given up, but in such a way that it appears to have been retained, and can therefore be asserted without qualification in other contexts. Sometimes there is a further complication: the supposed solution moves to and fro between, say, two of the constituent propositions, at one point asserting the first of these but covertly abandoning the second, at another point asserting the second but covertly abandoning the first. These fallacious solutions often turn upon some equivocation with the words "good" and "evil," or upon some vagueness about the way in which good and evil are opposed to one another, or about how much is meant by "omnipotence." I propose to examine some of these so-called solutions, and to exhibit their fallacies in detail. Incidentally, I shall also be considering whether an adequate solution could be reached by a minor modification of one or more of the constituent propositions, which would, however, still satisfy all the essential requirements of ordinary theism.

1. "Good cannot exist without evil" or "Evil is necessary as a counterpart to good."

It is sometimes suggested that evil is necessary as a counterpart to good, that if there were no evil there could be no good either, and that this solves the problem of evil. It is true that it points to an answer to the question "Why should there be evil?" But it does so only by qualifying some of the propositions that constitute the problem.

First, it sets a limit to what God can do, saying that God *cannot* create good without simultaneously creating evil, and this means either that God is not omnipotent or that there are *some* limits to what an omnipotent thing can do. It may be replied that these limits are always presupposed, that omnipotence has never meant the power to do what is logically impossible, and on the present view the existence of good without evil would be a logical impossibility. This interpretation of omnipotence may, indeed, be accepted as a modification of our original account which does not reject anything that is essential to theism, and I shall in general assume it in the subsequent discussion. It is, perhaps, the most common theistic view, but I think that some theists at least believe that God can do what is logically impossible. Many theists, at any rate, have held that logic itself is created and laid down by God, that logic is the way in which God arbitrarily chooses to think. (This is, of course, parallel to the ethical view that morally right actions are those which God arbitrarily chooses to command, and the two views encounter similar difficulties.) And *this* account of logic is clearly inconsistent with the view that God is bound by logical necessities—unless it is possible for an omnipotent being to bind himself, an issue which we shall consider later, when we come to the Paradox of Omnipotence. This solution of the problem of evil cannot, therefore, be consistently adopted along with the view that logic is itself created by God.

But, secondly, this solution denies that evil is opposed to good in our original sense. If good and evil are counterparts, a good thing will not "eliminate evil as far as it can." Indeed, this view suggests that good and evil are not strictly qualities of things at all. Perhaps the suggestion is that good and evil are related in much the same way as great and small. Certainly, when the term "great" is used relatively as a condensation of "greater than so-and-so," and "small" is used correspondingly, greatness and smallness are counterparts and cannot exist without each other. But in this sense greatness is not a quality, not an intrinsic feature of anything; and it would be absurd to think of a movement in favor of greatness and against smallness in this sense. Such a movement would be self-defeating, since relative greatness can be promoted only be by a simultaneous promotion of relative smallness. I feel sure that no theists would be content to regard God's goodness as analogous to this—

as if what he supports were not the good but the better, and as if he had the paradoxical aim that all things should be *better* than other things.

This point is obscured by the fact that "great" and "small" seem to have an absolute as well as a relative sense. I cannot discuss here whether there is absolute magnitude or not, but if there is, there could be an absolute sense for "great," it could mean of at least a certain size, and it would make sense to speak of all things getting bigger, of a universe that was expanding all over, and therefore it would make sense to speak of promoting greatness. But in *this* sense great and small are not logically necessary counterparts: either quality could exist without the other. There would be no logical impossibility in everything's being small or in everything's being great.

Neither in the absolute nor in the relative sense, then, of "great" and "small" do these terms provide an analogy of the sort that would be needed to support this solution of the problem of evil. In neither case are greatness and smallness *both* necessary counterparts *and* mutually opposed forces or possible objects for support and attack.

It may be replied that good and evil are necessary counterparts in the same way as any quality and its logical opposite: redness can occur, it is suggested, only if nonredness also occurs. But unless evil is merely the privation of good, they are not logical opposites, and some further argument would be needed to show that they are counterparts in the same way as genuine logical opposites. Let us assume that this could be given. There is still doubt of the correctness of the metaphysical principle that a quality must have a real opposite: I suggest that it is not really impossible that everything should be, say, red, that the truth is merely that if everything were red we should not notice redness, and so we should have no word "red"; we observe and give names to qualities only if they have real opposites. If so, the principle that a term must have an opposite would belong only to our language or to our thought, and would not be an ontological principle, and, correspondingly, the rule that good cannot exist without evil would not state a logical necessity of a sort that God would just have to put up with. God might have made everything good, though we should not have noticed it if he had.

But, finally, even if we concede that this *is* an ontological principle, it will provide a solution for the problem of evil only if one is prepared to say, "Evil exists, but only just enough evil to serve as a counterpart of good." I doubt whether any theist will accept this. After all, the *ontological* requirement that nonredness should occur would be satisfied even if all the universe, except a minute speck, were red, and if there were a corresponding requirement for evil as a counterpart to good, a minute dose of evil would presumably do. But theist are not usually willing to say, in all contexts, that all the evil that occurs is a minute and necessary dose.

2. "Evil is necessary as a means to good."

It is sometimes suggested that evil is necessary for good not as a counterpart but as a means. In its simple form this has little plausibility as a solution of the problem of evil, since it obviously implies a severe restriction of God's power. It would be a *causal* law that you cannot have a certain end without a certain means, so that if God has to introduce evil as a means to good, he must be subject to at least some causal laws. This certainly conflicts with what a theist normally means by omnipotence. This view of God as limited by causal laws also conflicts with the view that causal laws are themselves made by God, which is more widely held than the corresponding view about the laws of logic. This conflict would, indeed, be resolved if it were possible for an omnipotent being to bind himself, and this possibility has still to be considered. Unless a favorable answer can be given to this question, the suggestion that evil is necessary as a means to good solves the problem of evil only by denying one of its constituent propositions, either that God is omnipotent or that "omnipotent" means what it says.

3. "The universe is better with some evil in it than it could be if there were no evil."

Much more important is a solution which at first seems to be a mere variant of the previous one, that evil may contribute to the goodness of a whole in which it is found, so that the universe as a whole is better as it is, with some evil in it, than it would be if there were no evil. This solution may be developed in either of two ways. It may be supported by an aesthetic analogy, by the fact that contrasts heighten beauty, that in a musical work, for example, there may occur discords which somehow add to the beauty of the work as a whole. Alternatively, it may be worked out in connection with the notion of progress, that the best possible organization of the universe will not be static, but progressive, that the gradual overcoming of evil by good is really a finer thing than would be the eternal unchallenged supremacy of good.

In either case, this solution usually starts from the assumption that the evil whose existence gives rise to the problem of evil is primarily what is called physical evil, that is to say, pain. In Hume's rather half-hearted presentation of the problem of evil, the evils that he stresses are pain and disease, and those who reply to him argue that the existence of pain and disease makes possible the existence of sympathy, benevolence, heroism, and the gradually successful struggle of doctors and reformers to overcome these evils. In fact, theists often seize the opportunity to accuse those who stress the problem of evil of taking a low, materialistic view of good and evil, equating these with pleasure and pain, and of ignoring the more spiritual goods which can arise in the struggle against evils.

But let us see exactly what is being done here. Let us call pain and misery "first order evil" or "evil (1)." What contrasts with this, namely, pleasure and happiness, will be called "first order good" or "good (1)." Distinct from this is "second order good" or "good (2)" which somehow emerges in a complex situation in which evil (1) is a necessary component—logically, not merely causally, necessary. (Exactly *how* it emerges does not matter: in the crudest version of this solution good (2) is simply the heightening of happiness by the contrast with misery, in other versions it includes sympathy with suffering, heroism in facing danger, and the gradual decrease of first order evil and increase of first order good.) It is also being assumed that second order good is more important first order good or evil, in particular that it more than outweighs the first order evil it involves.

Now this is a particularly subtle attempt to solve the problem of evil. It defends God's goodness and omnipotence on the ground that (on a sufficiently long view) this is the best of all logically possible worlds because it includes the important second order goods, and yet it admits that real evils, namely first order evils, exist. But does it still hold that good and evil are opposed? Not, clearly, in the sense that we set out originally: good does not tend to eliminate evil in general. Instead, we have a modified, a more complex pattern. First order good (e.g., happiness) *contrasts with* first order evil (e.g., misery): these two are opposed in a fairly mechanical way; some second order goods (e.g., benevolence) try to maximize first order good and minimize first order evil; but God's goodness is not this, it is rather the will to maximize *second* order good. We might, therefore, call God's goodness an example of a third order goodness, or good (3). While this account is different from our original one, it might well be held to be an improvement on it, to give a more accurate description of the way in which good is opposed to evil, and to be consistent with the essential theist position.

There might, however, be several objections to this solution.

First, some might argue that such qualities as benevolence—and *a fortiori* the third order goodness which promotes benevolence—have merely derivative value, that they are not higher sorts of good, but merely means to good (1), that is, to happiness, so that it would be absurd for God to keep misery in existence in order to make possible the virtues of benevolence, heroism, etc. The theist who adopts the present solution must, of course, deny this, but he can do so with some plausibility, so I should not press this objection.

Secondly, it follows from this solution that God is not in our sense benevolent or sympathetic: he is not concerned to minimize evil (1), but only to promote good (2); and this might be a disturbing conclusion for some theists.

But, thirdly, the fatal objection is this. Our analysis shows clearly the possibility of the existence of a *second* order evil, an evil (2) contrasting with good (2) as evil (1) contrasts with good (1). This would include malevolence, cruelty, callousness, cowardice, and states in which good (1) is decreasing and evil (1) is increasing. And just as good (2) is held to be the important kind of good, the kind that God is concerned to promote, so evil (2) will, by analogy, be the important kind of evil, the kind which God, if he were ever wholly good and omnipotent, would eliminate. And yet evil (2) plainly exists, and indeed most theists (in other contexts) stress its existence more than that of evil (1). We should, therefore, state the problem of evil in terms of second order evil, and against this form of the problem the present solution is useless.

An attempt might be made to use this solution again, at a higher level, to explain the occurrence of evil (2): indeed the next main solution that we shall examine does just this, with the help of some new notions. Without any fresh notions, such a solution would have little plausibility: for example, we could hardly say that the really important good was a good (3), such as the increase of benevolence in proportion to cruelty, which logically required for its occurrence the occurrence of some second order evil. But even if evil (2) could be explained in this way, it is fairly clear that there would be third order evils contrasting with this third order good: and we should be well on the way to an infinite regress, where the solution of a problem of evil, stated in terms of evil (n), indicated the existence of an evil ($n + 1$), and a further problem to be solved.

4. "Evil is due to human free will."

Perhaps the most important proposed solution of the problem of evil is that evil is not to be ascribed to God at all, but to the independent actions of human beings, supposed to have been endowed by God with freedom of the will. This solution may be combined with the preceding one: first order evil (e.g., pain) may be justified as a logically necessary component in second order good (e.g. sympathy) while second order evil (e.g., cruelty) is not *justified*, but is so ascribed to human beings that God cannot be held responsible for it. This combination evades my third criticism of the preceding solution.

The free-will solution also involves the preceding solution at a higher level. To explain why a wholly good God gave men free will although it would lead to some important evils, it must be argued that it is better on the whole that men should act freely, and sometimes err, than that they should be innocent automata, acting rightly in a wholly determined way. Freedom, that is to say, is now treated as a third order good, and as being more valuable than second order goods (such as sympathy and heroism) would be if they were deterministically produced, and it is being assumed that second order evils, such as cruelty, are logically necessary accompaniments of freedom, just as pain is a logically necessary precondition of sympathy.

I think that this solution is unsatisfactory primarily because of the incoherence of the notion of freedom of the will: but I cannot discuss this topic adequately here, although some of my criticisms will touch upon it.

First I should query the assumption that second order evils are logically necessary accompaniments of freedom. I should ask this: if God has made men such that in their free choices they sometimes prefer what is good and sometimes what is evil, why could he not have made men such that they always freely choose the good? If there is no logical impossibility in a man's freely choosing the good on one, or on several occasions, there cannot be a logical impossibility in his freely choosing the good on every occasion. God was not, then, faced with a choice between making innocent automata and making beings who, in acting freely, would sometimes go wrong: there was open to him the obviously better possibility of making beings who would act freely but always go right. Clearly, failure to avail himself of this possibility is inconsistent with his being both omnipotent and wholly good.

If it is replied that this objection is absurd, that the making of some wrong choices is logically necessary for freedom, it would seem that "freedom" must here mean complete randomness or indeterminacy, including randomness with regard to the alternatives good and evil, in other words that men's choices and consequent actions can be "free" only if they are not determined by their characters. Only on this assumption can God escape the responsibility for men's actions; for if he made them as they are, but did not determine their wrong choices, this can only be because the wrong choices are not determined by men as they are. But then if freedom is randomness, how can it be a characteristic of *will*? And, still more, how can it be the most important good? What value or merit would there be in free choices if these were random actions which were not determined by the nature of the agent?

I conclude that to make this solution plausible two different senses of "freedom" must be confused, one sense which will justify the view that freedom is a third order good, more valuable than other goods would be without it, and another sense, sheer randomness, to prevent us from ascribing to God a decision to make men such that they sometimes go wrong when he might have made them such that they would always freely go right.

This criticism is sufficient to dispose of this solution. But besides this there is a fundamental difficulty in the notion of an omnipotent God creating men with free will, for if men's wills are really free this must mean that even God cannot control them, that is, that God is no longer omnipotent. It may be objected that God's gift of freedom to men does not mean that he *cannot* control their wills, but that he always *refrains* from controlling their wills. But why, we may ask, should God refrain from controlling evil wills? Why should he not leave men free to will rightly, but intervene when he sees them beginning to will wrongly? If God could do this, but does not, and if he is wholly good, the only explanation could be that even a wrong free act of will is not really evil, that its freedom is a value which outweighs its wrongness, so that there would be a loss of value if God took away the wrongness and the freedom together. But this is utterly opposed to what theists say about sin in other contexts. The present solutions of the problem of evil, then, can be maintained only in the form that God has made men so free that he cannot control their wills.

This leads us to what I call the "Paradox of Omnipotence": can an omnipotent being make things which he cannot subsequently control? Or, what is practically equivalent to this, can an omnipotent being make rules which then bind himself? (These are practically equivalent because any such rules could be regarded as setting certain things beyond his control and vice versa.) The second of these formulations is relevant to the suggestions that we have already met, that an omnipotent God creates the rule of logic or causal laws, and is then bound by them.

It is clear that this is a paradox: the question cannot be answered satisfactorily either in the affirmative or in the negative. If we answer "Yes," it follows that if God actually makes things which he cannot control, or makes rules which bind himself, he is not omnipotent once he had made them: there are *then* things which he cannot do. But if we answer "No," we are immediately asserting that there are things which he cannot do, that is to say that he is already not omnipotent.

It cannot be replied that the question which sets this paradox is not a proper question. It would make good sense to say that a human mechanic has made a machine which he cannot control: if there is any difficulty about the question it lies in the notion of omnipotence itself.

This, incidentally, shows that although we have approached this paradox from the free-will theory, it is equally a problem for a theological determinist. No one thinks that machines have free will, yet they may well be beyond the control of their makers. The determinist might reply that anyone who makes anything determines its ways of acting, and so determines its subsequent behavior: even the human mechanic does this by his *choice* of materials and structure for his machine, though he does not know all about either of these: the mechanic thus determines, though he may not foresee, his machine's actions. And since God is omniscient, and since his creation of things is total, he both determines and foresees the ways in which his creatures will act. We may grant this, but it is beside the point. The question is not whether God *originally* determined the future actions of his creatures, but whether he can *subsequently* control their actions, or whether he was able in his original creation to put things beyond his subsequent control. Even on determinist principles the answers "Yes" and "No" are equally irreconcilable with God's omnipotence.

Before suggesting a solution of this paradox, I would point out that there is a parallel Paradox of Sovereignty. Can a legal sovereign make a law restricting its own future legislative power? For example, could the British parliament make a law forbidding any future parliament to socialize banking, and also forbidding the future repeal of this law itself? Or could the British parliament, which was legally sovereign in Australia in, say, 1899, pass a valid law, or series of laws, which made it no longer sovereign in 1933? Again, neither the affirmative nor the negative answer is really satisfactory. If we were to answer "Yes," we should be admitting the validity of a law which, if it were actually made, would mean that parliament was no longer sovereign. If we were to answer "No," we should be admitting that there is a law, not logically absurd, which parliament cannot validly make, that is, that parliament is not now a legal sovereign. This paradox can be solved in the following way. We should distinguish between first order laws, that is, law governing the actions of individuals and bodies other than the legislature, and second order laws, that is, laws about laws, laws governing the actions of the legislature itself. Correspondingly, we should distinguish two orders of sovereignty, first order sovereignty (sovereignty (1)) which is unlimited authority to make first order laws, and second order sovereignty (sovereignty (2)) which is unlimited authority to make second order laws. If we say that parliament is sovereign we might mean that any parliament at any time has sovereignty (1), or we might mean that parliament has both sovereignty (1) and sovereignty (2) at present, but we cannot without contradiction mean both that the present parliament has sovereignty (2) and that parliament at every time has sovereignty (1), for if the present parliament has sovereignty (2) it may use it to take away the sovereignty (1) of later parliaments. What the paradox shows is that we cannot ascribe to any continuing institution legal sovereignty in an inclusive sense.

The analogy between omnipotence and sovereignty shows that the paradox of omnipotence can be solved in a similar way. We must distinguish between first order omnipotence (omnipotence (1)), that is, unlimited power to act, and second order omnipotence (omnipotence (2)), that is, unlimited power to determine what powers to act things shall have. Then we could consistently say that God all the time has omnipotence (1), but if so no beings at any time have powers to act independently of God. Or we could say that God at one time had omnipotence (2), and used it to assign independent powers to act to certain things, so that God thereafter did not have omnipotence (1). But what the paradox shows is that we cannot consistently ascribe to any continuing being omnipotence in an inclusive sense.

An alternative solution of this paradox would be simply to deny that God is a continuing being, that any times can be assigned to his actions at all. But on this assumption (which also has difficulties of its own) no meaning can be given to the assertion that God made men with wills so free that he could not control them. The paradox of omnipotence can be avoided by putting God outside time, but the free-will solution of the problem of evil cannot be saved in this way, and equally it remains impossible to hold that an omnipotent God *binds himself* by causal or logical laws.

Conclusion

Of the proposed solutions of the problem of evil which we have examined, none has stood up to criticism. There may be other solutions which require examination, but this study strongly suggests that there is no valid solution of the problem which does not modify at least one of the constituent propositions in a way which would seriously affect the essential core of the theistic position.

Quite apart from the problem of evil, the paradox of omnipotence has shown that God's omnipotence must in any case be restricted in one way or another, that unqualified omnipotence cannot be ascribed to any being that continues through time. And if God and his actions are not in time, can omnipotence, or power of any sort, be meaningfully ascribed to him?

PART FOUR

EPISTEMOLOGY

THE MODES OF SUSPENSION OF JUDGEMENT

Sextus Empiricus

CHAPTER XII
General Introduction to the Modes of Suspension of Judgment

We were saying that mental tranquillity follows on suspension of judgement in regard to all things. Next, it would be proper for us to state how we attain suspension of judgement. As a general rule, this suspension of judgement is effected by our setting things in opposition. We oppose appearances to appearances, or thoughts to thoughts, or appearances to thoughts. For example, when we say, "The same tower appears round from a distance, but square from close by,"[1] we are opposing appearances to appearances. When a person is trying to prove the existence of providence from the order of the celestial bodies, and we counter him with the observation that the good often fare ill while the evil prosper and then conclude from this that there is no providence, we are opposing thoughts to thoughts. And then appearances may be opposed to thoughts. Anaxagoras,[2] for instance, could oppose to the fact that snow is white his reasoning that "Snow is frozen water, and water is black, snow therefore is black also." And sometimes, from the point of view of a different concept, we oppose present things to present things, as in the foregoing, and sometimes present things to past or future things. An example of this is the following. Whenever someone propounds an argument that we are not able to dispose of, we make this reply: "Before the birth of the founder of the school to which you belong, this argument of your school was not yet seen to be a sound argument. From the point of view of nature, however, it existed all the while as such. In like manner it is possible, as far as nature is concerned, that an argument antithetical to the one now set forth by you is in existence, though as yet unknown to us. This being so, the fact that an argument seems valid to us now is not yet a sufficient reason why we must assent to it."

But for a better understanding of these antitheses, I shall now present also the modes by which suspension of judgement is induced. I cannot, however, vouch for their number or validity, since it is possible that they are unsound, and that there are more of them than the ones to be discussed.

CHAPTER XIV
The Ten Modes

With the older Sceptics the usual teaching is that the modes by which suspension of judgement seems to be brought about are ten in number, which they also term synonymously "arguments" and "forms." These are as follows. First is that in which suspension is caused by the variation in animals. In the

From Sectus Empiricus, *Selections from the Major Writings on Scepticism, Man, and God*, translated by Sanford Etheridge, 1985, Hackett Publishing Company, Inc., Indianapolis, IN and Cambridge, MA.

second it is caused by the differences in human beings. Third, by the differences in the construction of the organs of sense. Fourth, by the circumstances. Fifth, by the positions, distances, and places involved. Sixth, by the admixtures present. Seventh, by the quantities and compoundings of the underlying objects. Eighth, by the relativity of things. Ninth, by the frequency or rarity of occurrence. Tenth, by the institutions, customs, laws, mythical beliefs, and dogmatic notions. This order, however, is merely arbitrary.

Transcending these are three modes: the argument from the subject judging, the argument from the object judged, and that from both. The first four modes above are subordinate to the argument from the subject judging (for that which judges is either an animal or a human being or a sense, and is in some circumstance or other). The seventh and the tenth are referred to the argument from the object judged. The fifth, sixth, eighth, and ninth are referred to the argument from both combined. These three modes are in turn referred to the mode of relativity, so that the mode of relativity is the *summum genus*,[3] while the three are its species, and the ten are subordinate. This is the most plausible statement we can make concerning their number. In regard to their meaning, we have the following to say.[4]

The First Mode

As we were saying, the first argument is the argument from differences in animals. According to this mode, the same objects do not produce the same impression in different animals. This we conclude both from the fact that they have different origins and from the variety exhibited in the structure of their bodies. Now to consider origin. Some animals are produced without sexual union, others by coition. Of those which are produced without sexual union, some are generated out of fire, such as the little animals that appear in furnaces, others out of stagnant water, such as mosquitoes, and others from soured wine, such as ants. From the earth come earthworms, from mud come frogs, from dung, maggots. From asses come beetles, and from vegetables caterpillars. Other animals come from fruits, as the gall-insects from wild figs; and still others from rotting animals, as bees from bulls and wasps from horses. Of the animals produced by sexual union, some (most of them, in fact) are the offspring of parents of like kind, some of parents of different kinds, as are mules. Speaking of animals in general again, some are born alive, as are human beings, some are born as eggs, as are birds, and some are born as unformed flesh, as bears. It is reasonable,[5] then, to suppose that the dissimilarities and differences in their respective origins are a cause of greatly contrary affections in animals, and that the discordant, incongruous, and conflicting character of their affections is derived from their different origins.

Moreover, a very great conflict between sense-impressions can be produced even by differences in the most important parts of the body, especially the organs whose natural function is judging and perceiving. For instance, people suffering from jaundice [6] say that what appears to us as white is yellow, and those who have a bloodshot condition of the eyes say it is blood-red. Now, since some animals have yellow eyes, others bloodshot eyes, while others have eyes which are white, and others have eyes of still other colours, it is reasonable to suppose, I think, that their perception of colour is different. Moreover, if we fix our gaze on the sun for a long time and then look down into a book, the letters appear to be goldcoloured and going in circles. Also, some animals have a sort of natural brilliance in their eyes, and send off from them a fine light which travels easily, so that they even see at night. In view of this fact, we might well be right in supposing that the impressions they get of external objects are different from ours. [7] And jugglers, too, by smearing their lamp-wick with copper rust or with the ink of the cuttle-fish, make their onlookers appear to have a copper or black colour, as the case may be. This they effect by the application of only a small quantity of their preparation. It is surely much more reasonable to suppose that if the eyes of animals contain different mixtures of fluids, the impressions they receive of external objects will be different. Also, when we press one side of the eyeball, the objects viewed appear longish and narrow in form, figure, and size. It is probable, therefore, that those animals which have a slanting and elongated pupil, such as goats, cats, and the like, receive impressions of objects which are different from and unlike the impressions had of the same objects by animals with round pupils. And then mirrors: owing to differences in their construction, they sometimes show the external objects as being very small (concave mirror), sometimes as longish and narrow (convex mirror) . Some show the mirrored person's head at the bottom and his feet at the top. Now, there are similar differences in the organs of sight of animals. Some of these, owing to their convexity, protrude quite out of the sockets, while others are more concave, and others lie in a flat plane. It is natural [8] to suppose that these conditions also may cause differences in the sense-impressions. If this is so, when dogs and fishes and lions and humans and locusts look at the same objects, they would in each case see objects that are neither equal in size nor similar in shape. Rather, what each perceives would be the impression created by the particular sight that receives the object.

The same argument applies to the other senses. Take the sense of touch. One could hardly postulate a similarity of sensibility between hard-shelled animals, fleshy animals, thorny animals, and feathered or scaly ones. And as for perceptions conveyed through the sense of hearing, one could hardly say that they are the same in those animals which have a very narrow auditory passage as they are in those which have a very wide one, or the same in animals with hairy ears as in those with smooth ears. We can even see the truth of this assertion in ourselves, as far as the sense of hearing is concerned, for when we plug up our ears, our perception through this sense is different from our normal hearing. The sense of smell also would exhibit differences by virtue of the variety in animals. We ourselves, when we have a cold and the phlegm in us is excessive, are affected in one way; but when an excessive amount of blood is collected in the parts about the head, we are affected in another way, and turn away from things which to others seem fragrant, believing ourselves overpowered, as it were, by their smell. Some animals, too, are flaccid by nature and abound in phlegm, while others are very rich in blood; and in others yellow or black bile, present in an excessive amount, is the predominant element. Hence it would be reasonable to assume that this is another reason why objects of smell appear different to each severally. It is the same with objects of taste. In the first place, the tongues of animals are different, some being rough and without moisture, some very moist. In fever our tongues too become very dry, so that we think the food set before us has an earthy, ill-flavoured, and bitter taste; and this experience of ours is caused by the varying predominance of the juices we are said to have in us. Now, since the organs of taste of animals differ from each other, and have different juices in excess, it would follow that they also receive different ideas of the taste of things.

An analogous process is the distribution of food throughout the body. In one place it becomes a vein, in another an artery, a bone, a sinew, and so on. The difference in the power it displays corresponds with the differences between the parts which receive it. Water also, which is one and uniform when it is absorbed by trees, becomes in different places bark, branch, or fruit, and further, fig, pomegranate, or whatever it may be. The breath of the musician, also one and the same when it enters the flute, becomes in turn a high-pitched tone or a low one. Similarly, the same pressure of his hand upon the lyre sometimes produces a low tone, sometimes a high one. In the same manner it is a fair supposition that external objects appear different to the animals receiving the sense-impressions of the objects, and that this is due to differences of constitution in the different animals. But this can be seen more clearly from the preferences and aversions of animals. For example, perfume seems very agreeable to men, but intolerable to beetles and bees. Olive-oil is beneficial to men, but it kills wasps and bees if sprinkled on them. Sea-water is unpleasant for men to drink, even poisonous, but for fish most pleasant—and drinkable. Pigs would much rather wash in the most stinking mire than in clear and pure water. And then some animals subsist on herbs, others on shrubs, and others live in the woods; others live on seeds, flesh, or milk. Some enjoy putrefied food, while others like it prepared by cooking; and in general, what is pleasant to some is unpleasant to others, and may be undesirable, even fatal. Hemlock, for example, fattens quails, and henbane fattens sows. The latter even like to eat salamanders, just as deer eat venomous animals and swallows eat blister-beetles. Ants and wood-lice, if swallowed by humans, produce nausea and colic, while the bear, if he falls sick, licks them up and thus regains his strength. One touch of an oaktwig is sufficient to stun a viper. The leaf of a plane-tree has the same effect on bats. An elephant will run from a ram, a lion from a cock. Sea-monsters will flee from the crackling noise produced by the pounding of beans, [9] and a tiger will run from the mere sound of a drum. We could multiply these examples, but it would mean dwelling unduly long on the subject. In short, if the same things are unpleasant to some animals but pleasant to others, and pleasure and displeasure depend on sense-impression, then the sense-impressions that animals get from the objects are different.

But if the difference in animals is a cause of things appearing different, then we shall, it is true, be able to say what—in our view—a thing is; but on the question what it really is by nature, we shall suspend judgement. And as for acting ourselves as judges between our own sense-impressions and those of the other animals, that is out of the question, because we ourselves are a party to the disagreement. For this reason, in fact, we shall be more in need of a judge than capable ourselves of judging.[10] Moreover, we are unable, either without proof or with proof, to give the preference to our own sense-impressions over those of the irrational animals. For besides the possibility (which we shall mention) that proof is non-existent, the so-called proof itself will be either apparent to us or non-apparent. If it is non-apparent, we cannot even bring it forward with confidence. But suppose it is apparent to us. Then, since what is apparent to animals is the question at issue and we to whom the proof is apparent are animals, we still shall have to investigate whether the proof itself is in the same degree true as it is apparent. It is absurd to attempt to establish the question at issue by means of the question at issue, since that would involve believing and disbelieving the same thing at once—which is impossible. We should have to believe it in so far as it professes to furnish the proof, and disbelieve it in so far as it itself is the thing to be proved. We shall have, then, no proof which will enable us to give the preference to our own sense-impressions over those of the so-called irrational animals. If, therefore, the sense-impressions of animals differ as a consequence of the differences which exist between animals, and we cannot possibly sit in judgement over them, we must of necessity suspend judgement in regard to external objects.

We also allow ourselves the luxury of comparing the so-called irrational animals with man in respect of sense-impressions. For after our practical arguments have done their work, we feel not unqualified to make sport of those demented braggarts the dogmatists.[11] Now, the men of our school are wont to compare the generality of the irrational animals with man. But since the dogmatists sophistically assert that the comparison is unfair, we shall base our argument on one animal only—for instance, the dog, if you please, which seems to be the most worthless—and still continue our jesting at great advantage. Even so, we shall find that as far as the trustworthiness of appearances goes, the animals we speak of are not inferior to ourselves. Now, the dogmatists concede that this animal excels us in sense-perception. His perception by the sense of smell is superior to ours, and he also has a keen sense of hearing.

Let us now turn to the faculty of reason. One kind of reason is internal reason, and the other kind is uttered reason.[12] Let us look first at internal reason. According to those dogmatists whose doctrines are the most opposed to us, namely, the Stoics, it seems that internal reason is activated in the following cases: in the choice of congenial and the avoidance of alien things; in the knowledge of the arts that contribute to this; in the apprehension and alleviation of one's own sufferings; and in the acquisition of the virtues consistent with one's own nature. Now, the dog—the example we decided to take for the sake of the argument—makes a choice of the congenial when he seeks after food, and he avoids the harmful when he retires before a raised whip. What is more, he possesses an art by which he procures what is congenial to him, the art of hunting. He is not without virtue, either. Certainly, at any rate, if justice means to render each his due, the dog would not be without justice, for he exercises it by guarding and wagging his tail at those who are familiar to him and who treat him well, and by keeping strangers and those who harm him at a distance. But if he possesses this virtue, then, since the virtues are reciprocally implied, he possesses the other virtues also, which according to the claim of the wise men the majority of men do not possess. We see that he is brave from the way he defends us, and intelligent too, as Homer also testified when he represented Odysseus as going unrecognized by all the members of his household and as being recognized only by his dog Argus, who was not deceived by the changes that had come over the body of the man. Neither had his impression of the man lost its immediacy; in fact, it appeared that he had retained this immediacy of impression better than the humans did. But according to Chrysippus, who is hostile, if anybody is, to irrational animals, the dog even shares in the famous science of dialectic. At any rate, the aforesaid man is responsible for the statement that the dog knows intuitively the fifth complex indemonstrable syllogism.[13] He shows this knowledge whenever he is tracking an animal and comes to a meeting of three roads. After he has tried two of the roads and found that the animal has not passed that way, he rushes off immediately on the third without even stopping to pick up the scent. The old philosopher says that the dog virtually reasons this out, as follows: "The animal passed either this way, or this way, or this way; but it did not take this road, nor that; therefore it must have gone by the third road." Moreover, he is capable of apprehending his own sufferings and of relieving them. Thus, if there is a thorn stuck in his foot, he sets about removing it by rubbing his foot against the ground, or by means of his teeth. And if he has a sore anywhere, because dirty sores are slow to heal and clean ones heal easily, he gently wipes off the discharge that gathers. Why, he even observes the teaching of Hippocrates, and very well at that; for if he should receive an injury to his foot, he applies the general rule (that rest will cure it) and elevates the injured foot and keeps it as undisturbed as possible. And when he is troubled by unwholesome humours, he eats grass, which enables him to vomit up the unwholesome matter and get well.

Now, we based our observations on the dog as an example for the sake of the argument. If, then, it appears that he chooses what is good for him and avoids what is troublesome, if he possesses an art which enables him to procure the good things, if he is capable of apprehending and relieving his own sufferings, if he is not without virtue—these being the conditions on which the perfection of internal reason depends—then the dog will be, in this respect, perfect. This may be the reason why some philosophers have exalted themselves with the name of this animal.[14]

An inquiry concerning uttered reason is for the present unnecessary, since even some of the dogmatists have rejected it on the grounds that it is prejudicial to the acquisition of virtue. For the same reason they also used to practise silence during the time they were learners.[15] And besides, just supposing a man were dumb, no one is going to say that he is irrational. But leaving this consideration aside also, as our subject is animals, we certainly see some animals, jays among others, that can even utter human sounds. But leaving this point aside also, we note simply that even though we do not understand the sounds made by the so-called irrational animals, it is not altogether improbable that they do converse—without our understanding them. But then when we hear the speech of foreigners we do not understand that either; we think it monotonous. Also, the sounds we hear dogs utter are different: when they are keeping people off it is one sound, when they are howling it is another; and when they receive a beating, the sound is different from the sound they utter when they are fawning. And in general, if a person were to look into this matter carefully, he would find that the utterances of both this and the other animals vary greatly under different circumstances. On this account the so-called irrational animals might fairly be said to share in uttered reason also. But if these animals are inferior to humans neither in the accuracy of their perceptions, nor in internal reason, nor—needless to say—in uttered reason, then their sense-impressions will be no more untrustworthy than ours. It is perhaps even possible to prove this by basing our argument on each class of the irrational animals separately. Who, for example, would not admit that birds excel in quickness of wit and that they possess the use of uttered reason? Their understanding is not confined to the present but extends to future things as well, and to those who are able to understand them they show the future beforehand, both by their prophetic cry and by the other signs they give.

The comparison I have here drawn is given into the bargain as a bonus. This I have indicated before. I had previously shown sufficiently, I think, that we cannot give the preference to our own sense-impressions over those of the irrational animals. But then if the irrational animals, as judges of the sense-impressions, are not less reliable than we, and if the discrepancy in sense-impressions is due to the difference between animals, it is true that I shall be able to say what each object appears to me to be, but no more. As to what its real nature is, I shall be forced, for the reasons given above, to suspend judgement.

The Second Mode

Such, then, is the first mode of suspension. The second, as we said, is the argument from the difference between men. Let us make a concession for the sake of the argument and say that human beings are more to be believed than the irrational animals. Even so, inasmuch as we differ from one another, we shall find suspension of judgement being brought in. It is said that man is made up of two elements, soul and body. Well, in both of these we differ from one another.

As for the body, we have different figures and constitutional peculiarities. Now, the Scythian's figure is different from that of an Indian, and the difference is due, it is said, to the varying predominance of the humours. And according as different humours predominate in men, their sense-impressions also are different, as we showed in the first argument. That is why there is also much difference between them in their choice and avoidance of external things. Thus the Indian standard of taste is different from that in our country, and the fact that we enjoy different things is indicative of a difference in the sense-impressions that we get from the external objects. We differ also in our constitutional peculiarities: for some people, beef is easier to digest than rock-fish, and some suffer diarrhoea from inferior Lesbian wine. There used to be an old woman of Attica, they say, who could take thirty drams of hemlock with impunity, and Lysis used to take four drams of opium without harm. And Demophon, Alexander's butler, used to shiver when he was in the sun or in a hot bath, but when he was in the shade he felt warm. Athenagoras of Argos was not affected by the sting of scorpions and poisonous spiders; the tribe called the Psyllaeans are not injured by the bite of snakes and asps; and the Tentyritae, an Egyptian people, suffer no harm from the crocodiles. Also, the Ethiopians who live along the Astapous River on the other side of Lake Meroe eat scorpions and snakes and suchlike animals without ill effect. Rufinus of Chalcis would drink hellebore without vomiting and without any evacuation at all; he could simply take it and digest it like any of the usual beverages. Chrysermus, of the school of Herophilus, ran the risk of a heart attack whenever he took pepper, and Soterichus the surgeon used to suffer from diarrhoea whenever he caught the odour of fried sheat-fish. Andron of Argos was so unaffected by thirst that he even journeyed across the waterless part of Libya without requiring a drink. Tiberius Caesar could see in the dark, and Aristotle tells us of a certain Thracian who had the hallucination that a man was continually leading the way in front of him.

Now, we shall content ourselves with the recitation of these few examples from the many found in the writings of the dogmatists. Even so, it is clear that the bodily differences between men are great, and it is thus natural to assume that these differences extend also to the very soul of man, for the body is in a sense the stamped image of the soul, as the art of physiognomy shows us. But the greatest indication of the wide, indeed infinite, variety to be found in human intelligence is the discrepancy in the statements which the dogmatists make on every subject, particularly on the question what things it is proper to choose or avoid. The poets, too, have expressed themselves on this. Pindar says:

The honours and wreaths won by wind-swift
horses are the delight of one man,
Others delight in a life in gilded chambers;
Another man, too, finds joy in traversing
the salty main with a fast ship. [16]

And the Poet says:

Different men take delight in different deeds.[17]

Tragedy also is full of these sentiments. For example:

If fair and wise meant both the same to all,
Dispute and strife would be no more.[18]

And again:

Strange, to say the least, that what gives joy to some,
Is an object of hate to others.[19]

Now, since choice and avoidance depend on pleasure and displeasure, and pleasure and displeasure in turn depend on sensation and sense-impression, it is logical for us to conclude that whenever the same things are chosen by some and avoided by others they are not even affected in the same manner by the same objects, since otherwise they would agree in their choices and avoidances. But if it is because of the differences between men that the same objects affect us differently, then this would be another good reason for bringing in suspension of judgement. We are, perhaps, able to say what each external object appears to be from our several different points of view, but we are unable to give an account of its true essence. For we shall have to believe either all men or some of them; to believe all would be an impossible undertaking, as we should have to accept contradictory accounts, while if we are to believe some, let them tell us who it is we are supposed to agree with. The Platonist will say Plato, the Epicurean, Epicurus, and so on with the others. They cannot decide as between their own factions, and this only serves to bring us round to suspension again. Furthermore, to say that we should agree with the majority would be puerile, since it is in no one's power to make a survey of all mankind and determine statistically the majority opinion. It is quite possible that there are peoples unknown to us, to whom things rare with us are common occurrences and with whom the conditions obtaining with us are comparatively rare. It might turn out, for example, that those who feel no pain at the bite of spiders are in the majority, and that some feel pain only rarely; and this might be similarly the case with the other constitutional peculiarities mentioned above. The differences in men, therefore, are another compelling reason for invoking suspension of judgement.

The Third Mode

Now, the dogmatists are a rather conceited class of people, and they say that they must give themselves the preference over other men in the matter of judging things; but we know that their claim is absurd because they themselves form a party to the disagreement. Furthermore, if they are thus prejudiced in favour of themselves whenever they judge appearances, then they are begging the question before they even begin their judgement, because they are turning the decision over to themselves. Nevertheless, we can arrive at suspension of judgement even when basing the argument on a single man, for instance on the "wise man"[20] who is the product of their dreams. In order to do this we bring into play the mode which is third in order. This is the one we called the argument from the differences in the senses. And it is clear at the outset that the senses differ from one another. Take paintings, for example. To the eye they seem to have hollows and prominences, but certainly not to the sense of touch. And to some, honey appears to be pleasant to the tongue, but to the eyes it appears unpleasant; thus it is impossible to say whether it is in itself pleasant or unpleasant. With perfume the case is similar; it delights the sense of smell but is disgusting to the taste. Then there is the juice of the spurge. Since it is painful to the eyes but causes pain to no other part of the body, it will not be for us to say whether, as far as its own nature is concerned, it is in itself painful or painless to bodies. And rain-water is beneficial to the eyes, but irritates the windpipe and lungs just as olive-oil does, which to the skin is soothing. The electric ray produces stiffness if applied to the extremities, while application to the rest of the body is without ill effect. Therefore we are not in a position to say what each thing is by nature, although it is possible to say what it appears to be on each occasion.

We could easily cite more examples,[21] but to avoid waste of time, on account of the plan of the treatise, we need say just this. Each appearance that we perceive through the senses seems to present itself under many forms; an apple, for instance, seems smooth, fragrant, sweet, and yellow.[22] It is uncertain, however, whether these are really the only qualities it possesses, or whether it is of one quality only but appears in different forms because the various sense-organs are of different construction. It may also be that it has more qualities than are apparent, and that some of them are not perceived by us. Now, that the apple is of a single quality we can conclude, on the one hand, from our previous statements about the distribution of food throughout the body, of water throughout trees, and about the breathing of wind into flutes, pipes, and similar instruments. For the apple, like these, may well be of a uniform quality, yet still appear to possess several qualities by reason of the differences between the sense-organs through which its perception takes place. On the other hand, we can conclude that the apple possesses more qualities than those which are apparent to us, as follows. Let us imagine a man whose senses of touch, smell, and taste are intact, but who is congenitally deaf and blind. This man will have no idea at all that a thing is visible or audible, but will believe that only those three classes of qualities exist which he is capable of apprehending.[23] With us too it is possible that our apprehension of qualities in the apple is determined by the number of senses we possess—five only. And it is possible that there exist other qualities that fall within the province of other organs of sense. Our not possessing any such other organs of sense would be reason enough why we do not apprehend the type of sense-objects proper to them.

"But," one will say, "nature made the senses commensurate with their objects." In view of the great disagreement amongst the dogmatists on the unsettled question of the existence of nature, we can only reply, "Which nature?" On this question of the existence of nature the layman's judgement will carry no authority with the dogmatists. But a philosopher's judgement is no better, for he is not a judge, but a party to the disagreement, himself subject to judgement. However, given these possible alternatives, that there may subsist in the apple only those qualities which we seem to apprehend, likewise that there may subsist more than just these; or again that even the ones we perceive may not subsist at all; it follows that it will be non-evident to us what kind of thing the apple is. And the same argument holds for the other objects of sense. But then if the senses do not apprehend external objects, the intellect cannot apprehend them either, seeing that it is led astray by its guides, which is all the more reason why suspension of judgement in regard to the external underlying objects will be indicated.

The Fourth Mode

But we can also reach suspension by basing our argument on each sense separately, or even by disregarding the senses. To this end we employ the fourth mode of suspension, which we call the mode based on the circumstances. We understand by "circumstances" the states in which we are. This mode, we say, is seen in cases of natural or unnatural states, in states of waking or sleeping, in cases where age, motion or rest, hating or loving are involved; or where the determining factor is a state of want or satiety, drunkenness or soberness; in cases of predispositions, or when it is a question of confidence or fear, or grief or joy. For example, things appear dissimilar according to whether we are in a natural or unnatural state; delirious people, and those who are possessed by a god, think that they hear divine voices, while we do not. Often they claim that they perceive, among a number of other things, the odour of storax or frankincense, or something of that sort, where we perceive nothing. And the same water that seems hot to a person when poured on inflamed parts seems lukewarm to us. The coat which appears yellowish-orange to men with bloodshot eyes does not appear so to me, yet it is the same coat. And the same honey that appears sweet to me appears bitter to those suffering from jaundice.

Now, one might object that in those whose condition is unnatural it is the intermingling of certain humours that causes them to get unnatural impressions from the external objects. Our reply to this would be that it is possible that the external objects actually are in reality such as they appear to those who are said to be in an unnatural state; and that since persons in a state of good health also have mixed humours, it may be that it is these humours that make the objects appear different to them. For it would be a fabrication to attribute to the humours of sick people a power to to change external objects, and to deny this power to the humours of the healthy. After all, it is natural for the healthy to be in a healthy state, and unnatural for them to be in a sick state. By the same token it is unnatural for the sick to be in a healthy state, but natural for them to be in a sick state. Consequently, the sick warrant credence also, since they too are in some respect in a natural state. Whether one is in a sleeping or a waking state also makes a difference in the sense-impressions, since our manner of perception while awake differs from the perception we have in sleep; and our manner of perception in sleep is not like our waking perception. As a result, the existence or non-existence of our sense-impressions is not absolute but relative, since they bear a relation to our sleeping or waking state. It is probable, therefore, that although our dream-images are unreal in our waking state, they are nevertheless not absolutely unreal, for they do exist in our dreams.[24] In the same manner the realities of the waking state, even if they do not exist in dreams, nevertheless exist. Age also makes a difference. Old men, for example, may think the air is cold, but the same air seems mild to those who are in the prime of life. The same colour appears dim to older persons but full to those in their prime. And a sound, likewise the same, seems faint to the former but quite audible to the latter. The matter of choice and avoidance of things also provokes different reactions in people of different ages. Children, perhaps, take their ball-games and their hoops seriously, but grown men have different tastes, and old men prefer still other things. From this it follows that differences of age also can cause the sense-impressions to be different where the external objects are the same. Motion or rest may also be the determining factor when objects appear different. For instance, things which we see to be motionless when we are stationary seem to be moving when we are sailing past them. Loving or hating may also make the difference. For example, there are those to whom pork is extremely repugnant, while others eat it with gusto. Hence also Menander's lines:

> And then what does his face look like,
> Since he has come to be like this? Why, he's a beast!
> Fair dealing makes us fair as well.

There are also many who have ugly mistresses and yet think them very beautiful. Hunger or satiety may also be the cause, as the same food can seem very tasty to the hungry and yet disagreeable to those who have had their fill. Drunkenness or soberness is another cause, since what we think shameful when sober does not seem shameful to us when we are drunk. Predispositions are another cause, since the same wine seems to be sour if you have eaten dates or dried figs beforehand, and sweet if you have eaten nuts or chick-peas. Also, the vestibule of the bath-house is warming to those who come in from the outside, but chills those who are coming out, if they tarry in it. Fear or confidence is also a cause, as a thing may seem fearful and terrible to the coward, yet not at all so to the man who is more daring. Being in a state of grief or joy would also be a factor, since the same matters are at once burdensome to those who are in grief and pleasant to those who are rejoicing.

Now, considering the fact that so much discrepancy is due to the states we are in, and that men are in different states at different times, it is easy, perhaps, to state the nature of each object as it appears to this or that person, but difficult to say further what its real nature is. This is because the discrepancy does not lend itself to judgement. In fact, whoever attempts to resolve this discrepancy will find himself either in one or the other of the aforesaid states or else in no state at all. But now to say that he is in no state at all, that he is neither healthy nor sick, neither in motion nor at rest, that he is not of any particular age, and that he is free from the other states, is perfectly absurd. On the other hand, the fact of his being in some state or other while attempting to pass judgement will make him a party to the controversy. And moreover, he will be confused by the states in which he finds himself, and this will prevent him from being an absolute judge [25] in the matter. A person, therefore, who is in the waking state cannot compare the impressions of a sleeping person with those of waking persons, and a healthy person cannot compare the impressions of sick people with those of the healthy. We do, after all, tend to give our assent to those things which are present and have a present influence over us rather than to things which are not present.

The discrepancy between such impressions is irresolvable on other grounds also, for if a person prefers one sense-impression to another, and one circumstance to another, he does so either without judging and without proof or by judging and offering proof. But he cannot do so without judgement and proof, for then he will be discredited. Nor can he do so even with judgement and proof, for if he judges the impressions, he must at all events use a criterion in judging them. And this criterion he will declare to be either true or false. If false, he will not be worthy of belief; but if he claims it is true, then his statement that the criterion is true will be offered either without proof or with proof. If without proof, again he will not be worthy of belief; but if he offers proof for his statement, the proof must in any case be a true one, otherwise he will not be worthy of belief. Now, if he says that the proof employed for the confirmation of his criterion is true, will he say this after having passed judgement on the proof, or without having judged it? If he has not judged it, he will not be worthy of belief, but if he has, obviously he will say he has used a criterion in his judgement. We shall ask for a proof for this criterion, and for this proof another criterion. For the proof always needs a criterion to confirm it, and the criterion needs a proof to show that it is true. A proof cannot be sound without the pre-existence of a true criterion, and a criterion cannot be true either without prior confirmation of the proof. And so both the criterion and the proof fall into circular argument,[26] in which both are found to be untrustworthy. The fact that each expects confirmation from the other makes both of them equally untrustworthy. It is impossible, then, for a person to give the preference to one sense-impression over another. This being so, such differences in sense-impressions as arise from a disparity of states will be irresolvable. As a result, this mode also serves to introduce suspension of judgement with regard to the nature of external objects.

The Fifth Mode

The fifth argument is the one based on positions, distances, and places. Each of these can cause the same objects to appear different. Take a portico for example. When seen from either end, it appears tapered, yet the same portico viewed from the middle appears symmetrical on all sides. Also, the same boat appears small and stationary from a distance, and large and moving from close by. And the same tower appears round from afar but square from near by.

These differences are the result of the distances involved.[27] Then there are differences due to the places involved. For example, the light of a lamp appears dim in sunlight but bright in the dark, the same oar appears broken in the water but straight when out of the water,[28] and the egg is soft inside the bird but hard when exposed to the air. Amber is liquid when inside the lynx but hard when exposed to the air,[29] and coral is soft when in the sea but hard in the air. And a sound appears different according to whether it is produced in a pipe, a flute, or simply in the air.

Position also may be the cause of different appearances. The same picture appears smooth when inclined backwards, but seems to have hollows and prominences when inclined forward to a certain angle. Also, the necks of pigeons appear different in colour according to differences in inclination.

Thus all objects appearing to us are seen as being in some place or other, at a certain distance, and in a certain position, and each of these factors makes a great difference in the sense-impressions, as we have mentioned. Hence, by this mode also we shall be compelled to have recourse to suspension of judgement. In point of fact, anyone who wishes to give any of these sense-impressions the preference over the others will be undertaking an impossible task. For if he makes his judgement simply and without proof, he will be discredited; and if he wishes to employ a proof, then says his proof is false, he will be refuting himself; if he says the proof is true, he will be asked for a proof of its truth, and another proof for that one, and so on *ad infinitum.*[30] But it is impossible to present an infinite series of proofs; therefore he will not be able, even by the use of proofs, to prefer one sense-impression to another. And if a person is unable to pass judgement on the above-mentioned impressions either without proof or with proof, then the necessary result is suspension of judgement.

Thus, while we are perhaps able to state of what nature each object appears to be in one particular position, at one particular distance, and in one location, it is not in our power, for the reasons just given, to declare what its true nature is.

The Sixth Mode

The sixth mode is the one based on admixtures. By this mode we conclude that, since none of the external objects appears to us singly but always in conjunction with something else, it is perhaps possible to state the nature of the mixture resulting from the conjunction of the external object and that other thing which we perceive together with it, but we are not able to say what the real nature of the external object is in its unmixed state. That no external object is ever perceived singly but in all cases together with something else, and that this causes it to have a different appearance for us, I take as evident fact. Our skin, for instance, shows a different colour according to whether the air is warm or cold; and we cannot say what our true natural colour is, but only what it appears to be in conjunction with each of these conditions. And the same sound appears different according as it occurs in air which is rarefied or dense; and aromatic odours are rather more overpowering in the warm bath and in the sun than in chilled air; and if a body is enclosed by water, it is light, but if enclosed by air, it is heavy.

But to get away from external admixtures, the internal contents of our eyes consist of both membranes and fluid matter. Now, since visible objects, in order to be seen, require both of these, they will not be apprehended with accuracy. What we actually perceive is the mixture, and this is the reason why people sick with jaundice see everything yellow, and those with bloodshot eyes see everything blood-red. And since the same sound appears different according as it occurs in open places or in narrow and winding places, and according as the air is pure or foul, it is probable that our apprehension of the sound is not free from admixture. For the ears have winding, narrow passages and are fouled with vaporous discharges which are said to gather from various parts of the head. And since secreted matter is also present in the nostrils and in the places where the sense of taste is located, our apprehension of the objects of taste and smell is not without admixture but includes the apprehension of that matter as well. Consequently, the admixtures prevent our senses from apprehending with accuracy the true nature of external objects.

But neither can the intellect do this, the chief reason being that the senses, which are its guides, are deceived; though perhaps the intellect, too, produces some peculiar admixture of its own, which then also affects the reports communicated by the senses. For we can perceive the presence of certain humours in each place where the dogmatists think the ruling part of the soul is located, whether one wishes to regard it as located in the brain, in the heart, or in any part of the animal body whatever. We see, therefore, that according to this mode also we are unable to predicate anything about the nature of external objects. As a result, we are compelled to suspend judgement.

The Seventh Mode

The seventh mode, as we said, is based on the quantities and compoundings of the external objects. By their "compounding" we mean in general their composition. And it is evident that this mode too obliges us to suspend judgement as regards the nature of things. For example, the filings from a goat's horn appear white when they are seen by themselves and uncompounded, but when they are compounded so as to constitute a horn they appear black. And filings of silver appear black by themselves, but in conjunction with the whole they are perceived as white. And pieces of the marble of Taenarum look white when they are polished, but when together in the rough stone they appear yellow. Grains of sand appear rough when they are scattered apart, but when combined as a heap they produce the impression of softness. Hellebore causes suffocation if taken as a fine powder, but not if taken coarse. Wine strengthens us if drunk in moderate amounts, but if more than this is taken, it enervates the body. And with food the case is similar, for the efficacy it exhibits varies according to the quantity taken. For instance, taking food in large quantities often causes the body to be purged through attacks of indigestion and diarrhoea. Here also, then, we shall be in a position to state the nature of the small bit of horn and of the whole composed of the many fine parts, and the nature of the chip of Taenarean marble and of the whole composed of the many small pieces. We may also be able to state the nature, in relative terms, of the grains of sand, the hellebore, the wines, and the food. Yet we shall not be able to go further and state the absolute nature of the objects. This we are prevented from doing by the discrepancy in our sense-impressions caused by the varying compositions of things.

In fact, it seems generally true that even things beneficial to us become harmful through their use in immoderate quantities, and that things that seem harmful when taken in excessive quantity are not injurious in very small quantities. The best argument in support of this reasoning is the observation we make regarding the action of medicines. Here we find that an accurate mixing of the component drugs renders the compound beneficial, while sometimes the slightest inclination of the balance, if overlooked, can render the product not only ineffectual but often very harmful, even poisonous. Thus the argument based on the quantities and compoundings makes the question of the real properties of external objects a confused issue. Therefore, since we are unable to state in absolute terms the nature of external objects, this mode also will bring us round naturally to suspension of judgement.

The Eighth Mode

The eighth mode is the argument from relativity. By this mode we conclude that, since all things are relative, we shall suspend judgement as to what they are absolutely and in themselves. But there is one qualification we must realize, both here and elsewhere. This is that we employ the word "are" in place of the word "appear," so that what we are saying amounts virtually to this: "All things appear to be relative." And our statement about relativity has a double sense; in the first place, there is a relationship to the thing judging (for the external object being judged appears to the thing judging it), and there is a relationship—in another way—to the things which are perceived along with it, such as the relationship of right to left. But we have considered the relativity of all things in the foregoing also. With respect to the thing which judges, for instance, we said that each object appears relatively to some particular animal or man or sense, and to such and such a circumstance. With respect to the things perceived along with it, each object appears relatively to some particular admixture or manner or composition or quantity or position.

But it is also possible to prove separately that all things are relative. This is done in the following manner. Do absolutes differ from relatives or not? If they do not differ, then they are themselves relative. But if they do differ, since all things which differ are relative (for it is in relation to that from which it differs that it is said to differ), then absolute things are relative. Also, the dogmatists divide all existent things into three classes,[31] the highest genera, the lowest species, and the things which are both genera and species. But all these are relative; therefore all things are relative. A further statement which they themselves make is that some things are manifest, others non-evident; and they say that apparent things are significative and that it is the non-evident things that are made manifest by the apparent things, for according to them, "Things apparent are an aspect of the things not evident."[32] But that which makes manifest and that which is made manifest are relative; therefore all things are relative. In addition to this, existent things are divided into the similar and the dissimilar, and the equal and the unequal. But now these are relative; therefore all things are relative. But even he who denies that all things are relative confirms, by his opposition to us, the proposition that all things are relative; for he shows that the proposition itself (that all things are relative) is relative [33] to us, and not universal.

The result, however, is clear once we show in this manner that all things are relative. We shall not be able to say what each object is in its own nature and absolutely, but what it appears to be under the aspect of relativity. Hence follows the necessity of our suspending judgement concerning the nature of things.

The Ninth Mode

The mode concerned with frequency or rarity of occurrence, which we said was ninth in order, we expound as follows. The sun is surely a much more amazing thing than a comet. But the sun we see constantly, whereas we rarely see a comet. Hence our astonishment at the sight of a comet is such that we may even believe it to be a divine omen, while we are not at all astonished at the sight of the sun. If, however, we only imagine the sun as appearing rarely and setting rarely, illuminating everything at once and causing everything to be thrown suddenly into shadow, then we shall observe great astonishment at the occurrence. Earthquakes, also, do not cause a like degree of confusion in those who are experiencing one for the first time as they do in those who have become accustomed to them by habit. And how great is the astonishment the sea causes in a man who beholds it for the first time! But also the beauty of the human body, in a subject we see for the first time, and suddenly, excites us more than if the sight should become a common one. Rare things seem to be valuable; things familiar to us, and easily obtainable, not at all. For example, if we suppose water to be a rare thing, how much more valuable it will appear to us than all the things which are held to be valuable! Or if we ponder the thought of gold simply lying about in large quantities on the ground like stones, to whom shall we suppose it would be so valuable, or so much worth locking up? Since, therefore, according to the frequency or rarity of their occurrence, the same things seem sometimes to be astonishing or valuable, and sometimes not at all so, we conclude that we shall perhaps be able to say what the nature of each of these things appears to be in the context of its frequent or rare occurrence, but that it is not within our power to state the nature of each external object considered purely and simply in itself. And so this mode too causes us to suspend judgement concerning them.

The Tenth Mode

There is a tenth mode, this one concerned chiefly with ethics. This is the argument from disciplines, customs, laws, mythical beliefs, and dogmatic notions. Now, a "discipline" is a choice of a way of life or of some objective, made by one person or by many. A case in point would be Diogenes, or the Laconians. A law is a written covenant among men who live in organized states, the transgressor of which is punished. A custom or habit (there is no difference) is a common acceptance by many men of a certain thing. Here the transgressor is not punished at all. Examples: It is a law not to commit adultery, but a custom not to have intercourse with a woman publicly. Mythical belief is an acceptance of unhistorical and fictitious events, such as—among others—the tales told of Kronos (for there are many who are led to believe these tales). A dogmatic notion is acceptance of a thing in so far as the acceptance seems to be confirmed by a line of reasoning or by some proof, for example, that atoms [34] are the elements of existing things, or homoeomeries, or minimal bodies, or something else.

Each of these we oppose sometimes to itself, sometimes to each of the others. We oppose custom to custom, for instance, in this way. Some of the Ethiopians tattoo their babies, while we do not. And Persians think that the use of bright-coloured, dragging garments is seemly, while we think it is unbecoming. And the Indians have intercourse with their women in public, whereas most other peoples hold this to be shameful. We oppose law to law in the following manner. With the Romans, he who relinquishes claim to the property inherited from his father is not obliged to pay his father's debts, but with the Rhodians one must pay them in any event. And among the Tauri of Scythia there was a law that strangers should be sacrificed to Artemis, while with us the ritual killing of humans is forbidden. We oppose discipline to discipline when we set the discipline of Diogenes in opposition to that of Aristippus, or that of the Laconians to that of the Italians. We oppose mythical belief to mythical belief when we say that in one version Zeus is spoken of as the father of gods and men, while in another version it is Oceanus. To quote:

> Ocean, sire of the gods, and Tethys their mother.[35]

And we set dogmatic notions against one other when we say that some declare that there is only one element, while others assume that they are infinite in number. We do so also when we say that some believe the soul to be mortal, others immortal; and that some declare that human affairs are directed by divine providence, while others claim providence has no hand in them.

We oppose custom to the other things, as for example to a law, when we say that with Persian men it is a custom to indulge in homosexual practices, while with the Romans this practice is prohibited by law. This is also the case when we say that with us adultery is forbidden, while with the Massagetae the custom is traditionally an indifferent matter, as Eudoxus of Cnidos records in the first book of his *Voyage*. And whereas intercourse with our mothers is prohibited by our laws, with the Persians it is a custom to marry thus if one possibly can. Among the Egyptians men marry their sisters, a practice which with us is prohibited by law. The opposition of custom to discipline is seen in the fact that whereas most men have intercourse with their wives in private, Crates did so with Hipparchia in public.[36] And Diogenes went about with only a one-sleeved tunic, while we dress as is customary. Custom is opposed to mythical belief when the stories have it that Kronos devoured his own children, since it is our custom to provide for our children. And while it is habitual practice with us to venerate the gods as being good and unaffected by evils, the poets represent them as getting wounded and being envious of one another. And custom is opposed to dogmatic notion when Epicurus says, in opposition to our custom of begging favours of the gods, that the Divinity does not pay any attention to us; and when Aristippus thinks that dressing in women's clothes is a matter of indifference, whereas we consider this a shameful thing.

We have discipline opposed to law when in the face of a law which forbids the striking of a freeman or a well-born man, pancratiasts strike each other because of the discipline of the life they follow; and when gladiators, for the same reason, kill each other even though homicide is forbidden. We oppose mythical belief to discipline when we say that the myths tell of Heracles' that he

> carded wool and endured the lot of a slave,[37]

and that he did things that no one, exercising even a moderate choice, would have done, whereas Heracles' discipline of life was a noble one. Discipline is opposed to dogmatic notion when athletes pursue glory as something good, and for its sake take upon themselves a laborious discipline of life, while many philosophers have the dogmatic notion that glory is a trivial thing. We oppose law to mythical belief when the poets portray the gods as committing adultery and practising paederasty, whereas with us these practices are forbidden by law. And we oppose law to dogmatic notion when Chrysippus says that having intercourse with mothers or sisters is a matter of indifference, while the law forbids this. And we oppose mythical belief to dogmatic notion when the poets tell of Zeus coming down and having intercourse with mortal women, while with the dogmatists it is believed that this is impossible. And the Poet says that Zeus, in his grief over Sarpedon, "poured down showers of blood to the earth,"[38] yet it is a dogma of philosophers that the Deity is impassive; and philosophers confute the story of the horse-centaurs, and offer us the horse-centaur as an example of non-reality.

Now, it would be possible to take up many other examples for each of the antitheses mentioned above, but for a brief account these will be sufficient. However, since this mode too points out how great the discrepancy in things is, we shall not be able to say what quality an object possesses according to nature, but only what quality it appears to possess with reference to a particular discipline, a particular law, a particular custom, and so on with each of the others. This mode also, then, compels us to suspend judgement regarding the nature of external objects. And so in this manner, through the ten modes, we end with suspension of judgement.

NOTES

1. Bishop Berkeley, the great British Empiricist (1685-1753), used this example as part of his efforts to refute what he called "execrable Scepticism." And yet the Greek Sceptics did not differ from him as much as he thought they did: they and he were attacking the notion that we can have "absolute" knowledge of an object, knowledge not involved with our distance from it, or our visual capacities to perceive it, etc. They and he were insisting that all our knowledge is relative to the observer and to his relationship with the object. Of course, there were great differences between Berkeley's anti-materialist metaphysics and the Sceptics' non-metaphysical philosophy, but the similarities are far more striking and important than Berkeley ever suspected.

2. Anaxagoras of Clazomenae lived around 450 B.C. and was a friend of Euripides and Pericles. He taught that a supreme intelligence (*nus*) ruled all things by composing and decomposing numberless "seeds of all things," or basic, elemental, indivisible building blocks of the universe.

3. This general point must be kept in mind, because it shows how similar all philosophers are who argue for the relativity of human knowledge, from the *Theaetetus* of Plato through the British Empiricists to H. H. Price in our own day.

4. What follows are the modes of argument, the ways of putting arguments in opposition, supposedly set up by Aenesidemus. The single philosopher who drew most heavily from them was Michel de Montaigne (1533-1592) in his "Apology for Raymond Sebond."

5. One could ask here: Is it reasonable to "suppose" all that follows? What sort of notion of "reason" or the "reasonable" can a Sceptic use in such speculative matters if he is out to show what a "rogue" reason is when she deals with such matters?

6. This example, too, was to become famous in modern philosophy as an indication of the relativity of sense-perception to one's physiological condition.

7. But if "we might well be right in supposing" this, is this supposition enough to bring about a suspension of judgement on this matter? Later Descartes, in his *Discourse on Method* and his *Meditations,* would (as he put it in Part IV of the *Discourse)* simply "suppose" that all of his perceptions are illusory, without giving any really sound evidence for their being illusory, and this would suit his over-all project of doubting "anything of which I *could* have the *least* doubt." But with the Greeks, suppositions are not enough: doubts must be based on evidence as weighty as the belief we are putting in doubt, the balance-scale was the symbol of the Sceptics, not of Descartes. How could a *supposition* have "equality of force" with a given, firmly entrenched belief in the blackness and

whiteness of books, for example? The Sceptic might respond to all this by pointing out that we use all ten modes in order to cast a given belief into doubt, and the total weight of these modes could be said to counterbalance the beliefs we are putting into doubt. Still, it is the duty of the critical, sceptical reader to ask: What solid evidence do the Sceptics put forward in order to induce doubt, and just how solid is it?

8. Again, in the light of the last note, how can a Sceptic use "natural" reason on such suppositious matters?

9. This, it is quite possible, is a bit of humour on the part of Sextus, the hard-headed physician.

10. Here is a turning-point in the argument: where, Sextus is asking, is the standard, the universally persuasive, universally cogent *criterion* for deciding whose sense-impressions are "true to nature"? All of our standards are *our* standards, relative to us, to our prejudices, our condition, etc. To set them up as judicial criteria is to beg the whole question of which impressions are right. Or to put it slightly differently, it is to perpetuate the dispute by putting forward mutually warring or opposing "criteria," that is to say, standards that are not decisive *criteria* at all, since a criterion is a universally acceptable standard.

11. Here Sextus is referring especially to the favourite enemies of the Sceptics, the Stoics, whose belief in the cognitive powers of Sage (see below, fn. 20) in particular is as strong as their belief in the great power of human reason in general, "sovereign reason."

12. i.e., thought and speech. (—Tr.)

13. Stoic logic is at least as important in the history of logic as Aristotle's logic, especially as far as developing certain notions important to "symbolic" or "mathematical" logic is concerned. For a smattering of it see the life of Zeno in the *Lives* of Diogenes Laertius. For a fuller study see *Stoic Logic,* by Benson Mates. They used five forms of inference as "primitives," unprovable "anapodeictic" forms of argument; they used these forms in the proving of other, provable forms of argument. The fifth of these five argument-forms was: "Either X or Y or Z is the case; neither X nor Y is the case; therefore Z is the case."

14. An ironic reference to the Cynics, a sect founded by Antisthenes, who used to meet in the *kynosarges,* a gymnasium outside of Athens dedicated to the use of those who were not of pure Athenian blood. It seems just as likely that their name is derived from their place of meeting as that it is from the Greek word for "dog" *(kyon).* See Windelband, *A History of Philosophy.*

15. This is a reference to the Pythagoreans, whose rule of silence was famous. The most powerful dogmatical opponents of the Sceptics, the Stoics, apparently influenced a first-century B.C. form of Pythagoreanism. See the *Lives* of Diogenes Laertius, Bk. VIII, Ch. 10.

16. Pindar, fragment 221 (242). (—Tr.)

17. Homer, *Odyssey* XIV 228. (—Tr.)

18. Euripides, *Phoenissae* 499 f. (—Tr.)

19. Author unknown. (—Tr.)

20. The much discussed Sage of the Stoics (who was never found) often was the subject of Sceptical assault and humorous irony. He was to be the arbiter, the judge whose experiences and judgements were to give men the final truth about the universe, and about man's role in it. Supposedly, of course, he would confirm, when he finally did arrive, what the Stoics had said about these matters.

21. The richness of the examples Sextus gives us on these physiological matters reminds us that he was a physician.

22. This smooth, sweet apple turns up again in Montaigne's "Apology for Raymond Sebond," and in the same context, though after thirteen centuries it ripened and was red for Montaigne.

23. Montaigne and the British Empiricists (especially Locke and Berkeley) were to discuss the differences between the senses at great length, and to try to show how, despite them (or rather using them), knowledge by way of the senses was still possible. See Bk. II, Ch. 9, of Locke's *Essay Concerning Human Understanding.*

24. This belief has been much discussed by twentieth-century philosophers. See Norman Malcolm's little book, *Dreaming.*

25. The word "absolute" is important in this sentence. There are relative judges, or practical criteria—standards of action, as Sextus puts it in Ch. XI. In the area of action these judges (common-sense men) and criteria do have competence; they can help us live successfully amongst relative phenomena.

26. Actually, if one would be strict in classifying the modes of argument, this one would appear in Ch. XV with Agrippa's five modes, specifically the one on circular reasoning.

27. In the example of the portico, both position and distance seem to be involved. Note also that Sextus' use of terms is not exact: "tapered" is not asymmetrical. (—Tr.)

28. Another example that was to be much used by subsequent philosophers seeking to prove the relativity of sense-knowledge.

29. *Lyngurion,* amber or a type of amber, thought to be the solidified urine of the lynx; from the Greek words for "lynx" and "urine." (—Tr.)

30. Here again Agrippa's modes will cover the same point in Ch. XV.

31. The highest class, or *summum genus,* has meaning not only relatively to lower genera but also depends upon what sort of thing you are trying to classify. If you are talking about everything, then the *summum genus* would be "being" or "entity"; the *infimae species* or lowest species, the one that cannot be subdivided further, would be the class that contains only one individual, say, "Socrates." In between are genera that are both species of higher genera and classes containing individuals, like the genus "man," which is lower than "entity" but higher than "Socrates." However, if you are talking about these nine modes, for example, the *summum genus* is "relativity," and there are ten *infimae species,* as Sextus pointed out before he started to present them. See the beginning of Chapter XIV.

32. A dictum of Anaxagoras. (—Tr.)

33. The word "relative" is suffering various changes in meaning throughout this paragraph; he is equivocating, and so the "relativity" he is defending here is not as clear as the ten modes themselves make it out to be.

34. Democritus, Epicurus, and Lucretius the Epicurean held the first view; Anaxagoras believed in the homoeomeries; and Diodorus Cronos, whose school was absorbed into the Stoics, believed in the minimal bodies.

35. Homer, *Iliad* XIV 201. (—Tr.)

36. While this seems to us the very opposite of what we call "discipline," the point is that Crates' "discipline," or way of life, permitted this. (—Tr.)

37. Homer, *Odyssey* XXII 423 (the passage in Homer does not refer to Heracles). (—Tr.)

38. Homer, *Iliad* XVI 459. (—Tr.)

MEDITATION ONE: CONCERNING THOSE THINGS THAT CAN BE CALLED INTO DOUBT

René Descartes

Several years have now passed since I first realized how many were the false opinions that in my youth I took to be true, and thus how doubtful were all the things that I subsequently built upon these opinions. From the time I became aware of this, I realized that for once I had to raze everything in my life, down to the very bottom, so as to begin again from the first foundations, if I wanted to establish anything firm and lasting in the sciences. But the task seemed so enormous that I waited for a point in my life that was so ripe that no more suitable a time for laying hold of these disciplines would come to pass. For this reason, I have delayed so long that I would be at fault were I to waste on deliberation the time that is left for action. Therefore, now that I have freed my mind from all cares, and I have secured for myself some leisurely and carefree time, I withdraw in solitude. I will, in short, apply myself earnestly and openly to the general destruction of my former opinions.

Yet to this end it will not be necessary that I show that all my opinions are false, which perhaps I could never accomplish anyway. But because reason now persuades me that I should withhold my assent no less carefully from things which are not plainly certain and indubitable than I would to what is patently false, it will be sufficient justification for rejecting them all, if I find a reason for doubting even the least of them. Nor therefore need one survey each opinion one after the other, a task of endless proportion. Rather—because undermining the foundations will cause whatever has been built upon them to fall down of its own accord—I will at once attack those principles which supported everything that I once believed.

Whatever I had admitted until now as most true I took in either from the senses or through the senses; however, I noticed that they sometimes deceived me. And it is a mark of prudence never to trust wholly in those things which have once deceived us.

But perhaps, although the senses sometimes deceive us when it is a question of very small and distant things, still there are many other matters which one certainly cannot doubt, although they are derived from the very same senses; that I am sitting here before the fireplace wearing my dressing gown, that I feel this sheet of paper in my hands, and so on. But how could one deny that these hands and that my whole body exist? Unless perhaps I should compare myself to insane people whose brains are so impaired by a stubborn vapor from a black bile that they continually, insist that they are kings when they are in utter poverty, or that they are wearing purple robes when they are naked, or that they have a head made of clay, or that they are gourds, or that they are made of glass. But they are all demented; and I would appear no less demented if I were to take their conduct as a model for myself.

All of this would be well and good, were I not a man who is accustomed to sleeping at night, and to undergoing in my sleep the very same things—or now and then even less likely ones—as do these insane people when they are awake. How often has my evening slumber persuaded me

René Descartes, Meditations on First Philosphy, translated by Donald A. Cress, 1979, Hackett Publishing Co., Inc. Indianapolis, IN and Cambridge, MA.

of such customary things as these: that I am here, clothed in my dressing govern, seated at the fireplace, when in fact I am lying undressed between the blankets! But right now I certainly am gazing upon this piece of paper with eyes wide awake. This head which I am moving is not heavy with sleep. I extend this hand consciously and deliberately and I feel it. These things would not be so distinct for one who is asleep. But this all seems as if I do not recall having been deceived by similar thoughts on other occasions in my dreams. As I consider these cases more intently, I see so plainly that there are no definite signs to distinguish being awake from being asleep that I am quite astonished, and this astonishment almost convinces me that I am sleeping.

Let us say, then, for the sake of argument, that we are sleeping and that such particulars as these are not true: that we open our eyes, move our heads, extend our hands. Perhaps we do not even have these hands or any such body at all. Nevertheless, it really must be admitted that things seen in sleep are, as it were, like painted images, which could have been produced only in the likeness of true things. Therefore at least these general things (eyes, head, hands, the whole body) are not imaginary things, but are true and exist. For indeed when painters wish to represent sirens and satyrs by means of bizarre and unusual forms they surely cannot ascribe utterly new natures to these creatures. Rather, they simply intermingle the members of various animals. And even if they concoct something so utterly novel that its likes have never been seen before (being utterly fictitious and false), certainly, at the very minimum the colors from which the painters compose the thing ought to be true. And for the same reason, although even these general things (eyes, head, hands, and the like) can be imaginary, still one must necessarily admit that at least other things that are even more simple and universal are true, from which, as from true colors, all these things—be they true or false—which in our thought are images of things, are constructed.

To this class seems to belong corporeal nature in general, together with its extension; likewise the shape of extended things, their quantity or size, their number; as well as the place where they exist, the time of their duration, and other such things.

Hence perhaps we do not conclude improperly that physics, astronomy, medicine, and all the other disciplines that are dependent upon the consideration of composite things are all doubtful. But arithmetic, geometry, and other such disciplines—which treat of nothing but the simplest and most general things and which are indifferent as to whether these things do or do not exist—contain something certain and indubitable. For whether I be awake or asleep, two plus three makes five, and a square does not have more than four sides; nor does it seem possible that such obvious truths can fall under the suspicion of falsity.

All the same, a certain opinion of long standing has been fixed in my mind, namely that there exists a God who is able to do anything and by whom I, such as I am, have been created. How do I know that he did not bring it about that there be no earth at all, no heavens, no extended thing, no figure, no size, no place, and yet all these things should seem to me to exist precisely as they appear to do now? Moreover—as I judge that others sometimes make mistakes in matters that they believe they know most perfectly—how do I know that I am not deceived every time I add two and three or count the sides of a square or perform an even simpler operation, if such can be imagined? But perhaps God has not willed that I be thus deceived, for it is said that he is supremely good. Nonetheless, if it were repugnant to his goodness that he should have created me such that I be deceived all the time, it would seem, from this same consideration, to be foreign to him to permit me to be deceived occasionally. But we cannot make this last assertion.

Perhaps there are some who would rather deny such a powerful God, than believe that all other matters are uncertain. Let us not put these people off just yet; rather, let us grant that everything said here about God is fictitious. Now they suppose that I came to be what I am either by fate or by chance or by a continuous series of events or by some other way. But because being deceived and being mistaken seem to be imperfections, the less powerful they take the author of my being to be, the more probable it will be that I would be so imperfect as to be deceived perpetually. I have nothing to say in response to these arguments. At length I am forced to admit that there is nothing, among the things I once believed to be true, which it is not permissible to doubt—not for reasons of frivolity or a lack of forethought, but because of valid and considered arguments. Thus I must carefully withhold assent no less from these things than from the patently false; if I wish to find anything certain.

But it is not enough simply to have made a note of this; I must take care to keep it before my mind. For long-standing opinions keep coming back again and again, almost against my will; they seize upon my credulity, as if it were bound over to them by long use and the claims of intimacy. Nor will I get out of the habit of assenting to them and believing in them, so long as I take them to be exactly what they are, namely, in some respects doubtful as by now is obvious, but nevertheless highly probable, so that it is much more consonant with reason to believe them than to deny them. Hence, it seems to me, I would do well to turn my will in the opposite direction, to deceive myself and pretend for a considerable period that they are wholly false and imaginary, until finally, as if with equal weight of prejudice[1] on both sides, no bad habit should turn my judgment from the correct perception of things. For indeed I know that no danger or error will follow and that it is impossible for me to indulge in too much distrust, since I now am concentrating only on knowledge, not on action.

Thus I will suppose not a supremely good God, the source of truth, but rather an evil genius, as clever and deceitful as he is powerful, who has directed his entire effort to misleading me. I will regard the heavens, the air, the earth, colors, shapes, sounds, and all external things as nothing but the deceptive games of my dreams, with which he lays snares for my credulity. I will regard myself as having no hands, no eyes, no flesh, no blood, no senses, but as nevertheless falsely believing that I possess all these things. I will remain resolutely fixed in this meditation, and, even if it be out of my power to know anything true, certainly it is within my power to take care resolutely to withhold my assent to what is false, lest this deceiver, powerful and clever as he is, have an effect on me. But this undertaking is arduous, and laziness brings me back to my customary way of living. I am not unlike a prisoner who might enjoy an imaginary freedom in his sleep. When he later begins to suspect that he is sleeping, he fears being awakened and conspires slowly with these pleasant illusions. In just this way, I spontaneously fall back into my old beliefs, and dread being awakened, lest the toilsome wakefulness which follows upon a peaceful rest, have to be spent hence forward not in the light but among the inextricable shadows of the difficulties now brought forward.

NOTES

1. A "prejudice" is a prejudgment, that is, an adjudication of an issue without having first reviewed the appropriate evidence.

THE NATURE OF OUR IDEAS

John Locke

Of Ideas in General, and Their Original

Every man being conscious to himself that he thinks; and that which his mind is applied about whilst thinking being the *ideas* that are there, it is past doubt that men have in their minds several ideas—such as are those expressed by the words *whiteness, hardness, sweetness, thinking, motion, man, elephant, army, drunkenness,* and others: it is in the first place then to be inquired, *How he comes by them?*

I know it is a received doctrine, that men have native ideas, and original characters, stamped upon their minds in their very first being. This opinion I have at large examined already; and, I suppose what I have said in the foregoing Book will be much more easily admitted, when I have shown whence the understanding may get all the ideas it has; and by, what ways and degrees they may come into the mind—for which I shall appeal to everyone's own observation and experience.

Let us then suppose the mind to be, as we say, white paper, void of all characters, without any ideas:—How comes it to be furnished? Whence comes it by that vast store which the busy and boundless fancy of man has painted on it with an almost endless variety? Whence has it all the *materials* of reason and knowledge? To this I answer, in one word, from EXPERIENCE. In that all our knowledge is founded; and from that it ultimately derives itself. Our observation employed either, about external sensible objects, or about the internal operations of our minds perceived and reflected on by ourselves, is that which supplies our understandings with all the *materials* of thinking. These two are the fountains of knowledge, from whence all the ideas we have, or can naturally have, do spring.

First, our Senses, conversant about particular sensible objects, do convey into the mind several distinct perceptions of things, according to those various ways wherein those objects do affect them. And thus we come by those ideas we have of *yellow, white, heat, cold, soft, hard, bitter, sweet,* and all those which we call sensible qualities; which when I say the senses convey into the mind, I mean, they from external objects convey into the mind what produces there those perceptions. This great source of most of the ideas we have, depending wholly upon our senses, and derived by them to the understanding, I call SENSATION.

Secondly, the other fountain from which experience furnisheth the understanding with ideas is,—the perception of the operations of our own mind within us, as it is employed about the ideas it has got;—which operations, when the soul comes to reflect on and consider, do furnish the understanding with another set of ideas, which could not be had from things without. And such are *perception, thinking, doubting, believing, reasoning, knowing, willing,* and all the different actings

This selection consists of excerpts from Chapters 1, 2, 8, and 23 of Book 11 of Locke's *Essay Concerning Human Understanding*, first published in 1690.

of our own minds;—which we being conscious of, and observing in ourselves, do from these receive into our understandings as distinct ideas as we do from bodies affecting our senses. This source of ideas every man has wholly in himself; and though it be not sense, as having nothing to do with external objects, yet it is very like it, and might properly enough be called *internal sense*. But as I call the other Sensation, so I call this REFLECTION, the ideas it affords being such only as the mind gets by reflecting on its own operations within itself. By reflection then, in the following part of this discourse, I would be understood to mean, that notice which the mind takes of its own operations, and the manner of them, by reason whereof there come to be ideas of these operations in the understanding. These two, I say, viz. external material things, as the objects of SENSATION, and the operations of our own minds within, as the objects of REFLECTION, are to me the only originals from whence all our ideas take their beginnings. The term *operations* here I use in a large sense, as comprehending not barely the actions of the mind about its ideas, but some sort of passions arising sometimes from them, such as is the satisfaction or uneasiness arising from any thought.

The understanding seems to me not to have the least glimmering of any ideas which it doth not receive from one of these two. *External objects* furnish the mind with the ideas of sensible qualities, which are all those different perceptions they produce in us; and *the mind* furnishes the understanding with ideas of its own operations.

These, when we have taken a full survey of them, and their several modes, combinations, and relations, we shall find to contain all our whole stock of ideas; and that we have nothing in our minds which did not come in one of these two ways.

Of Simple Ideas

The better to understand the nature, manner, and extent of our knowledge, one thing is carefully to be observed concerning the ideas we have; and that is, that some of them are *simple* and some *complex*.

Though the qualities that affect our senses are, in the things themselves, so united and blended, that there is no separation, no distance between them; yet it is plain, the ideas they produce in the mind enter by the senses simple and unmixed. For, though the sight and touch often take in from the same object, at the same time, different ideas;—as a man sees at once motion and color; the hand feels softness and warmth in the same piece of wax: yet the simple ideas thus united in the same subject, are as perfectly distinct as those that come in by different senses. The coldness and hardness which a man feels in a piece of ice being as distinct ideas in the mind as the smell and whiteness of a lily; or as the taste of sugar, and smell of a rose. And there is nothing can be plainer to a man than the clear and distinct perception he has of those simple ideas; which, being each in itself uncompounded, contains in it nothing but *one uniform appearance, or conception in the mind,* and is not distinguishable into different ideas.

These simple ideas, the materials of all our knowledge, are suggested and furnished to the mind only by those two ways above mentioned, viz. sensation and reflection. When the understanding is once stored with these simple ideas, it has the power to repeat, compare, and unite them, even to an almost infinite variety, and so can make at pleasure new complex ideas. But it is not in the power of the most exalted wit, or enlarged understanding, by any quickness or variety of thought, to *invent* or *frame* one new simple idea in the mind, not taken in by the ways before mentioned; nor can any force of the understanding *destroy* those that are there. The dominion of man, in this little world of his own understanding being much what the same as it is in the great world of visible things; wherein his power, however managed by, art and skill, reaches no farther than to compound and divide the materials that are made to his hand; but can do nothing toward the making the least particle of new matter, or destroying one atom of what is already in being. The same inability will everyone find in himself, who shall go about to fashion in his understanding one simple idea, not received in by his senses from external objects, or by reflection from the operations of his own mind about them. I would have anyone try to fancy any taste which had never affected his palate; or frame the idea of a scent he had never smelt: and when he can do this, I will also conclude that a blind man hath ideas of colors, and a deaf man true distinct notions of sounds.

Some Further Considerations Concerning our Simple Ideas of Sensation

Concerning the simple ideas of Sensation, it is to be considered,—that whatsoever is so constituted in nature as to be able, by affecting our senses, to cause any perception in the mind, doth thereby produce in the understanding a simple idea; which, whatever be the external cause of it, when it comes to be taken notice of by our discerning faculty, it is by the mind looked on and considered there to be a real positive idea in the understanding, as much as any other whatsoever; though, perhaps, the cause of it be but a privation of the subject.

Thus the ideas of heat and cold, light and darkness, white and black, motion and rest, are equally clear and positive ideas in the mind; though, perhaps, some of the causes which produce them are barely privations, in those subjects from whence our senses derive those ideas. These the understanding, in its view of them, considers all as distinct positive ideas, without taking notice of the causes that produce them: which is an inquiry not belonging to the idea, as it is in the understanding, but to the nature of the things existing without us. These are two very different things, and carefully to be distinguished; it being one thing to perceive and know the idea of white or black, and quite another to examine what kind of particles they must be, and how ranged in the superficies, to make any object appear white or black.

* * * *

To discover the nature of our *ideas* the better, and to discourse of them intelligibly, it will be convenient to distinguish them *as they are ideas or perceptions in our minds;* and *as they are modifications of matter in the bodies that cause such perceptions in us:* that so we may not think (as perhaps usually is done) that they are exactly the images and resemblances of something inherent in the subject; most of those of sensation being in the mind no more the likeness of something existing without us, than the names that stand for them are the likeness of our ideas, which yet upon hearing they are apt to excite in us.

Whatsoever the mind perceives *in itself*; or is the immediate object of perception, thought, or understanding, that I call *idea;* and the power to produce any idea in our mind, I call *quality* of the subject wherein that power is. Thus a snowball having the power to produce in us the ideas of white, cold. and round,—the power to produce those ideas in us, as they are in the snowball, I call qualities; and as they are sensations or perceptions in our understandings, I call them ideas; which *ideas,* if I speak of sometimes as in the things themselves, I would be understood to mean those qualities in the objects which produce them in us.

Qualities thus considered in bodies are,

First, such as are utterly inseparable from the body, in what state soever it be; and such as in all the alterations and changes it suffers, all the force can be used upon it, it constantly keeps; and such as sense constantly finds in every particle of matter which has bulk enough to be perceived; and the mind finds inseparable from every particle of matter, though less than to make itself singly be perceived by our senses: v.g. Take a grain of wheat, divide it into two parts; each part has still solidity, extension, figure, and mobility: divide it again, and it retains still the same qualities; and so divide it on, till the parts become insensible: they must retain still each of them all those qualities. For division (which is all that a mill, or pestle, or any other body, does upon another, in reducing it to insensible parts) can never take away either solidity, extension, figure, or mobility from any body, but only makes two or more distinct separate masses of matter, of that which was but one before; all which distinct masses, reckoned as so many distinct bodies, after division, make a certain number. These I call *original* or *primary qualities* of body, which I think we may observe to produce simple ideas in us, viz. [namely] solidity, extension, figure, motion or rest, and number.

Secondly, such qualities which in truth are nothing in the objects themselves but powers to produce various sensations in us by their primary qualities, i.e. by the bulk, figure, texture, and motion of their insensible parts, as colors, sounds, tastes, etc. These I call *secondary qualities.* To these might be added a *third* sort, which are allowed to be barely powers; though they are as much real qualities in the subject as those which I, to comply with the common way of speaking, call qualities, but for distinction, secondary qualities. For the power in fire to produce a new color, or consistency, in *wax* or *clay,*—by its primary qualities, is as much a quality in fire, as the power it has to produce in *me* a new idea or sensation of warmth or burning, which I felt not before,— by the same primary qualities, viz. the bulk, texture, and motion of its insensible parts.

The next thing to be considered is, how bodies produce ideas in us; and that is manifestly by impulse, the only way which we can conceive bodies to operate in.

If then external objects be not united to our minds when they produce ideas therein; and yet we perceive these *original* qualities in such of them as singly fall under our senses, it is evident that some motion must be thence continued by our nerves, or animal spirits, by some parts of our bodies, to the brains or the seat of sensation, there to produce in our minds the particular ideas we have of them. And since the extension, figure, number, and motion of bodies of an observable bigness, may be perceived at a distance by the sight, it is evident some singly imperceptible bodies must come from them to the eyes, and thereby convey to the brain some motion; which produces these ideas which we have of them in us.

After the same manner that the ideas of these original qualities are produced in us, we may conceive that the ideas of *secondary* qualities are also produced, viz. by the operation of insensible particles on our senses. For, it being manifest that there are bodies and good store of bodies, each whereof are so small, that we cannot by any of our senses discover either their bulk, figure, or motion,—as is evident in the particles of the air and water, and others extremely smaller than those; perhaps as much smaller than the particles of air and water, as the particles of air and water are smaller than peas or hailstones;—let us suppose at present that the different motions and figures, bulk and number, of such particles, affecting the several organs of our senses, produce in us those different sensations which we have from the colors and smells of bodies; v.g. [for example] that a violet, by the impulse of such insensible particles of matter, of peculiar figures and bulks, and in different degrees and modifications of their motions, causes the ideas of the blue color, and sweet scent of that flower to be produced in our minds. It being no more impossible to conceive that God should annex such ideas to such motions, with which they have no similitude, than that he should annex the idea of pain to the motion of a piece of steel dividing our flesh, with which that idea hath no resemblance.

What I have said concerning colors and smells may be understood also of tastes and sounds, and other the like sensible qualities: which, whatever reality we by mistake attribute to them, are in truth nothing in the objects themselves, but powers to produce various sensations in us; and depend on those primary qualities, viz. bulk, figure, texture, and motion of parts.

From whence I think it easy to draw this observation,—that the ideas of primary qualities of bodies are resemblances of them, and their patterns do really exist in the bodies themselves, but the ideas produced in us by these secondary qualities have no resemblance of them at all. There is nothing like our ideas, existing in the bodies themselves. They are, in the bodies we denominate from them, only a power to produce those sensations in us: and what is sweet, blue, or warm in idea, is but the certain bulk, figure, and motion of the insensible parts, in the bodies themselves, which we call so.

Flame is denominated hot and light; snow, white and cold: and manna, white and sweet, from the ideas they produce in us. Which qualities are commonly thought to be the same in those bodies that those ideas are in us, the one the perfect resemblance of the other, as they are in a mirror, and it would by most men be judged very extravagant if one should say otherwise. And yet he that will consider that the same fire that, at one distance produces in us the sensation of warmth, does, at a nearer approach, produce in us the far different sensation of pain, ought to bethink himself what reason he has to say—that this idea of warmth, which was produced in him by the fire, is *actually in the fire;* and his idea of pain, which the same fire produced in him the same way, is *not* in the fire. Why are whiteness and coldness in snow, and pain not, when it produces the one and the other idea in us: and can do neither, but by the bulk, figure, number, and motion of its solid parts?

The particular bulk, number, figure, and motion of the parts of fire or snow are really in them,—whether anyone's senses perceive them or no: and therefore they may be called *real* qualities, because they really exist in those bodies. But light, heat, whiteness, or coldness, are no more really in them than sickness or pain is in manna. Take away the sensation of them; let not the eyes see light or colors, nor the cars hear sounds; let the palate not taste, nor the nose smell, and all colors, tastes, odors, and sounds, *as they are such particular ideas,* vanish and cease, and are reduced to their causes, i.e. bulk, figure, and motion of parts.

Let us consider the red and white colors in porphyry. Hinder light from striking on it, and its colors vanish; it no longer produces any such ideas in us: upon the return of light it produces these appearances on us again. Can anyone think any real alterations are made in the porphyry by the presence or absence of light; and that those ideas of whiteness and redness are really in porphyry in the light, when it is plain it *has no color in the dark?* It has, indeed, such a configuration of particles, both night and day, as are apt, by the rays of light rebounding from some parts of that hard stone, to produce in us the idea of redness, and from others the idea of whiteness; but whiteness or redness are not in it at any time, but such a texture that hath the power to produce such a sensation in us.

Ideas being thus distinguished and understood, we may be able to give an account how the same water, at the same time, may produce the idea of cold by one hand and of heat by the other: whereas it is impossible that the same water, if those ideas were really in it, should at the same time be both hot and cold. For, if we imagine *warmth,* as it is in our hands, to be nothing but a certain sort and degree of motion in the minute particles of our nerves or animal spirits, we may understand how it is possible that the same water may, at the same time, produce the sensations of heat in one hand and cold in the other: which yet *figure* never does, that never producing the idea of a square by one hand which has produced the idea of a globe by another. But if the sensation of heat and cold be nothing but the increase or diminution of the motion of the minute parts of our bodies, caused by the corpuscles of any other body, it is easy to be understood, that if that motion be greater in one hand than in the other; if a body be applied to the two hands, which has in its minute particles a greater motion than in those of one of the hands, and a less than in those of the other, it will increase the motion of the one hand and lessen it in the other; and so cause the different sensations of heat and cold that depend thereon.

I have in what just goes before been engaged in physical inquiries a little further than perhaps I intended. But, it being necessary to make the nature of sensation a little understood; and to make the difference between the *qualities* in bodies, and the *ideas* produced by them in the mind, to be distinctly conceived, without which it were impossible to discourse intelligibly of them;— I hope I shall be pardoned this little excursion into natural philosophy; it being necessary in our present inquiry to distinguish the *primary* and *real* qualities of bodies, which are always in them (viz. solidity, extension, figure, number, and motion, or rest, and are sometimes perceived by us, viz. when the bodies they are in are big enough singly to be discerned), from those *secondary* and *imputed* qualities, which are but the powers of several combinations of those primary ones, when they operate without being distinctly discerned;— whereby we may also come to know what ideas are, and what are not, resemblances of something really existing in the bodies we denominate from them.

The qualities, then, that are in bodies, rightly considered, are of three sorts:—

First, The bulk, figure, number, situation, and motion or rest of their solid parts. Those are in them, whether we perceive them or not; and when they are of that size that we can discover them, we have by these an idea of the thing as it is in itself; as is plain in artificial things. These I call *primary qualities.*

Secondly, The power that is in any body, by reason of its insensible primary qualities, to operate after a peculiar manner on any of our senses, and thereby produce in us the different ideas of several colors, sounds, smells, tastes, etc. These are usually called *sensible qualities.*

Thirdly, The power that is in any body, by reason of the particular constitution of its primary qualities, to make such a change in the bulk, figure, texture, and motion of *another body,* as to make it operate on our senses differently from what it did before. Thus the sun has a power to make wax white, and fire to make lead fluid. These are usually called *powers.*

The first of these, as has been said, I think may be properly called real, original, or primary qualities; because they are in the things themselves, whether they are perceived or not: and upon their different modifications it is that the secondary qualities depend.

The other two are only powers to act differently upon other things: which powers result from the different modifications of those primary qualities.

To conclude. Beside those forementioned primary qualities in bodies, viz. bulk, figure, extension, number, and motion of their solid parts; all the rest, whereby we take notice of bodies, and distinguish them one from another, are nothing else but several powers in them, depending on those primary qualities; whereby they are fitted, either by immediately operating on our bodies to produce several different ideas in us; or else, by operating on other bodies, so to change their primary qualities as to render them capable of producing ideas in us different from what before they did. The former of these, I think, may be called secondary qualities *immediately perceivable:* the latter, secondary qualities, *mediately perceivable.*

Of Our Complex Ideas of Substances

The mind being, as I have declared, furnished with a great number of the simple ideas, conveyed in by the senses as they are found in exterior things, or by reflection on its own operations, takes notice also that a certain number of these simple ideas go constantly together; which being presumed to belong to one thing, and words being suited to common apprehensions, and made use of for quick dispatch, are called, so united in one subject, by one name; which, by inadvertency, we are apt afterward to talk of and consider as one simple idea, which indeed is a complication of many ideas together: because, as I have said, not imagining how these simple ideas *can* subsist by themselves, we accustom ourselves to suppose some *substratum* wherein they do subsist, and from which they do result, which therefore we call *substance.*

So that if anyone will examine himself concerning his notion of pure substance in general, he will find he has no other idea of it at all, but only a supposition of he knows not what *support* of such qualities which are capable of producing simple ideas in us; which qualities are commonly called accidents. If anyone should be asked, what is the subject wherein color or weight inheres, he would have nothing to say, but the solid extended parts; and if he were demanded, what is it that solidity and extension adhere in, he would not be in a much better case than the Indian before mentioned who, saying that the world was supported by a great elephant, was asked what the elephant rested on; to which his answer was—a great tortoise: but being again pressed to know what gave support to the broad-backed tortoise, replied—*something, he knew not what.* And thus here, as in all other cases where we use words without having clear and distinct ideas, we talk like children: who, being questioned what such a thing is, which they know not, readily give this satisfactory answer, that it is *something:* which in truth signifies no more, when so used, either by children or men, but that they know not what; and that the thing they pretend to know, and talk of, is what they have no distinct idea of at all, and so are perfectly ignorant of it, and in the dark. The idea then we have, to which we give the *general* name substance, being nothing but the supposed, but unknown, support of those qualities we find existing, which we imagine cannot subsist *sine re substante,* without something to support them, we call that support *substantia;* which, according to the true import of the word, is, in plain English, standing under or upholding.

An obscure and relative idea of *substance in general* being thus made we come to have the ideas of *particular sorts of substances,* by collecting *such* combinations of simple ideas as are, by experience and observation of men's senses, taken notice of to exist together; and are therefore supposed to flow from the particular internal constitution, or unknown essence of that substance. Thus we come to have the ideas of a man, horse, gold, water, etc.; of which substances, whether anyone has any other *clear* idea, further than of certain simple ideas co-existent together, I appeal to everyone's own experience. It is the ordinary qualities observable in iron, or a diamond, put together, that make the true complex idea of those substances, which a smith or a jeweler commonly knows better than a philosopher; who, whatever *substantial forms* he may talk of, has no other idea of those substances, than what is framed by a collection of those simple ideas which are to be found in them: only we must take notice, that our complex ideas of substances, besides all those simple ideas they are made up of, have always the confused idea of something to which they belong, and in which they subsist: and therefore when we speak of any sort of substance, we say it is a thing having such or such qualities: as body is a thing that is extended, figured, and capable of motion; spirit, a thing capable of thinking; and so hardness, friability, and power to draw iron, we say, are qualities to be found in a loadstone. These, and the like fashions of speaking, intimate that the substance is supposed always *something besides* the extension, figure, solidity, motion, thinking, or other observable ideas, though we know not what it is.

Hence, when we talk or think of any particular sort of corporeal substances, as horse, stone, etc., though the idea we have of either of them be but the complication or collection of those several simple ideas of sensible qualities, which we used to find united in the thing called horse or stone; yet, *because we cannot conceive how they should subsist alone, nor one in another,* we suppose them existing in and supported by some common subject; which support we denote by the name substance, though it be certain we have no clear or distinct idea of that thing we suppose a support.

The same thing happens concerning the operations of the mind, viz. thinking, reasoning, fearing, etc., which we concluding not to subsist of themselves, nor apprehending how they can belong to body, or be produced by it, we are apt to think these the actions of some other *substance,* which we call spirit; whereby yet it is evident that, having no other idea or notion of matter, but something wherein those many sensible qualities which affect our senses do subsist; by supposing a substance wherein thinking, knowing, doubting, and a power of moving, etc., do subsist, we have as clear a notion of the substance of spirit, as we have of body; the one being supposed to be (without knowing what it is) the *substratum* to those simple ideas we have from without; and the other supposed (with a like ignorance of what it is) to be the *substratum* to those operations we experiment in ourselves within. It is plain then, that the idea of *corporeal substance* in matter is as remote from our conceptions and apprehensions, as that of *spiritual substance*, or spirit: and therefore, from our not having any notion of the substance of spirit, we can no more conclude its non-existence, than we can, for the same reason, deny the existence of body; it being as rational to affirm there is no body, because we have no clear and distinct idea of the substance of matter, as to say there is no spirit, because we have no clear and distinct idea of the substance of a spirit.

OF THE PRINCIPLES OF HUMAN KNOWLEDGE

George Berkeley

It is evident to anyone who takes a survey of the *objects* of human knowledge that they are either ideas actually imprinted on the senses, or else such as are perceived by attending to the passions and operations of the mind, or lastly, ideas formed by help of memory and imagination—either compounding, dividing, or barely representing those originally perceived in the aforesaid ways. By sight I have the ideas of light and colors, with their several degrees and variations. By touch I perceive, for example, hard and soft, heat and cold, motion and resistance, and of all these more and less either as to quantity or degree. Smelling furnishes me with odors, the palate with tastes, and hearing conveys sounds to the mind in all their variety of tone and composition. And as several of these are observed to accompany each other, they come to be marked by one name, and so to be reputed as one thing. Thus, for example, a certain color, taste, smell, figure, and consistence having been observed to go together, are accounted one distinct thing signified by the name "apple;" other collections of ideas constitute a stone, a tree, a book, and the like sensible things—which as they are pleasing or disagreeable excite the passions of love, hatred, joy, grief, and so forth.

2. But, besides all that endless variety of ideas or objects of knowledge, there is likewise something which knows or perceives them and exercises divers operations, as willing, imagining, remembering, about them. This perceiving, active being is what I call "mind," "spirit," "soul," or "myself." By which words I do not denote any one of my ideas, but a thing entirely distinct from them, wherein they exist or, which is the same thing, whereby they are perceived—for the existence of an idea consists in being perceived.

3. That neither our thoughts, nor passions, nor ideas formed by the imagination exist without the mind is what everybody will allow. And it seems no less evident that the various sensations or ideas imprinted on the sense, however blended or combined together (that is, whatever objects they compose), cannot exist otherwise than in a mind perceiving them.—I think an intuitive knowledge may be obtained of this by anyone that shall attend to what is meant by the term "exist" when applied to sensible things. The table I write on I say exists, that is, I see and feel it; and if I were out of my study I should say it existed—meaning thereby that if I was in my study I might perceive it, or that some other spirit actually does perceive it. There was an odor, that is, it was smelled; there was a sound, that is to say, it was heard; a color or figure, and it was perceived by sight or touch. This is all that I can understand by these and the like expressions. For as to what is said of the absolute existence of unthinking things without any relation to their being perceived, that seems perfectly unintelligible. Their *esse* is *percipi,* nor is it possible they should have any existence out of the minds or thinking things which perceive them.

From George Berkeley, *A Treatise Concerning the Principles of Human Knowledge*, first published in 1710.

4. It is indeed an opinion strangely prevailing amongst men that houses, mountains, rivers, and, in a word, all sensible objects have an existence, natural or real, distinct from their being perceived by the understanding. But with how great an assurance and acquiescence soever this principle may be entertained in the world, yet whoever shall find in his heart to call it in question may, if I mistake not, perceive it to involve a manifest contradiction. For what are the forementioned objects but the things we perceive by sense? And what do we perceive besides our own ideas or sensations? And is it not plainly repugnant that any one of these, or any combination of them, should exist unperceived?

5. If we thoroughly examine this tenet it will, perhaps, be found at bottom to depend on the doctrine of *abstract ideas*. For can there be a nicer strain of abstraction than to distinguish the existence of sensible objects from their being perceived, so as to conceive them existing unperceived? Light and colors, heat and cold, extension and figures—in a word, the things we see and feel—what are they but so many sensations, notions, ideas, or impressions on the sense? And is it possible to separate, even in thought, any of these from perception? For my part, I might as easily divide a thing from itself. I may, indeed, divide in my thoughts, or conceive apart from each other, those things which, perhaps, I never perceived by sense so divided. Thus I imagine the trunk of a human body without the limbs, or conceive the smell of a rose without thinking on the rose itself. So far, I will not deny, I can abstract—if that may properly be called "abstraction" which extends only to the conceiving separately such objects as it is possible may really exist or be actually perceived asunder. But my conceiving or imagining power does not extend beyond the possibility of real existence or perception. Hence, as it is impossible for me to see or feel anything without an actual sensation of that thing, so it is impossible for me to conceive in my thoughts any sensible thing or object distinct from the sensation or perception of it.

6. Some truths there are so near and obvious to the mind that a man need only open his eyes to see them. Such I take this important one to be, to wit, that all the choir of heaven and furniture of the earth, in a word, all those bodies which compose the mighty frame of the world, have not any subsistence without a mind—that their *being* is to be perceived or known, that, consequently, so long as they are not actually perceived by me or do not exist in my mind or that of any other created spirit, they must either have no existence at all or else subsist in the mind of some eternal spirit—it being perfectly unintelligible, and involving all the absurdity of abstraction, to attribute to any single part of them an existence independent of a spirit. To be convinced of which, the reader need only reflect, and try to separate in his own thoughts, the *being* of a sensible thing from its being perceived.

7. From what has been said it follows there is not any other substance than *spirit,* or that which perceives. But, for the fuller proof of this point, let it be considered the sensible qualities are color, figure, motion, smell, taste, and such like—that is, the ideas perceived by sense. Now, for an idea to exist in an unperceiving thing is a manifest contradiction, for to have an idea is all one as to perceive; that, therefore, wherein color, figure, and the like qualities exist must perceive them; hence it is clear there can be no unthinking substance or *substratum* of those ideas.

8. But, say you, though the ideas themselves do not exist without the mind, yet there may be things like them, whereof they are copies or resemblances, which things exist without the mind in an unthinking substance. I answer, an idea can be like nothing but an idea; a color or figure can be like nothing but another color or figure. If we look but ever so little into our thoughts, we shall find it impossible for us to conceive a likeness except only between our ideas. Again, I ask whether those supposed originals or external things, of which our ideas are the pictures or representations, be themselves perceivable or no? If they are, then they are ideas and we have gained our point; but if you say they are not, I appeal to anyone whether it be sense to assert a color is like something which is invisible; hard or soft, like something which is intangible; and so of the rest.

9. Some there are who make a distinction betwixt *primary* and *secondary* qualities.[1] By the former they mean extension, figure, motion, rest, solidity or impenetrability, and number; by the latter they denote all other sensible qualities, as colors, sounds, tastes, and so forth. The ideas we have of these they acknowledge not to be the resemblances of anything existing without the mind, or unperceived, but they will have our ideas of the primary qualities to be patterns or images of things which exist without the mind, in an unthinking substance which they call "matter." By "matter," therefore, we are to understand an inert, senseless substance, in which extension, figure, and motion do actually subsist. But it is evident from what we have already shown that extension, figure, and motion are only ideas existing in the mind, and that an idea can be like nothing but another idea, and that consequently neither they nor their archetypes can exist in an unperceiving substance. Hence it is plain that the very notion of what is called "matter" or "corporeal substance" involves a contradiction in it.

10. They who assert that figure, motion, and the rest of the primary or original qualities do exist without the mind in unthinking substances do at the same time acknowledge that colors, sounds, heat, cold, and suchlike secondary qualities do not—which they tell us are sensations existing in the mind alone, that depend on and are occasioned by the different size, texture, and motion of the minute particles of matter. This they take for an undoubted truth which they can demonstrate beyond all exception. Now, if it be certain that those original qualities are inseparably united with the other sensible qualities, and not, even in thought, capable of being abstracted from them, it plainly follows that they exist only in the mind. But I desire anyone to reflect and try whether he can, by any abstraction of thought, conceive the extension and motion of a body without all other sensible qualities. For my own part, I see evidently that it is not in my power to frame an idea of a body extended and moved, but I must withal give it some color or other sensible quality which is acknowledged to exist only in the mind. In short, extension, figure, and motion, abstracted from all other qualities, are inconceivable. Where therefore the other sensible qualities are, there must these be also, to wit, in the mind and nowhere else.

11. Again, *great* and *small, swift* and *slow* are allowed to exist nowhere without the mind, being entirely relative, and changing as the frame or position of the organs of sense varies. The extension, therefore, which exists without the mind is neither great nor small, the motion neither swift nor slow; that is, they are nothing at all. But, say you, they are extension in general, and motion in general: thus we see how much the tenet of extended movable substances existing without the mind depends on that strange doctrine of *abstract ideas*. And here I cannot but remark how nearly the vague and indeterminate description of matter or corporeal substance, which the modern philosophers are run into by their own principles, resembles that antiquated and so much ridiculed notion of *material prima*, to be met with in Aristotle and his followers. Without extension, solidity cannot be conceived; since, therefore, it has been shown that extension exists not in an unthinking substance, the same must also be true of solidity.

12. That number is entirely the creature of the mind, even though the other qualities be allowed to exist without, will be evident to whoever considers that the same thing bears a different denomination of number as the mind views it with different respects. Thus the same extension is one, or three, or thirty-six, according as the mind considers it with reference to a yard, a foot, or an inch. Number is so visibly relative and dependent on men's understanding that it is strange to think how anyone should give it an absolute existence without the mind. We say one book, one page, one line; all these are equally units, though some contain several of the others. And in each instance it is plain the unit relates to some particular combination of ideas arbitrarily put together by the mind.

13. Unity I know some will have to be a simple or uncompounded idea accompanying all other ideas into the mind. That I have any such idea answering the word "unity" I do not find; and if I had, methinks I could not miss finding it; on the contrary, it should be the most familiar to my understanding, since it is said to accompany all other ideas and to be perceived by all the ways of sensation and reflection. To say no more, it is an *abstract idea.*

14. I shall further add that, after the same manner as modern philosophers prove certain sensible qualities to have no existence in matter, or without the mind, the same thing may be likewise proved of all other sensible qualities whatsoever. Thus, for instance, it is said that heat and cold are affections only of the mind, and not at all patterns of real beings existing in the corporeal substances which excite them, for that the same body which appears cold to one hand seems warm to another. Now, why may we not as well argue that figure and extension are not patterns or resemblances of qualities existing in matter, because to the same eye at different stations, or eyes of a different texture at the same station, they appear various and cannot, therefore, be the images of anything settled and determinate without the mind? Again, it is proved that sweetness is not really in the sapid thing, because, the thing remaining unaltered, the sweetness is changed into bitter, as in case of a fever or otherwise vitiated palate. Is it not as reasonable to say that motion is not without the mind, since if the succession of ideas in the mind become swifter, the motion, it is acknowledged, shall appear slower without any alteration in any external object?

15. In short, let anyone consider those arguments which are thought manifestly to prove that colors and tastes exist only in the mind, and he shall find they may with equal force be brought to prove the same thing of extension, figure, and motion. Though it must be confessed this method of arguing does not so much prove that there is no extension or color in an outward object as that we do not know by sense which is the true extension or color of the object. But the arguments foregoing plainly show it to be impossible that any color or extension at all, or other sensible quality whatsoever, should exist in an unthinking subject without the mind, or, in truth, that there should be any such thing as an outward object.

16. But let us examine a little the received opinion.—It is said extension is a mode or accident of matter, and that matter is the *substratum* that supports it. Now I desire that you would explain what is meant by matter's "supporting" extension. Say you, I have no idea of matter and, therefore, cannot explain it. I answer, though you have no positive, yet, if you have any meaning at all, you must at least have a relative idea of matter; though you know not what it is, yet you must be supposed to know what relation it bears to accidents, and what is meant by its supporting them. It is evident "support" cannot here be taken in its usual or literal sense—as when we say that pillars support a building; in what sense therefore must it be taken?

17. If we inquire into what the most accurate philosophers[2] declare themselves to mean by "material substance," we shall find them acknowledge they have no other meaning annexed to those sounds but the idea of being in general together with the relative notion of its supporting accidents. The general idea of being appears to me the most abstract and incomprehensible of all other; and as for its supporting accidents, this, as we have just now observed, cannot be understood in the common sense of those words; it must, therefore, be taken in some other sense, but what that is they do not explain. So that when I consider the two parts or branches which make the signification of the words "material substance," I am convinced there is no distinct meaning annexed to them. But why should we trouble ourselves any further in discussing this material *substratum* or support of figure and motion and other sensible qualities? Does it not suppose they have an existence without the mind? And is not this a direct repugnancy and altogether inconceivable?

18. But, though it were possible that solid, figured, movable substances may exist without the mind, corresponding to the ideas we have of bodies, yet how is it possible for us to know this? Either we must know it by sense or by reason. As for our senses, by them we have the knowledge only of our sensations, ideas, or those things that are immediately perceived by sense, call them what you will; but they do not inform us that things exist without the mind, or unperceived, like to those which are perceived. This the materialists themselves acknowledge. It remains therefore that if we have any knowledge at all of external things, it must be by reason, inferring their existence from what is immediately perceived by sense. But what reason can induce us to believe the existence of bodies without the mind, from what we perceive, since the very patrons of matter themselves do not pretend there is any necessary connection betwixt them and our ideas? I say it is granted on all hands (and what happens in dreams, frenzies, and the like, puts it beyond dispute) that it is possible we might be affected with all the ideas we have now, though no bodies existed *without* resembling them. Hence it is evident the supposition of external bodies is not necessary for the producing our ideas; since it is granted they are produced sometimes, and might possibly be produced always in the same order we see them in at present, without their concurrence.

19. But though we might possibly have all our sensations without them, yet perhaps it may be thought easier to conceive and explain the manner of their production by supposing external bodies in their likeness rather than otherwise; and so it might be at least probable there are such things as bodies that excite their ideas in our minds. But neither can this be said, for, though we give the materialists their external bodies, they by their own confession are never the nearer knowing how our ideas are produced, since they own themselves unable to comprehend in what manner body can act upon spirit, or how it is possible it should imprint any idea in the mind. Hence it is evident the production of ideas or sensations in our minds can be no reason why we should suppose matter or corporeal substances, since that is acknowledged to remain equally inexplicable with or without this supposition. If therefore it were possible for bodies to exist without the mind, yet to hold they do so must needs be a very precarious opinion, since it is to suppose, without any reason at all, that God has created innumerable beings that are entirely useless and serve to no manner of purpose.

20. In short, if there were external bodies, it is impossible we should ever come to know it; and if there were not, we might have the very same reasons to think there were that we have now. Suppose—what no one can deny possible—an intelligence without the help of external bodies, to be affected with the same train of sensations or ideas that you are, imprinted in the same order and with like vividness in his mind. I ask whether that intelligence has not all the reason to believe the existence of corporeal substances, represented by his ideas and exciting them in his mind, that you can possibly have for believing the same thing? Of this there can be no question—which one consideration is enough to make any reasonable person suspect the strength of whatever arguments he may think himself to have for the existence of bodies without the mind.

21. Were it necessary to add any further proof against the existence of matter after what has been said, I could instance several of those errors and difficulties (not to mention impieties) which have sprung from that tenet. It has occasioned numberless controversies and disputes in philosophy, and not a few of far greater moment in religion. But I shall not enter into the detail of them in this place as well because I think arguments a posteriori are unnecessary for confirming what has been, if I mistake not, sufficiently demonstrated a priori, as because I shall hereafter find occasion to speak somewhat of them.

22. I am afraid I have given cause to think me needlessly prolix in handling this subject. For to what purpose is it to dilate on that which may be demonstrated with the utmost evidence in a line or two to anyone that is capable of the least reflection? It is but looking into your own thoughts, and

so trying whether you can conceive it possible for a sound, or figure, or motion, or color to exist without the mind or unperceived. This easy trial may make you see that what you contend for is a downright contradiction. Insomuch that I am content to put the whole upon this issue: if you can but conceive it possible for one extended movable substance, or, in general, for any one idea, or anything like an idea, to exist otherwise than in a mind perceiving it, I shall readily give up the cause. And, as for all that compares of external bodies which you contend for, I shall grant you its existence, though you cannot either give me any reason why you believe it exists, or assign any use to it when it is supposed to exist. I say the bare possibility of your opinion's being true shall pass for an argument that it is so.

23. But, say you, surely there is nothing easier than to imagine trees, for instance, in a park, or books existing in a closet, and nobody by to perceive them. I answer you may so, there is no difficulty in it; but what is all this, I beseech you, more than framing in your mind certain ideas which you call books and trees, and at the same time omitting to frame the idea of anyone that may perceive them? But do not you yourself perceive or think of them all the while? This therefore is nothing to the purpose; it only shows you have the power of imagining or forming ideas in your mind; but it does not show that you can conceive it possible the objects of your thought may exist without the mind. To make out this, it is necessary that you conceive them existing unconceived or unthought of, which is a manifest repugnancy. When we do our utmost to conceive the existence of external bodies, we are all the while only contemplating our own ideas. But the mind, taking no notice of itself, is deluded to think it can and does conceive bodies existing unthought of or without the mind, though at the same time they are apprehended by or exist in itself. A little attention will discover to anyone the truth and evidence of what is here said, and make it unnecessary to insist on any other proofs against the existence of *material substance*.

24. It is very obvious, upon the least inquiry into our own thoughts, to know whether it be possible for us to understand what is meant by "the absolute existence of sensible objects in themselves, or without the mind." To me it is evident those words mark out either a direct contradiction or else nothing at all. And to convince others of this, I know no readier or fairer way than to entreat they would calmly attend to their own thoughts; and if by this attention the emptiness or repugnancy of those expressions does appear, surely nothing more is requisite for their conviction. It is on this, therefore, that I insist, to wit, that "the absolute existence of unthinking things" are words without a meaning, or which include a contradiction. This is what I repeat and inculcate, and earnestly recommend to the attentive thoughts of the reader.

25. All our ideas, sensations, or the things which we perceive, by whatsoever names they may be distinguished, are visibly inactive—there is nothing of power or agency included in them. So that one idea or object of thought cannot produce or make any alteration in another. To be satisfied of the truth of this, there is nothing else requisite but a bare observation of our ideas. For since they and every part of them exist only in the mind, it follows that there is nothing in them but what is perceived; but whoever shall attend to his ideas, whether of sense or reflection, will not perceive in them any power or activity; there is, therefore, no such thing contained in them. A little attention will discover to us that the very being of an idea implies passiveness and inertness in it, insomuch that it is impossible for an idea to do anything or, strictly speaking, to be the cause of anything; neither can it be the resemblance or pattern of any active being, as is evident from sec. 8. Whence it plainly follows that extension, figure, and motion cannot be the cause of our sensations. To say, therefore, that these are the effects of powers resulting from the configuration, number, motion, and size of corpuscles must certainly be false.

26. We perceive a continual succession of ideas, some are anew excited, others are changed or totally disappear. There is, therefore, some cause of these ideas, whereon they depend and which produces and changes them. That this cause cannot be any quality or idea or combination of ideas is clear from the preceding section. It must therefore be a substance; but it has been shown that there is no corporeal or material substance: it remains, therefore, that the cause of ideas is an incorporeal, active substance or spirit.

27. A spirit is one simple, undivided, active being—as it perceives ideas it is called "the understanding," and as it produces or otherwise operates about them it is called "the will." Hence there can be no *idea* formed of a soul or spirit; for all ideas whatever, being passive and inert *(vide* sec. 25), they cannot represent unto us, by way of image or likeness, that which acts. A little attention will make it plain to anyone that to have an idea which shall be like that active principle of motion and change of ideas is absolutely impossible. Such is the nature of spirit, or that which acts, that it cannot be of itself perceived, but only by the effects which it produces. If any man shall doubt of the truth of what is here delivered, let him but reflect and try if he can frame the idea of any power or active being, and whether he has ideas of two principal powers marked by the names "will" and "understanding," distinct from each other as well as from a third idea of substance or being in general, with a relative notion of its supporting or being the subject of the aforesaid powers—which is signified by the name "soul" or "spirit." This is what some hold; but, so far as I can see, the words "will," "soul," "spirit" do not stand for different ideas or, in truth, for any idea at all, but for something which is very different from ideas, and which, being an agent, cannot be like unto, or represented by, any idea whatsoever. [Though it must be owned at the same time that we have some notion of soul, spirit, and the operations of the mind, such as willing, loving, hating—in as much as we know or understand the meaning of those words.][3]

28. I find I can excite ideas in my mind at pleasure, and vary and shift the scene as oft as I think fit. It is no more than willing, and straightway this or that idea arises in my fancy; and by the same power it is obliterated and makes way for another. This making and unmaking of ideas does very properly denominate the mind active. Thus much is certain and grounded on experience; but when we talk of unthinking agents or of exciting ideas exclusive of volition, we only amuse ourselves with words.

29. But, whatever power I may have over my own thoughts, I find the ideas actually perceived by sense have not a like dependence on my will. When in broad daylight I open my eyes, it is not in my power to choose whether I shall see or no, or to determine what particular objects shall present themselves to my view; and so likewise as to the hearing and other senses; the ideas imprinted on them are not creatures of my will. There is therefore some *other will* or spirit that produces them.

NOTES

1. e.g. Locke, p. 139 ff.

2. e.g. Locke, p. 144: "If anyone will examine himself concerning his notion of pure substance in general, he will find he has no other idea of it all but only a supposition of he knows not what support of such qualities which are capable of producing simple ideas in us; which qualities are commonly called accidents."

3. This sentence was added to the second edition of 1734 and introduces the technical term "notion", but it is doubtful whether it marks a change of doctrine.

SCEPTICAL DOUBTS CONCERNING THE OPERATIONS OF THE UNDERSTANDING

David Hume

PART I

ALL the objects of human reason or enquiry may naturally be divided into two kinds, to wit, *Relations of Ideas,* and *Matters of Fact.* Of the first kind are the sciences of Geometry, Algebra, and Arithmetic; and in short, every affirmation which is either intuitively or demonstratively certain. *That the square of the hypothenuse is equal to the square of the two sides,* is a proposition which expresses a relation between these figures. *That three times five is equal to the half of thirty,* expresses a relation between these numbers. Propositions of this kind are discoverable by the mere operation of thought, without dependence on what is anywhere existent in the universe. Though there never were a circle or triangle in nature, the truths demonstrated by Euclid would for ever retain their certainty and evidence.

Matters of fact, which are the second objects of human reason, are not ascertained in the same manner; nor is our evidence of their truth, however great, of a like nature with the foregoing. The contrary of every matter of fact is still possible; because it can never imply a contradiction, and is conceived by the mind with the same facility and distinctness, as if ever so conformable to reality. *That the sun will not rise to-morrow* is no less intelligible a proposition, and implies no more contradiction, than the affirmation, *that it will rise.* We should in vain, therefore, attempt to demonstrate its falsehood. Were it demonstratively false, it would imply a contradiction, and could never be distinctly conceived by the mind.

It may, therefore, be a subject worthy of curiosity to enquire what is the nature of that evidence which assures us of any real existence and matter of fact, beyond the present testimony of our senses, or the records of our memory. This part of philosophy, it is observable, has been little cultivated, either by the ancients or moderns; and therefore our doubts and errors, in the prosecution of so important an enquiry, may be the more excusable; while we march through such difficult paths without any guide or direction. They may even prove useful, by exciting curiosity, and destroying that implicit faith and security, which is the bane of all reasoning and free enquiry. The discovery of defects in the common philosophy, if any such there be, will not, I presume, be a discouragement, but rather an incitement, as is usual, to attempt something more full and satisfactory than has yet been proposed to the public.

All reasonings concerning matter of fact seem to be founded on the relation of *Cause and Effect.* By means of that relation alone we can go beyond the evidence of our memory and senses. If you were to ask a man, why he believes any matter of fact, which is absent; for instance, that his friend is in the country, or in France; he would give you a reason; and this reason would be some other fact; as a letter received from him, or the knowledge of his former resolutions and promises. A man finding a watch or any other machine in a desert island, would conclude that there had once been men

From David Hume: *Enquiry Concerning the Human Understanding*, posthumous edition of 1777.

in that island. All our resasonings concerning fact are of the same nature. And here it is constantly supposed that there is a connexion between the present fact and that which is inferrred from it. Were there nothing to bind them together, the inference would be entirely precarious. The hearing of an articulate voice and rational discourse in the dark are the effects of the human make and fabric, and closely connected with it. If we anatomize all the other reasonings of this nature, we shall find that they are founded on the relation of cause and effect, and that this relation is either near or remote, direct or collateral. Heat and light are collateral effects of fire, and the one effect may justly be inferred from the other.

If we would satisfy ourselves, therefore, concerning the nature of that evidence, which assures us of matters of fact, we must enquire how we arrive at the knowledge of cause and effect.

I shall venture to affirm, as a general proposition, which admits of no exception, that the knowledge of this relation is not, in any instance, attained by reasonings *a priori;* but arises entirely from experience, when we find that any particular objects are constantly conjoined with each other. Let an object be presented to a man of ever so strong natural reason and abilities; if that object be entirely new to him, he will not be able, by the most accurate examination of its sensible qualities, to discover any of its causes or effects. Adam, though his rational faculties be supposed, at the very first, entirely perfect, could not have inferred from the fluidity and transparency of water that it would suffocate him, or from the light and warmth of fire that it would consume him. No object ever discovers, by the qualities which appear to the senses, either the causes which produced it, or the effects which will arise from it; nor can our reason, unassisted by experience, ever draw any inference concerning real existence and matter of fact.

This proposition, *that causes and effects are discoverable, not by reason but by experience*, will readily be admitted with regard to such objects, as we remember to have once been altogether unknown to us; since we must be conscious of the utter inability, which we then lay under, of foretelling what could arise from them. Present two smooth pieces of marble to a man who has no tincture of natural philosophy; he will never discover that they will adhere together in such a manner as to require great force to separate them in a direct line, while they make so small a resistance to a lateral pressure. Such events, as bear little analogy to the common course of nature, are also readily confessed to be known only by experience; nor does any man imagine that the explosion of gunpowder, or the attraction of a loadstone, could ever be discovered by arguments *a priori*. In like manner, when an effect is supposed to depend upon an intricate machinery or secret structure of parts, we made too difficulty in attributing all our knowledge of it to experience. Who will assert that he can give the ultimate reason, why milk or bread is proper nourishment for a man, not for a lion or a tiger?

But the same truth may not appear, at first sight, to have the same evidence with regard to events, which have become familiar to us from our first appearance in the world, which bear a close analogy to the whole course of nature, and which are supposed to depend on the simple qualities of objects, without any secret structure of parts. We are apt to imagine that we could discover these effects by the mere operation of our reason, without experience. We fancy, that were we brought on a sudden into this world, we could at first have inferred that one Billiard ball would communicate motion to another upon impulse; and that we needed not to have waited for the event, in order to pronounce with certainty concerning it. Such is the influence of custom, that, where it is strongest, it not only covers our natural ignorance, but even conceals itself, and seems not to take place, merely because it is found in the highest degree.

But to convince us that all the laws of nature, and all the operations of bodies without exception, are known only by experience, the following reflections may, perhaps, suffice. Were any object presented to us, and were we required to pronounce concerning the effect, which will result from it, without consulting past observation; after what manner, I beseech you, must the mind proceed in this operation? It must invent or imagine some event, which it ascribes to the object as its effect; and it is plain that this invention must be entirely arbitrary. The mind can never possibly find the effect in the supposed cause, by the most accurate scrutiny and examination. For the effect is totally different from the cause, and consequently can never be discovered in it. Motion in the second Billiard-ball is a quite distinct event from motion in the first; nor is there anything in the one to suggest the smallest hint of the other. A stone or piece of metal raised into the air, and left without any support, immediately falls: but to consider the matter *a priori,* is there anything we discover in this situation which can beget the idea of a downward, rather than an upward, or any other motion, in the stone or metal?

And as the first imagination or invention of a particular effect, in all natural operations, is arbitrary, where we consult not experience; so must we also esteem the supposed tie or connexion between the cause and effect, which binds them together, and renders it impossible that any other effect could result from the operation of that cause. When I see, for instance, a Billiard-ball moving in a straight line towards another; even suppose motion in the second ball should by accident be suggested to me, as the result of their contact or impulse; may I not conceive, that a hundred different events might as well follow from that cause? May not both these balls remain at absolute rest? May not the first ball return in a straight line, or leap off from the second in any line or direction? All these suppositions are consistent and conceivable. Why then should we give the preference to one, which is no more consistent or conceivable than the rest? All our reasonings *a priori* will never be able to show us any foundation for this preference.

In a word, then, every effect is a distinct event from its cause. It could not, therefore, be discovered in the cause, and the first invention or conception of it, *a priori,* must be entirely arbitrary. And even after it is suggested, the conjunction of it with the cause must appear equally arbitrary; since there are always many other effects, which, to reason, must seem fully as consistent and natural. In vain, therefore, should we pretend to determine any single event, or infer any cause or effect, without the assistance of observation and experience.

Hence we may discover the reason why no philosopher, who is rational and modest, has ever pretended to assign the ultimate cause of any natural operation, or to show distinctly the action of that power, which produces any single effect in the universe. It is confessed, that the utmost effort of human reason is to reduce the principles, productive of natural phenomena, to a greater simplicity, and to resolve the many particular effects into a few general causes, by means of reasonings from analogy, experience, and observation. But as to the causes of these general causes, we should in vain attempt their discovery; nor shall we ever be able to satisfy ourselves, by any particular explication of them.These ultimate springs and principles are totally shut up from human curiosity and enquiry. Elasticity, gravity, cohesion of parts, communication of motion by impulse; these are probably the ultimate causes and principles which we shall ever discover in nature; and we may esteem ourselves sufficiently happy, if, by accurate enquiry and reasoning, we can trace up the particular phenomena to, or near to, these general principles. The most perfect philosophy of the natural kind only staves off our ignorance a little longer: as perhaps the most perfect philosophy of the moral or metaphysical kind serves only to discover larger portions of it. Thus the observation of human blindness and weakness is the result of all philosophy, and meets us at every turn, in spite of our endeavours to elude or avoid it.

Nor is geometry, when taken into the assistance of natural philosophy, ever able to remedy this defect, or lead us into the knowledge of ultimate causes, by all that accuracy of reasoning for which it is so justly celebrated. Every part of mixed [applied] mathematics proceeds upon the supposition that certain laws are established by nature in her operations; and abstract reasonings are employed, either to assist experience in the discovery of these laws, or to determine their influence in particular instances, where it depends upon any precise degree of distance and quantity. Thus, it is a law of motion, discovered by experience, that the moment or force of any body in motion is in the compound ratio or proportion of its solid contents and its velocity; and consequently, that a small force may remove the greatest obstacle or raise the greatest weight, if, by any contrivance or machinery, we can increase the velocity of that force, so as to make it an overmatch for its antagonist. Geometry assists us in the application of this law, by giving us the just dimensions of all the parts and figures which can enter into any species of machine; but still the discovery of the law itself is owing merely to experience, and all the abstract reasonings in the world could never lead us one step towards the knowledge of it. When we reason *a priori,* and consider merely any object or cause, as it appears to the mind, independent of all observation, it never could suggest to us the notion of any distinct object, such as its effect; much less, show us the inseparable and inviolable connexion between them. A man must be very sagacious who could discover by reasoning that crystal is the effect of heat, and ice of cold, without being previously acquainted with the operation of these qualities.

PART II

But we have not yet attained any tolerable satisfaction with regard to the question first proposed. Each solution still gives rise to a new question as difficult as the foregoing, and leads us on to farther enquiries. When it is asked, *What is the nature of all our reasonings concerning matter of fact?* the proper answer seems to be, that they are founded on the relation of cause and effect. When again it is asked, *What is the foundation of all our reasonings and conclusions concerning that relation?* it may be replied in one word, Experience. But if we still carry on our sifting humour, and ask, *What is the foundation of all conclusions from experience?* this implies a new question, which may be of more difficult solution and explication. Philosophers, that give themselves airs of superior wisdom and sufficiency, have a hard task when they encounter persons of inquisitive dispositions, who push them from every corner to which they retreat, and who are sure at last to bring them to some dangerous dilemma. The best expedient to prevent this confusion, is to be modest in our pretensions; and even to discover the difficulty ourselves before it is objected to us. By this means, we may make a kind of merit of our very ignorance.

I shall content myself, in this section, with an easy task, and shall pretend only to give a negative answer to the question here proposed. I say then, that, even after we have experience of the operations of cause and effect, our conclusions from that experience are *not* founded on reasoning, or any process of the understanding. This answer we must endeavour both to explain and to defend.

It must certainly be allowed, that nature has kept us at a great distance from all her secrets, and has afforded us only the knowledge of a few superficial qualities of objects; while she conceals from us those powers and principles on which the influence of these objects entirely depends. Our senses inform us of the colour, weight, and consistence of bread; but neither sense nor reason can ever inform us of these qualities which fit it for the nourishment and support of a human body. Sight or feeling conveys an idea of the actual motion of bodies; but as to that wonderful force or power, which would carry on a moving body for ever in a continued change of place, and which bodies never lose but by communicating it to others; of this we cannot form the most distant conception. But notwithstanding this ignorance of natural powers* and principles, we always presume, when we see like sensible qualities, that they have like secret powers, and expect that effects, similar to those which we have experienced, will follow from them. If a body of like colour and consistence with that bread, which we have formerly eat, be presented to us, we make no scruple of repeating the experiment, and foresee, with certainty, like nourishment and support. Now this is a process of the mind or thought, of which I would willingly know the foundation. It is allowed on all hands that there is no known connexion between the sensible qualities and the secret powers; and consequently, that the mind is not led to form such a conclusion concerning their constant and regular conjunction, by anything which it knows of their nature. As to past *Experience,* it can be allowed to give *direct* and *certain* information of those precise objects only, and that precise period of time, which fell under its cognizance: but why this experience should be extended to future times, and to other objects, which for aught we know, may be only in appearance similar; this is the main question on which I would insist. The bread, which I formerly eat, nourished me; that is, a body of such sensible qualities was, at that time, endued with such secret powers: but does it follow, that other bread must also nourish me at another time, and that like sensible qualities must always be attended with like secret powers? The consequence seems nowise necessary. At least, it must be acknowledged that there is here a consequence drawn by the mind; that there is a certain step taken; a process of thought, and an inference, which wants to be explained. These two propositions are far from being the same, I *have found that such an object has always been attended with such an effect,* and *I foresee, that other objects, which are, in appearance, similar, will be attended with similar effects.* I shall allow, if you please, that the one proposition may justly be inferred from the other: I know, in fact, that it always is inferred. But if you insist that the inference is made by a chain of reasoning, I desire you to produce that reasoning. The connexion between these propositions is not intuitive. There is required a medium, which may enable the mind to draw such an inference, if indeed it be drawn by reasoning and argument. What that medium is, I must confess, passes my comprehension; and it is incumbent on those to produce it, who assert that it really exists, and is the origin of all our conclusions concerning matter of fact.

This negative argument must certainly, in process of time, become altogether convincing, if many penetrating and able philosophers shall turn their enquiries this way and no one be ever able to discover any connecting proposition or intermediate step, which supports the understanding in this conclusion. But as the question is yet new, every reader may not trust so far to his own penetration, as to conclude, because an argument escapes his enquiry, that therefore it does not really exist. For this reason it may be requisite to venture upon a more difficult task; and enumerating all the branches of human knowledge, endeavour to show that none of them can afford such an argument.

*The word *Power,* is here used in a loose and popular sense. The more accurate explication of it would give additional evidence to this argument.

All reasonings may be divided into two kinds, namely, demonstrative reasoning, or that concerning relations of ideas, and moral reasoning, or that concerning matter of fact and existence. That there are no demonstrative arguments in the case seems evident; since it implies no contradiction that the course of nature may change, and that an object, seemingly like those which we have experienced, may be attended with different or contrary effects. May I not clearly and distinctly conceive that a body, falling from the clouds, and which, in all other respects, resembles snow, has yet the taste of salt or feeling of fire? Is there any more intelligible proposition than to affirm, that all the trees will flourish in December and January, and decay in May and June? Now whatever is intelligible, and can be distinctly conceived, implies no contradiction, and can never be proved false by any demonstrative argument or abstract reasoning *a priori*.

If we be, therefore, engaged by arguments to put trust in past experience, and make it the standard of our future judgement, these arguments must be probable only, or such as regard matter of fact and real existence, according to the division above mentioned. But that there is no argument of this kind, must appear, if our explication of that species of reasoning be admitted as solid and satisfactory. We have said that all arguments concerning existence are founded on the relation of cause and effect; that our knowledge of that relation is derived entirely from experience; and that all our experimental conclusions proceed upon the supposition that the future will be conformable to the past. To endeavour, therefore, the proof of this last supposition by probable arguments, or arguments regarding existence, must be evidently going in a circle, and taking that for granted, which is the very point in question.

In reality, all arguments from experience are founded on the similarity which we discover among natural objects, and by which we are induced to expect effects similar to those which we have found to follow from such objects. And though none but a fool or madman will ever pretend to dispute the authority of experience, or to reject that great guide of human life, it may surely be allowed a philosopher to have so much curiosity at least as to examine the principle of human nature, which gives this mighty authority to experience, and makes us draw advantage from the similarity which nature has placed among different objects. From causes which appear *similar* we expect similar effects. This is the sum of all our experimental conclusions. Now it seems evident that, if this conclusion were formed by reason, it would be as perfect at first, and upon one instance, as after ever so long a course of experience. But the case is far otherwise. Nothing so like as eggs; yet no one, on account of this appearing similarity, expects the same taste and relish in all of them. It is only after a long course of uniform experiments in any kind, that we attain a firm reliance and security with regard to a particular event. Now where is that process of reasoning which, from one instance, draws a conclusion, so different from that which it infers from a hundred instances that are nowise different from that single one? This question I propose as much for the sake of information, as with an intention of raising difficulties. I cannot find, I cannot imagine any such reasoning. But I keep my mind still open to instruction, if any one will vouchsafe to bestow it on me.

Should it be said that, from a number of uniform experiments, we *infer* a connexion between the sensible qualities and the secret powers; this, I must confess, seems the same difficulty, couched in different terms. The question still recurs, on what process of argument this *inference* is founded? Where is the medium, the interposing ideas, which join propositions so very wide of each other? It is confessed that the colour, consistence, and other sensible qualities of bread appear not, of themselves, to have any connexion with the secret powers of nourishment and support. For otherwise we could infer these secret powers from the first appearance of these sensible qualities, without the aid of experience; contrary to the sentiment of all philosophers, and contrary to plain matter of fact. Here, then, is our natural state of ignorance with regard to the powers and influence of all objects.

How is this remedied by experience? It only shows us a number of uniform effects, resulting from certain objects, and teaches us that those particular objects, at that particular time, were endowed with such powers and forces. When a new object, endowed with similar sensible qualities, is produced, we expect similar powers and forces, and look for a like effect. From a body of like colour and consistence with bread we expect like nourishment and support. But this surely is a step or progress of the mind, which wants to be explained. When a man says, I *have found, in all past instances, such sensible qualities conjoined with such secret powers:* And when he says, *Similar sensible qualities will always be conjoined with similar secret powers,* he is not guilty of a tautology, nor are these propositions in any respect the same. You say that the one proposition is an inference from the other. But you must confess that the inference is not intuitive; neither is it demonstrative: Of what nature is it, then? To say it is experimental, is begging the question. For all inferences from experience suppose, as their foundation, that the future will resemble the past, and that similar powers will be conjoined with similar sensible qualities. If there be any suspicion that the course of nature may change, and that the past may be no rule for the future, all experience becomes useless, and can give rise to no inference or conclusion. It is impossible, therefore, that any arguments from experience can prove this resemblance of the past to the future; since all these arguments are founded on the supposition of that resemblance. Let the course of things be allowed hitherto ever so regular; that alone, without some new argument or inference, proves not that, for the future, it will continue so. In vain do you pretend to have learned the nature of bodies from your past experience. Their secret nature, and consequently all their effects and influence, may change, without any change in their sensible qualities. This happens sometimes, and with regard to some objects: Why may it not happen always, and with regard to all objects? What logic, what process of argument secures you against this supposition? My practice, you say, refutes my doubts. But you mistake the purport of my question. As an agent, I am quite satisfied in the point; but as a philosopher, who has some share of curiosity, I will not say skepticism, I want to learn the foundation of this inference. No reading, no enquiry has yet been able to remove my difficulty, or give me satisfaction in a matter of such importance. Can I do better than propose the difficulty to the public, even though, perhaps, I have small hopes of obtaining a solution? We shall at least, by this means, be sensible of our ignorance, if we do not augment our knowledge.

I must confess that a man is guilty of unpardonable arrogance who concludes, because an argument has escaped his own investigation, that therefore it does not really exist. I must also confess that, though all the learned, for several ages, should have employed themselves in fruitless search upon any subject, it may still, perhaps, be rash to conclude positively that the subject must, therefore, pass all human comprehension. Even though we examine all sources of our knowledge, and conclude them unfit for such a subject, there may still remain a suspicion, that the enumeration is not complete, or the examination not accurate. But with regard to the present subject, there are some considerations which seem to remove all this accusation of arrogance or suspicion of mistake.

It is certain that the most ignorant and stupid peasants—nay infants, nay even brute beasts—improve by experience, and learn the qualities of natural objects, by observing the effects which result from them. When a child has felt the sensation of pain from touching the flame of a candle, he will be careful not to put his hand near any candle; but will expect a similar effect from a cause which is similar in its sensible qualities and appearance. If you assert, therefore, that the understanding of the child is led into this conclusion by any process of argument or ratiocination, I may justly require you to produce that argument; nor have you any pretence to refuse so equitable a demand. You cannot say that the argument is abstruse, and may possibly escape your enquiry; since you confess that it is obvious to the capacity of a mere infant. If you hesitate, therefore, a moment, or if, after reflection, you produce any intricate or profound argument, you, in a manner, give up the question, and confess that it is not reasoning which engages us to suppose the past resembling the future, and to expect similar effects from causes which are, to appearance, similar. This is the proposition which I intended to enforce in the present section. If I be right, I pretend not to have made any mighty discovery. And if I be wrong, I must acknowledge myself to be indeed a very backward scholar; since I cannot now discover an argument which, it seems, was perfectly familiar to me long before I was out of my cradle.